KU-092-695

# Essence of Edinburgh

## An Eccentric Odyssey

JENNI CALDER

**Luath** Press Limited

EDINBURGH

www.luath.co.uk

| WEST DUNBARTONSHIRE LIBRARIES | |
| --- | --- |
| C 03 0280911 | |
| Askews & Holts | 21-Mar-2019 |
| 914.134 | £12.99 |
| AL | |

First published 2018

ISBN: 978-1-912147-54-0

The author's right to be identified as author of this book
under the Copyright, Designs and Patents Act 1988 has been asserted.

The paper used in this book is recyclable.
It is made from low chlorine pulps produced in a low energy,
low emission manner from renewable forests.

Printed and bound by Bell & Bain Ltd, Glasgow

Typeset in 11 point Sabon by Main Point Books, Edinburgh

Text © Jenni Calder 2018

Photographs by Alan Daiches © the Estate of Alan Daiches
Photographs by Rachel Calder © Rachel Calder

# Contents

This book is dedicated to the memory of my grandparents, Salis Daiches and Flora Levin, and William Mackay and Janet Lauder. Unknown to each other, both couples came to Edinburgh in 1919 to start new chapters of their lives, which in due course led to me in 1971 taking up residence in the city where my parents grew up. It is also dedicated to my now wonderfully extended family: Rachel, Gowan, Gideon, Paul, Arabella, Kristian, Megan, Leon, Arthur, Thomas, Susan, Gwen, Craig, Naomi, Alex, Torben, Dave, Rachel, Bella, George, Anna, Danna, John, Ben, Katy, Sonny, Wilfred and Juniper.

The Vennel and the Flodden Wall. Alan Daiches. Courtesy National Library of Scotland.

# Prologue

*This then is Edinburgh?*
Sir Walter Scott, *The Abbott*

*All Edinburgh is ours – and it's personal!*
Ron Butlin, 'The Magicians of Edinburgh'

*City of everywhere, broken necklace in the sun,*
*you are caves of guilt, you are pinnacles of jubilation.*
Norman MacCaig, 'Drop-out in Edinburgh'

CHICAGO IS THE city of my birth, Edinburgh the city in my bloodstream. My parents both grew up in Edinburgh and my earliest memories are woven with their stories about the city of their youth. I first visited Edinburgh when I was four years old, and have lived in or near the city for nearly half a century. Gradually my own experience has built on my parents' foundations, although I have always retained that early imprint of Edinburgh as an almost mythical place.

For many, the first impression of Edinburgh is of castle walls rising from solid rock, and the city has a stony reality that reinforces a history full of clashes and contradictions. And perhaps because of this blend of the stubborn and the volatile, the thrawn and the thoughtful, the bloodily destructive and the boldly inventive, Edinburgh is a city of the mind and the imagination that has fed many versions of its past and much fictional drama. Not unique, perhaps, but nevertheless distinctive.

If my response to Edinburgh is coloured by my inheritance, by the memories of others as well as by my own experience, it is equally influenced by the words of those who over the centuries have described it. I have borrowed from a wealth of documentation and interpretation of the city, set down by travellers, novelists, poets, journalists, the writers of letters.

As the title suggests, this book is a personal journey – an eccentric odyssey – exploring aspects of past and present, people and places. It is an evocation rather than a history. There are tangents and diversions, but a timeline at the end of the book provides some historical coherence. I am accompanied at times by friends and family, by my dog, and always by those who have gone before. Two literary heroes, Walter Scott and Robert Louis Stevenson, are frequently at my elbow. I cannot conceive of Edinburgh without them.

Edinburgh is a wonderfully walkable city and most of my exploration has been on foot. The most rewarding journeys are often those that don't stick to a plan, that follow serendipitous associations and are open to the unexpected. You turn a corner and there is a surprising vista of hills or water or trees or impressive buildings and curious monuments, sometimes all at once – 'an eyeful of amazing', as novelist Val McDermid puts it. In a similar way, you turn corners of the past which break away from conventional chronology and suggest unexpected connections.

The photographs reveal some of this unpredictability, and I hope will encourage readers to see beyond the image. They have been taken by my brother, the late Alan Daiches, who began his photographic career in Edinburgh in the 1960s, and my daughter Rachel Calder, who has been filming and photographing professionally for nearly 20 years. Many of Alan's photographs were taken for a television programme featuring Sydney Goodsir Smith's long poem *Kynd Kittock's Land* (1964), itself a memorable and still relevant evocation of Edinburgh.

The Heart of Midlothian. Rachel Calder.

I

# The Heart of Midlothian

*The cruikit spell o' her backbane,*
*Yon shadow-mile o' spire and vane,*
*Wad ding them a'! Wad ding them a'*
Lewis Spence, 'The Prows o' Reekie'

*Yonder stands Auld Reekie… the heart of Scotland, and each throb that*
*she gives is felt from the edge of the Solway to Duncansby Head.*
Sir Walter Scott, *The Abbot*

IT IS EASY to miss the Heart of Midlothian. If you don't cast your eyes down you can tramp without noticing over the heart shape set into the pavement close to the entrance of the High Kirk of St Giles. But of course it's not the real heart. The original Heart of Midlothian is long gone, leaving the 21st century with a heart underfoot and a football team.

Edinburgh is a city of contradiction and paradox, as all who have written about the city acknowledge, and the heart underfoot is an emblem of paradox. It marks the site of the Tolbooth, a grim, multi-purpose building constructed in 1561, the year after the Flodden Wall was completed in an effort to keep out the English. Here it is as described by Walter Scott in *The Heart of Midlothian* (1818), the novel that takes its name from the Tolbooth itself:

> Reuben Butler stood now before the Gothic entrance of the ancient prison, which… rears its ancient front in the very middle of the High Street forming… the termination to a huge pile of buildings called the Luckenbooths, which, for some inconceivable reason, our ancestors had jammed into the midst of the principal street of the town, leaving for passage a narrow street on the north, and on the south, into which the prison opens, a narrow crooked lane, winding between the high and sombre walls of the Tolbooth and the adjacent houses upon the one side, and the buttresses and projections of the old Cathedral upon the other.

According to Robert T Skinner, the heart in the street marks the approximate position of the door to the Tolbooth, and was placed there in honour of Scott.

Initially the Tolbooth housed the Scottish parliament, as well as the courts of justice and a prison, but in 1639 parliament moved to a new building just to the south of St Giles. This came about at the insistence of Charles I, who also demanded that the city pay for the construction. Charles did not otherwise take much interest in Scotland.

The Heart of Midlothian was, according to Henry Cockburn, 'a most atrocious jail... the very breath of which almost struck down any stranger who entered its dismal door'. Its walls were 'black and horrid', the small dark cells 'airless, waterless, drainless; a living grave'. It was a 'dirty, fetid, cruel torture-house... more dreadful in its sufferings, more certain in its corruption, overwhelming the innocent with a more tremendous sense of despair, provoking the guilty to more audacious defiance'. Yet when it was eventually demolished Cockburn was sorry to see it go. In his view, nothing justified the destruction of the repository of so much history.

The Tolbooth went in 1817 – it had been in a bad state of repair for many decades which can't have made the experience of its inmates any easier – and Scott, who was passionately interested in evidence of the past, was able to secure parts of it for Abbotsford, the splendidly eclectic house he built on the banks of the Tweed 40-odd miles away. The gateway and the door to the prison were, in Scott's words, 'employed in decorating the entrance of his kitchen court at Abbotsford', and he adds:

the application of these relics of the Heart of Midlothian to serve as the postern gate to a court of modern offices, may be justly ridiculed as whimsical; but yet it is not without interest, that we see the gateway through which so much of the stormy politics of a rude age, and the vice and misery of later times, had found their passage, now occupied in the service of rural economy.

In 1817 Scott also began work on the novel, which was published the following year. The two events are clearly connected. Scott would in his fiction have quite a lot to say about stormy politics.

But let's return to Reuben Butler. He is not the hero of Scott's novel, who is undoubtedly Jeanie Deans, one of Scott's most impressive creations, but he is a crucial figure. He is, in a sense, our guide to the Edinburgh of 1736, when the novel is set. Why is he standing in front of the entrance to the Tolbooth? He is hoping to visit one of the inmates, Jeanie's sister Effie, imprisoned for infanticide for which the punishment is death. Butler is a

Grassmarket. Alan Daiches. Courtesy National Library of Scotland.

not quite fully fledged minister, a modest and mild and, it has to be said, rather boring man, who hopes to marry Jeanie, whom he has known since childhood. Butler is denied a meeting with Effie and, disappointed, sets out to make his way home to Liberton through the city's West Port at the west end of the Grassmarket. The gate takes him into a suburb called Portsburgh (the existing Portsburgh Square is a reminder), 'chiefly inhabited,' Scott tells us, 'by the lower order of citizens and mechanics'. There he encounters 'a considerable mass' of people moving rapidly towards the gate he has just come through. Butler is recognised as a clergyman and his services are demanded for what is about to happen. He is swept along back to the Tolbooth. The mob now numbers several thousand. The rioters attack the door with sledge-hammers and eventually set it alight. They charge through the flames and hunt down their victim, Captain John Porteous. Butler's role is to prepare Porteous for death.

Scott's description of the Porteous Riots of 1736 is vivid, detailed and precise. He makes it clear that he has drawn on contemporary evidence and takes pains to assure his readers that his narrative is as authentic as it can be. He knows the streets and buildings intimately. Captain Porteous is dragged from the Tolbooth and taken to the Grassmarket where he is hanged from a dyer's pole. Butler, whose attempts to restrain the mob are ineffectual, slips away through the crowd but glances back to see:

> by the red and dusky light of the torches... a figure wavering and struggling as it hung suspended above the heads of the multitude... The sight was of a nature to double his horror and to add wings to his flight.

According to Alexander Carlyle, the hanging was carried out in silence.

I walk from the heart under my feet west up the High Street. As always, at any time of the year, it is busy. There are tourists, a crocodile of schoolchildren, researchers heading for the National Library, council employees heading for the City Chambers, lawyers, mothers with buggies, dogs on strings. The lights at George IV Bridge pause the traffic only briefly and plenty of pedestrians ignore the red. I wait, and then follow the route of the rioters who made their way along the High Street and down the steep curve of the West Bow into the Grassmarket, an ominous torch-lit procession. Behind the doors and windows of the tall buildings on either side, people must have heard voices and the tramp of feet and known what was about to happen.

The Porteous Riots were an extraordinary episode in Edinburgh's history, which had seen plenty of mob protest – notably 30 years earlier at the time when the Union of Parliaments was being debated – and would see more. John Porteous was a captain of the Town Guard who had been convicted of causing the deaths of spectators at the execution of a smuggler for whom there was considerable public sympathy. The place of execution was the Grassmarket, where a gallows was erected. These events drew enormous crowds. Porteous and his men were nervous, suspecting an attempt to rescue the convicted man, and when the crowd grew hostile they opened fire, leaving six or seven dead and many wounded. Porteous was found to be responsible for the deaths, but on the appointed day of his execution a reprieve arrived from Queen Caroline – the king, George II, was abroad at the time. The Edinburgh mob responded by taking matters into their own hands. They wanted justice, but they also resented interference from London.

Public executions had at one time taken place beside the Tolbooth, virtually on the doorstep of St Giles, and for a while these were carried out by a specially designed beheading machine built in 1564. Known as 'the Maiden', it despatched around one hundred men and women. The heads of those designated 'traitors' were displayed over the building's north gable, uncomfortably close to the crowds who passed in the narrow street below. Among the heads was that of James Douglas, Earl of Morton, regent on behalf of the young James VI after the death of his mother Mary, Queen of Scots. Morton, who had been instrumental in the introduction of the Maiden, was convicted of complicity in the death of Mary's husband Darnley. He was executed on 2 June 1581 by means that he himself regarded as clean and efficient.

Over a hundred years later the Maiden despatched Archibald Campbell, 9th Earl of Argyll, a prominent political figure in the 1640s who had been a leader of the Covenanting rebellion against Charles I but later supported the king. He had been tried for treason in 1681 but escaped to Holland. Four years later he returned, led an attempt to displace James VII and II and put the Duke of Monmouth on the throne. He was captured on the island of Inchinnan in the Clyde. Twelve days later, on 30 June 1685, the Maiden claimed his head. He met his end with 'much calmness and serenity of soul', according to Robert Wodrow, author of *The History of the Sufferings of the Church of Scotland*. His head was also displayed on the Tolbooth, on the same spike, it is said, occupied 30 years earlier by the head of his rival and critic James Graham, Marquis of Montrose, who had also changed sides. Montrose, however, escaped the Maiden – he was hanged. In James Robertson's novel *The Fanatic* (2000) James Mitchel, in 1656, stands in the High Street and looks up at a skull picked clean by the gulls, the 'stripped bone' looking more 'like part of the stonework, a defective gargoyle, than something human'. It is Montrose, 'the empty head of a vain and prideful villain' according to a neighbour who stops to speak to Mitchell. The neighbour is Major Weir who might have been described in the same terms. His was 'a life characterised externally by all the graces of devotion, but polluted in secret by crimes of the most revolting nature'. These revolting crimes, according to Sir John Lauder, included witchcraft, bestiality and incest. Major Weir admitted his guilt and was 'brunt'. His sister, also implicated, 'a very lamentable object', was hanged. Major Weir has both a solid and a phantom presence in Robertson's novel.

The Maiden still exists and you can see it in the Scottish galleries of the National Museum of Scotland. It came to the Museum through the Society of Antiquaries, of which Walter Scott was a member. He was present when the beheading machine was handed over to the Society by the Lord Provost in 1797. It was a time of revolution in France and radicalism at home, and the ceremony may have caused a certain frisson among the Society's members. Scott himself in *Rob Roy* (1817) invokes the Maiden as a means of bringing Highland feuding to an end: 'it will be a time to sharp the maiden for shearing o' craigs and thrapples. I hope to see the auld rusty lass linking at a bluidy harst again.' This is the comment of an associate of Baillie Nichol Jarvie, the canny Glasgow merchant with a keen eye for commercial possibilities.

A bloody harvest. Midlothian's heart is unequivocally associated with misery and violence. Standing among the throng of tourists moving up and down the High Street, with the sun shining (it often does) and pubs and cafés and tartanry beckoning, it is hard to recreate the intimacy of life and death that characterised so much of the city's past. For most of its history the smell of death was inescapable. More so than in other cities? It is the particular concentration of Edinburgh's Old Town that suggests this may have been so. From a dwelling high up in an Old Town tenement, built high because of the lack of space, you might find yourself eyeball to eyeball with a dead head. The intimacy is held in the stone. That intimacy between life and death, light and dark, openness and secrecy, pleasure and suffering, will be a recurrent theme of this book.

I have not been able to discover at what point the Tolbooth, or the site of the Tolbooth, began to be called the Heart of Midlothian, or why. It is a roughly central point between the city ports, the gates in the city wall: Bristo and Potterrow Ports to the south, the West Port, Netherbow and Cowgate Ports to the east, and the New Port, just to the east of where Waverley Station now is. It is perhaps the approximate centre of the old county of Midlothian. Was the name intended to signify the pulse of the burgh? Was it an ironic comment on crime and the dispensing of justice? Or on the close proximity between sin and the church? For us today the heart embedded in the High Street may seem to be saying 'I heart Midlothian', or suggest football rather than punishment, or be nothing more than a bit of quirky street decoration. In fact, its resonance is profound.

In the introductory chapter to *The Heart of Midlothian* some of this is explored by two Edinburgh lawyers in conversation with a character called Peter Pattieson, a conversation that acts as a conduit to the narrative that is to follow. The lawyers reflect on the fact that the Tolbooth is about to be demolished. On learning that it is known as 'the Heart of Midlothian', Peter Pattieson comments, 'it could be said to have a sad heart'. 'And a close heart, and a hard heart… a wicked heart and a poor heart' add the lawyers. But also 'a strong heart, and a high heart'. One of the lawyers suggests that as the Tolbooth is a condemned building it should be granted its 'Last Speech, Confession, and Dying Words'. It would be a tale 'of unvaried sorrow and guilt,' says Pattieson. But the lawyer disagrees, pointing out that a prison is 'a world within itself, and has its own business, griefs, and joys, peculiar to its circle'. It is a world of infinite incident and emotion, and crammed full of stories. 'The true thing will triumph over the brightest inventions of the most ardent imagination.' So the heart of Midlothian contains all of human life, the engine, perhaps, of the city's, as well as the novel's pulse. Perhaps we can push the metaphor further, and suggest that the sad, hard, wicked, poor, strong and high heart is an emblem of much of Scotland's past.

Whatever its origins, the designation in Scott's narrative has, I think, another meaning. Effie Deans is a beautiful and vulnerable young woman who has been taken advantage of by a man she will not name. She may or may not be guilty, but in the town there is sympathy for her predicament. The justice system may be relentless, but Edinburgh has a heart. Perhaps it is the town's populace who are Edinburgh's beating heart. Or perhaps it is Jeanie Deans herself, who refuses to lie to save her sister, but sets off to walk barefoot to London to plead for Effie's life – barefoot, because she needs to keep her shoes and stockings decent for her audience with the Duke of Argyll.

The metaphorical resonance of the Heart of Midlothian has another dimension. The novel is set nearly 30 years after the 1707 Union of the Scottish and English Parliaments. Scott believed that the Union was good for Scotland, though his views were not without ambivalence, and that ambivalence is expressed in this novel and elsewhere. When Jeanie tells Effie that she is going to London to plead for her, Effie is disbelieving – how can she possibly go to London, so far away and across the ocean? Jeanie points out that you can get there by land. But 400 miles was still a great distance, and Effie's disbelief reflects that sense of the British capital occupying an alien world. London, the centre of government and the usual home of the royal family, was not easy to reach, especially on foot. And it was not easy to bridge the gulf of understanding between south and north. The Duke of Argyll is the essential bridge between Jeanie and justice. Argyll, Scott says, was seen by his countrymen as their defender and advocate. Jeannie's simple trust in his role and his authority both cuts through and highlights the murkier complications of the post-Union relationship between Edinburgh and London. That the two capitals could be brought together by a barefoot lass from the edge of Edinburgh defined by her simple integrity has resonance for the politics of the 21$^{st}$ century.

The connection between Jeanie and the Duke is crucial to the comment Scott is making on the legacy of the Union. The Porteous Riots were a response to the interference of government with Scottish law – the reprieve of Captain Porteous is seen as an offence to the Scottish people. When parliament proposed vindictive measures to punish Edinburgh for allowing the Riots to occur, Argyll vehemently objected, describing the measures as cruel and unjust and counter to both the articles and the spirit of the Treaty of Union. The bill, which proposed abolishing the city guard and destroying the city gates – 'rather a Hibernian mode of enabling them better to keep the peace' was Scott's heavily ironic comment – was amended and the gates and the guard escaped destruction.

A few hundred yards from Edinburgh's stone heart, as the ubiquitous pigeons fly, is the spot where in 1771 Walter Scott was born. I retrace my steps from the Grassmarket (to which I will return) and then walk south along George IV Bridge, past the Elephant House café where JK Rowling is said to have written parts of her first Harry Potter novel. Perhaps the ghost of Scott, the 'Wizard of the North', was hovering at her elbow as she conjured Harry into existence. I turn into Chambers Street. The houses in College Wynd were pulled down – or 'unbuilt' to use Lord Cockburn's word – to make way for the University of Edinburgh's Old College, which looms dark and solid beyond the imposing Venetian façade of the National Museum. Cockburn got a half holiday from school to see the College's foundation stone laid, 'which was done with great civic and masonic pomp'. He watched from the original Royal Infirmary building in Infirmary Street, and pointed out in his memoir that the space between was empty of all but 'grass fields and gardens'. The university was founded by James VI in 1582, 21 years before James's departure from Scotland to become James I of a united kingdom depleted the country of much of its cultural life. Founded but not paid for by James, who left it to the town to provide funds for the 'the Tounis College'. This was to become a Stewart habit.

The scheme for a new university complex was designed by Robert Adam. The foundation stone was laid in 1789, but work came to a halt four years later with the outbreak of the French wars. Robert Adam died and there was a long hiatus before it was agreed to proceed with a revised plan supervised by William Playfair. The Scott family had earlier moved to the newly built George Square, much of which would in due course be unbuilt to make way for more university expansion. The nearest you can get now to Scott's birthplace is the narrow and uninviting cavern of South College Street which divides the Museum from Old College. At the corner of Chambers Street and Guthrie Street, opposite Old College, a plaque marks the spot 'near which' Scott was born.

Scott's early experience of disappearing Edinburgh may have sparked his life-long interest in preserving the evidence of the past. He was growing up at a time when the town was changing and expanding. The school he attended, the Royal High School, was a new building at the end of Infirmary Street, a stone's throw from College Wynd and no distance from George Square. Every new building brought the destruction of something old, but sometimes it brought discovery. The last decades of the 18th century and early decades of the 19th saw an unprecedented degree of disturbance of the earth, as the city expanded, canals dug, roads and railways built. The past was uncovered in a way it had never been before. Scott was a keen member of the Society of Antiquaries, founded in 1780 with the object of preserving the evidence. Scott's novels also aimed to recover and explain Scotland's past.

I walk down Chambers Street past the Museum, a building once very familiar to me as I worked there for 23 years. For the first 20 or so of those years I entered each day up the broad steps and crossed the lofty, light-filled main hall to my office at the back of the building. It was a good way to start the working day. But with the completion of the new Museum of Scotland, staff were required to enter at the back and could spend the whole day without setting foot in the Museum's most inspiring space. Today I don't go into the building, but continue my walk, up South College Street and through the underpass to the newer part of the university. I am heading for George Square, and the house at number 25 where the Scott family moved shortly after Walter's birth.

George Square, what is left of it, marks Edinburgh's first Georgian expansion, begun in 1766 when George III was on the throne, although the square was named for George Brown, brother of its architect James Brown. But you can't go far in the centre of Edinburgh without encountering reminders of the Hanoverian monarchs and their families. We'll meet them all over the New Town, the second and hugely ambitious phase of Georgian development. Scott would eventually live in the New Town, in Castle Street, while he worked energetically to preserve the past in his splendid Abbotsford home. The North Bridge, constructed to connect the Old Town with the proposed New, was completed in 1763, eight years before Scott's birth.

When George Square first went up, it must have been peaceful, at a distance from the overcrowded, noisy, insalubrious High Street yet a short walk from the history the High Street contained, as well as from everything that mattered in the city's professional life. It is not surprising that Scott himself became a bridge between past and present, and in his frequent crossings from one to the other he wasn't always sure which was his favoured direction.

Henry Cockburn was born eight years later than Walter Scott. He wasn't exactly sure where his birth took place, but believed it to have been in 'one of the many lofty ranges of dwelling-houses which then formed the east side of Parliament Close'. At the northwest corner of Parliament Square was the room where the town council met, described by Cockburn many years later as a 'low, dark blackguard-looking room... very dirty, with some small dens off it for clerks'. The gentlemen who gathered there were considered by Cockburn to be 'omnipotent, corrupt, impenetrable'; they had charge of street paving and lighting, water, education, trade, provision (or not) for the poor, and the police. They were 'silent, powerful, submissive, mysterious and irresponsible'. Cockburn goes on to say that Edinburgh's town council was probably no worse – and possibly better – than any other. Many were 'sinks of political and municipal iniquity'.

One of Edinburgh's many tartan gift shops. Alan Daiches. Courtesy National Library of Scotland.

The Edinburgh that the young Cockburn witnessed was changing, and in his view not always for the better. He was scathing about 'improvements' to the parliament building. 'I cannot doubt that King Charles tried to spur his horse against the Vandals when he saw the profanation begin,' he wrote indignantly, referring to the equestrian statue of Charles II that stands beside the building. He added that 'there was such an absence of public spirit in Edinburgh then, that the building might have been painted scarlet without anybody objecting'. Vandalism against the fabric of the city is a recurring theme in Cockburn's memoirs. The stalls and booths in Parliament Close, and ranged along the north flank of St Giles, were occupied by jewellers, cutlers, toymakers and booksellers and had once been like a bazaar out of the Arabian Nights, but in 1817 the last of them was swept away along with the Heart of Midlothian itself. Today's gift shops are a poor reminder. By the time the Tolbooth was demolished the life of Edinburgh's High Street had profoundly changed. To the north of the castle's hill, on the far side of the North Loch, a transformation was taking place.

The New Town was under construction as Scott was growing up, so just as he was absorbing evidence of old Edinburgh, he had before him a prospect of the new. Cockburn describes the effect of the New Town on the Old Town life.

It was the rise of the new town that obliterated our old peculiarities with the greatest rapidity and effect. It not only changed our scenes and habits of life, but, by the mere inundation of modern population, broke up and, as then thought, vulgarised our prescriptive gentilities.

He went on to cite St Cecilia's Hall in the Cowgate as an example of decay – 'the best and most beautiful concert room I have ever yet seen', where literary and fashionable people congregated:

gentlemen... with their side curls, and frills, and ruffles, and silver buckles; and our stately matrons stiffened in hoops, and gorgeous satin; and our beauties with high heeled shoes, powdered and pomatomed hair, and lofty and composite head dresses. All this was in the Cowgate! the last retreat nowadays of destitution and disease.

And he goes on to say that when he last saw St Cecilia's Hall it 'seemed to be partly an old-clothesman's shop, and partly a brazier's'. The hall had only been built in 1762. It is now restored and functioning again as a concert hall.

This illustrates the rapidity of change. Edinburgh itself became an emblem of possibility at the same time as a location of decline. Just as Scotland's capital was drained of its cultural life blood when James VI went south, so the Old Town was abandoned by those whose personal, professional and creative lives had been anchored in its wynds and closes. The Heart of Midlothian was gone, in more ways than one. The nearby Mercat Cross was no longer a gathering point. But there was still plenty of activity, although the 19th-century 'rage for improvement' – Charles Kirkpatrick Sharp writing in the *Edinburgh Observer* in 1827 – continued to make inroads. An Improvement Act initiated a wave of removal and rebuilding. The West Bow, once a sharply angled street linking the Grassmarket with Castlehill, was partly demolished, removing what James Ballantine considered to be one of the noisiest quarters of the city:

the clinking of coppersmiths' hammers, the bawling of speech criers, ballad-singers, and vendors of street merchandise, were mingled with the scraping of fiddles, the beating of drums, and the squeaking of cracked clarionets.

The demolition included the house of the infamous Major Weir. The equally infamous Burke and Hare also resided in West Bow. The upper section of West Bow became Victoria Street with Victoria Terrace above, completed in 1834. If you walk along the terrace today during a summer lunchtime you can covertly examine the food and drink of the patrons of the eateries that have spilled into the open air.

But feet continue to tramp over the heart on the street, appropriate perhaps, given that the 19th century gave it a new incarnation in which feet featured prominently. Heart of Midlothian was the name given to a dancing club, some of whose members enjoyed playing football. What started out as a kick-about in the High Street became more organised when they began playing on the Meadows, a grassy expanse half a mile to the south which had once been under water. By 1874 a football team had evolved from these informal beginnings, and the following year the Heart of Mid-Lothian Football Club joined the Scottish Football Association. In that year they played in the Scottish Cup for the first time, against the 3rd Edinburgh Rifle Volunteers. It wasn't a promising start – the game ended in a scoreless draw – but Hearts, as they soon became known, went on to considerable early success, winning the league championship in 1895 and 1896, and the Scottish Cup four times in the period up to 1906. In 1902 they were declared World Champions. Hearts continued to play on the Meadows and also at Powburn and Powderhall until in 1881 they moved to Gorgie. Five years later they played their first match on their current ground at Tynecastle Park. Soon after the outbreak of war in 1914, 16 Hearts first team players enlisted in a volunteer battalion which became the 16th Royal Scots. They were joined by Hearts supporters, as well as players and supporters from other clubs. The seven players who lost their lives are commemorated on the Heart of Midlothian war memorial at Haymarket.

So the dancing feet on the High Street went on to dance their way around Edinburgh, Scotland and a large part of the globe, with varying success. But the shift westward of Edinburgh's heart did not depend on winning matches. The 19th-century popularity of Walter Scott's *The Heart of Midlothian*, once read all over the world, is now overshadowed by a very different resonance. Now the phrase is more likely to signify football than fiction. Similarly, few among the thousands who pass through Waverley Station every day are likely to have read the novel that gave it its name, although reminders of the station's connection with Scott placed in the

Tourists at the Mercat Cross. Rachel Calder.

station to commemorate the bicentenary of the publication of *Waverley* (1814) may change that. (My friend John Burnett finds them 'charming and ludicrous at the same time'.)

Scott's story of Jeannie and Effie Deans is bound into the topography of the Old Town and its immediate vicinity. And Scott's fiction generally is bound into my childhood reading and understanding of Scotland's past. He and Robert Louis Stevenson will make frequent appearances in what follows. For anyone acquainted with their books, it is impossible not to absorb the city through their eyes. The Deans family, the two sisters and their elderly Covenanting father, live in a small lonely farm at St Leonard's Crags, 'between Edinburgh and the mountain called Arthur's Seat'. It is only half a mile from the town – and even by Scott's time it had been built on – but it is rural and distant. The walk to the town links a struggling rural existence with urban life, providing a sense of both connection and contrast. At the time of her downfall, Effie is employed at the Saddletrees' High Street establishment, a harness shop at the sign of the Golden Nag. It is an urban environment full of risk and temptation. But Jeanie remains a country lass, milking cows and running the dairy and looking after her father. She seems not to be comfortable in the Edinburgh streets, negotiating the Edinburgh rabble, conversing with Edinburgh folk. By the time we see Jeanie and her father entering the town to attend Effie's trial we already know that Edinburgh is a place of dark spaces and dark deeds, of violence both judicial and criminal, with the Tolbooth, the Heart of Midlothian, looming over the daily lives of merchants and traders, lawyers and malefactors, rich and poor. Scott created a narrative embedded in Edinburgh that grew out of the town itself. It demonstrates gentility and sleaze cheek by jowl, comedy and tragedy, justice and exploitation, villainy and decency. It acts as a key to the city's contradictions, as relevant today as it was when it was first read.

Edinburgh Castle. Alan Daiches. Courtesy National Library of Scotland.

The native rock breaks through the Castle's stone

*The native rock breaks through*
*the Castle's stone: and we are bonded*
*to our human past*
George Bruce, 'City Inscape'

*Towering blackly, like iron upon the indomitable rock*
Eric Linklater, *Magnus Merriman*

APPROACHING EDINBURGH FROM almost any direction, the castle at some point appears. It can be seen from the Pentland Hills to the south of the city, and from smaller Lothian hills. The stone of its structure seems organic to the rock upon which it is built. From a distance its uncompromising outline can be dark and grim, but it is transformed when it catches the golden light of sunset, or when it appears to float in early morning mist. Close to, it is a brooding presence, incongruous perhaps, 'a Bass Rock upon dry land rooted in a garden' as Robert Louis Stevenson described it, 'shaken by passing trains, carrying a crown of battlements and turrets, and describing its warlike shadow over the liveliest and brightest thoroughfare of the new town'. This was written in the 1870s. Now the contrast is perhaps even greater as the ancient storehouse of history looks down on the banality of cut-price commerce spread along Princes Street.

Cities dominated by hilltop castles or cathedrals have a particular allure. Building on a hill is an uncompromising statement of power and dominance, as well as of defence, and a reminder of the smallness of ordinary lives. Even when distance renders the outline of Edinburgh's castle a minor if distinctive excrescence on the landscape, it conveys unequivocally a sense of human construction and an endeavour to command. The castle brings to an abrupt and craggy end the dramatic skyline of spires and towers and rooftops that stretches west from the palace of Holyrood. It was part of Edinburgh's beginning. 'Fortress of the hill slope' is the meaning of its original name, Dunedin. It was there when the Romans invaded the north of Britain, although they ignored it and built instead a port at Cramond on the Firth of Forth. At that time the fortress was probably little more than a rough outer wall of turf and stones guarding a cluster of turf dwellings. Later, this became a more solid wall surrounding a stone keep. But whatever the structures that topped the great mass of volcanic rock it was a natural stronghold. Although through its history the castle rock would be scaled more than once, and the castle itself bombarded and burned, it survived all attack.

The rock's height commands views to the south and the east, to the Pentland Hills, the Lammermuirs and the Moorfoot Hills and the southern approaches that edge the Firth of Forth, the route that successive invading English armies usually took. To the north and west are vistas across the Forth, to Fife and towards the Highlands. On a clear day you can see beyond the Highland Line. David Masson described the prospect as it was in the 1860s:

> Beneath you, paralleled and rectangle over a succession of slopes, the whole of the new city and its gardens, so that the cannon from where you stood could blast it into ruins at a descending angle, and so that always, when they do fire on peaceful gala-days, the windows of the city rattle and shiver with the far-going reverberations; beyond this city the villa studded banks of the Forth; again, beyond these the Firth's own flashing waters; and, still beyond even these, the towns, villages, and heights of the opposite Fifeshire coast. On either side… other views… till you could make out, on a clear day, that the risings in the amethystine distance… were really the summits of the far Highland hills.

This commanding view is embedded in the castle's character. It gives it a centrality rivalled only by Stirling castle to the north and west, which guards the upper crossing of the Forth and the divide between Highland and Lowland.

Caught in a throng of tourists spilling into the Lawnmarket and beating a way slowly up Castlehill, it is easy to lose touch with the past although it is the allure of the past that brings people here. Down at the foot of the rock Edinburgh citizens waiting for a bus or threading in and out of familiar stores may feel, like David Daiches, that the castle is 'too much always there, too permanent and accepted and matter-of-course a feature of the skyline to arouse romantic suggestions'. But even the most complacent citizen will surely have moments of astonishment when they lift their eyes to the castle's lofty presence.

When Chiang Yee, exiled from China and a dedicated traveller, visited Edinburgh in the 1940s he wrote that he liked to imagine that the original fortress on the rock was built at the same time as the Great Wall, which like the castle was constructed over many centuries, with its most substantial origins being around 200BC. Chiang Yee writes about Edinburgh with an empathetic warmth, a tenderness almost. For him the castle was not forbidding, but rather 'kindly… [it] attracts people to its friendly walls'.

In Alice Munro's story 'The view from castle rock' (2006), ten-year-old Andrew visits Edinburgh for the first time from his home in the Borders. They climb 'a slippery black street' until they reach a courtyard paved with blocks of stone. His father tells him that the stones have run with blood. Andrew can see nothing 'but enormous stone walls, barred gates, a redcoat soldier marching up and down'. They go through an archway and keep climbing, until they pause to look out to the north.

> The sun was out now, shining on the stone heap of houses and streets below them, and the churches whose spires did not reach to this height, and some little trees and fields, then a wide silvery stretch of water. And beyond that a pale green and gray-ish blue land, part in sunlight and part in shadow, a land as light as mist, sucked into the sky.

'America,' says Andrew's father, who has had a drink or two. Andrew knows better, though he doesn't know that what he is looking at is Fife. Some years later, in 1818, Andrew, grown-up and married, with his father and family embark in Leith to cross the Atlantic. Their destination is Canada, or British North America as it then was. It may not have been America that Andrew saw from Edinburgh castle, but it was a vision that planted in him the possibility of another life.

On a sunny April day in 2015, I am climbing towards the castle up Ramsay Garden with my two grandsons, aged nine and six. Kristian, the elder, reckons that it wouldn't be *that* difficult to scale the castle rock and in the course of our visit figures out ways it could be done. There is a long snaking queue at the ticket office and the boys are impatient. I wonder at the interest of all these people prepared to pay a hefty price (that for many others must be prohibitive) to spend time wandering through an ancient structure whose historic resonance can often be no more than vague. But that perhaps is the appeal. An imprecise sense of antiquity with a few highlighted details is enough. The stone walls, the cobbles underfoot, dark entries and narrow twisting stairways, cannon thrusting aggressively outwards, and a dazzling prospect of the city below, the hills beyond, the firth and its islands, a glimpse of the rail bridge that I see every day from my own back windows. It is a connection with place and the past which can be felt and relished. It is a trigger for the imagination, for those who allow themselves the space and time to let it loose.

The boys locate Mons Meg and run their hands over its shiny surface. It has been recently restored and gleams with fresh paint. They want to know why it has a name and why all the castle's cannon aren't as big. In Kristian's view, the castle would be better defended by a few very large cannon rather than a lot of small ones. I explain that the name comes from where it was made, Mons in Belgium, a present in 1457 from the Duke of Burgundy to his nephew James II. They examine the huge, heavy stones the cannon fired – they weigh 550 pounds. How far can they be fired? A mile? Kristian suggests. Surely not that far, I say, but a label tells me that its range is nearly two miles. I think he is impressed.

James was keen on guns, and Mons Meg was an impressive status symbol. But heavy artillery was hugely cumbersome and expensive to move about. Historian Rosalind Mitchison tells us that, in addition to the large number of 'skilled foreign gunners and smiths' needed to fire and maintain Mons Meg, 'a host of unskilled workmen with mattocks, spades, horses, and tows were needed to move it about'. The progress of Mons Meg down Castle Hill must have been a sight to behold, the equivalent of the power spectacles of a Chinese or North Korean military parade. When in 1497 Mons Meg set off on a journey to lay siege to Norham Castle on the south bank of the Tweed, the cannon was accompanied down the High Street by a band of minstrels.

The 'Auld Murderess' (Scott's words) was removed to London in 1754 and it was Scott who urged her return. In March 1829 he witnessed the cannon brought 'in solemn procession to reoccupy her ancient place on the Argyll Battery'. In his journal he commented:

Mons Meg is a monument of our pride and poverty. The size is immense but six smaller guns would have been made at the same expense and done six times as much execution as she could have done.

The drama of the cannon's return was much enhanced when rockets were let off, one of which set Scott's daughter's bonnet on fire. She remained calm – Scott was 'proud of her presence of mind'. I didn't mention this episode to the boys, who would have loved such a spectacle.

We go into St Margaret's Chapel, the oldest surviving part of the castle. Leon is intrigued – he goes to St Margaret's Primary School. The same St Margaret? I tell him yes and point out the little boat inscribed in the stone, a reminder of Margaret's frequent crossings of the Forth as she commuted between Dunfermline in Fife and the place that in the latter part of the 11th century was beginning to become a focal point for power and religious influence in Scotland. Dates and centuries mean little to six-year-old boys, but Leon knows about olden days and is on the lookout for knights and princesses. Castles are the location of good guys and bad guys. Somewhere there must be a dungeon. Perhaps even dragons.

Both boys are keen to see the Honours of Scotland. They are not particularly impressed by the tableaux that lead us to the crown jewels themselves – the kings and queens are patently unalive – but are fascinated when we reach the real thing. Are they real? Real gold? Real jewels? What was the sceptre for? Was the sword used to kill people? Kristian casts a practical eye on the security arrangements. He is not convinced they are adequate. Before we leave the castle we have hot chocolate in the café and visit the gift shop, where Leon purchases a plastic knight's helmet and Kristian a Scottish saltire key ring. He knows about flags. He doesn't know, five months before Scotland will be asked to vote for or against independence, that the saltire in April 2014 has a particular resonance. But he is hoping that it won't be too long before he is allowed his own front door key.

As the fortress on the rock became stronger, the growing huddle of turf huts straggled further down the craggy spine of the hill's gentlest slope. But Edinburgh didn't begin to become important until Kenneth McAlpin united Picts and Scots in the ninth century, and even then it remained only one of a series of fortresses. Stirling, poised between Highlands and Lowlands, was a more vital stronghold. In the reign of Malcolm Canmore, the 'big-headed' slayer of Macbeth, Edinburgh received more attention. Malcolm's court was on the other side of the Forth at Dunfermline, but his wife Margaret liked Edinburgh, which Malcolm used as a base for hunting in the great forest that stretched south and west from the rock, and he built for his pious wife a chapel, now the oldest building in the castle. Their son, David 1, founded the abbey of Holyrood a mile east of the castle in 1128. The twin outposts of what would become Edinburgh's Old Town were now in existence.

Over the next centuries much of Scotland's turbulent history was focused on Edinburgh, and the town itself was as turbulent as the history. James Hogg, attempting to transport himself back several hundred years, was sure that the promise of greatness was there in the beginning.

> See yon hamlet, o'ershadowed with smoke;
> See yon hoary battlement throned on the rock;
> Even there shall a city in splendour break forth,
> The haughty Dun-Edin, the Queen of the North;
> There learning shall flourish, and liberty smile,
> The awe of this world, and the pride of the isle.

His friend Scott writing about medieval Edinburgh was less predictive but also less restrained.

> For on the smoke-wreaths, huge and slow,
> That round her sable turrets flow,
>   The morning beams were shed,
>   And tinged them with a lustre proud,
>   Like that which streaks a thunder-cloud.
> Such dusky grandeur clothed the height,
> Where the huge castle holds its state,
>   And all the steep slope down,
> Whose ridgy back heaves to the sky,
> Piled deep and massy, close and high,
>   Mine own romantic town!

But these centuries of Edinburgh's history were not so much romantic as ruthless. Her castle stronghold was besieged and assaulted, bombarded and fired, most often by the English. The most renowned and relentless foe of Scotland was Edward I, who attacked the castle with three great assault engines that thundered against the walls for a week. In 1296 Edward took possession, and looted all the castle's valuables before heading north for further pacification. It was at this time that William Wallace, 'the Hammer and Scourge of England', appeared on the scene, harrying the English forces and waging guerrilla warfare until in 1305 he was captured and gruesomely executed in London.

As claimant to the Scottish throne, Robert the Bruce took up the fight, and in 1314 defeated Edward II's army of 15–20,000 men at Bannockburn, the year that saw the daring recapture of Edinburgh castle by Randolph, Earl of Moray, Bruce's nephew. Moray scaled the rock with a handful of men and deliberately destroyed the fortifications so they would be of no further use to the English. But 20 years later it was back in English hands, with by this time Edward III on the throne. He rebuilt the castle and held it for six years as the base for his subjection of the Scots. It was retaken by David II, Bruce's son. David made Edinburgh his centre, and built the great keep, King David's Tower, within the castle walls.

The solidity of stone and of the rock upon which it sits may today suggest safety, but the castle did not necessarily protect all who sheltered within it, and it certainly wasn't able to protect those outwith its walls. In 1385 the English were back, burning much of Edinburgh, including the original St Giles Cathedral, and besieging the castle. Fifteen years later they were battering at the gates again. The castle survived both sieges, but thought had to be given to the defences of the town. In 1450 James II instigated the construction of a wall starting at the southeast corner of the castle rock and running parallel with the High Street before bending north to reach the North Loch, an artificial lake created by the damning of a burn. At five feet high, the King's Wall, as it became known, may not have been much of a deterrent. It took 25 years to complete, and nearly 40 years later there would be another burst of wall construction.

The Stewart kings, descendants of Robert I, had made Edinburgh Castle their main residence. Their reigns tended to have inauspicious beginnings. The first three Jameses were young boys when they became king. James I was a prisoner of the English at the time, and James IV was only 16. His son was an infant when his father died. James V died when his daughter Mary was only six days old, and her son, James VI, became king at the age of one year, although his mother lived for another 20 years, most of that time as a captive of the English. The young monarchs were vulnerable, subject not only to threats from England but to the manipulations of rival factions in Scotland, the Douglases prominent among them. These power struggles often proved their undoing. In 1437, James I was murdered in Perth. Some 23 years later his son also met a violent end, when he was killed by an exploding cannon while laying siege to Roxburgh Castle which had been captured by the English, perhaps not a surprising demise for a man so enthusiastic about weapon technology. The Douglases may well have considered it just retribution.

In such volatile circumstances, punishment, execution and assassination were almost commonplace events, though not necessarily public. The castle was the scene of many dark and private deaths. Notorious among these was the murder of the youthful Earl of Douglas, seen as a danger to the crown. In 1440 he was invited by James II to Edinburgh. 'The noble youth,' wrote David Hume of Godscroft in 1644, set off 'in the innocency of his heart'. In the castle he and other nobles and courtiers gathered for dinner. 'At last about the end of dinner, they compasse him about with armed men, and cause present a bulls head before him on the board: the bulls head was in those days a token of death.' The armed men 'laid hold' of Douglas 'in the King's presence at the King's table'.

> As so without regard of King, or any duty, and without any further processe, without order, assise (or jury), no crime objected, he not being convicted at all; a young man of that age that was not liable to the law in regard of his youth, a Nobleman of that place, a worthy Gentleman of such expectation, a guest of that acceptation, one who had reposed upon their credit, who had committed himself to them, a friend in mind, who looked for friendship, to whom all friendship was promised; against dutie, law, friendship, faith, honesty, humanitie; against nature, against humane society, against Gods Law, against mans law, and the law of nature, is cruelly executed, and put to death.

During the reign of James III there was another attack from England and an English army occupied Edinburgh in 1482. The third James was not a popular king, and came to a mysterious end after a battle with rebellious nobles at Sauchieburn. James IV was in many ways accomplished as a ruler but had a somewhat extravagant notion of his own potential. In July 1513, 17 great guns pulled by 400 oxen and accompanied by too few experienced gunners, began a journey south from Edinburgh that would end in disaster. James was attempting an invasion of England. On 10 September news came back to Edinburgh: James and around 10,000 of his men had fallen on the field of Flodden, just south of the border, and an English army was making its way north. At once, the town council issued a proclamation requiring all those who could bear arms to prepare for the defence of the town and work was begun on the famous Flodden Wall. The city's women were ordered to

Flodden Wall, detail. Alan Daiches. Courtesy National Library of Scotland.

pray, possibly an effective strategy as the English army, this time, did not follow up their success. The attack never came, which was just as well as the wall took 47 years to complete. Some of it survives. Nearly 30 years after Flodden came another defeat of the Scots by the English, at Solway Moss. Three weeks later James v died, shortly after hearing the news that his wife, Mary of Guise, had borne a daughter at Linlithgow palace.

From the castle ramparts you can look south towards grey-green hills, and east, the direction from which an English invasion was most likely to come. And you can look west and north to locations of more home-grown troubles. How many of the Jameses gazed out in the four directions and reflected on potential threats, from England, from the Douglases in the Borders and the southwest, from the Campbells, from the Lords of the Isles? How safe did they feel, how protected by the formidable stone walls and the steep, unforgiving rock?

It was perhaps inevitable that Robert Louis Stevenson would find a place for the castle in his fiction. In *St Ives* (1898) he goes back to the year 1813, when Britain was at war with Napoleon and French prisoners of war were incarcerated there. One of these is our hero, St Ives himself, who plans to escape. From the battlements he looks down on 'the long terrace of Princes Street which serves as a promenade to the fashionable people of Edinburgh'. 'A singularity,' he adds, 'in a military prison, that it should command a view on the chief thoroughfare!' He plans his escape, but with considerable trepidation. The only safe exit is through the guarded main gate. 'In all other directions an abominable precipice surrounds it, down the face of which (if anywhere at all) we must regain our liberty.' The southwest corner seems the best route, 'a place they call the *Devil's Elbow*'.

> From the hell of masonry, the rascally, breakneck precipice descended sheer among waste lands, scattered suburbs of the city, and houses in the building. I had never the heart to look for any length of time – the thought that I must make the descent in person some dark night robbing me of breath; and, indeed, on anybody not a seaman or a steeple-jack, the mere sight of the *Devil's Elbow* wrought like an emetic.

St Ives and his fellow escapees acquire a rope and wait for a starless and moonless night to make their descent. The rope, however, seemed to hold 'a personal malignity against myself'. It swings erratically and dangerously, 'kept me all the time in the most outrageous fury of exertion; and dashed me at intervals against the face of the rock'. The darkness is total: 'the whole forces of my mind were so consumed with losing hold and getting it again, that I could scarce have told whether I was going up or coming down'. He makes it down, and heads for what he has been led to believe will be a temporary place of safety on a slope of the Pentland Hills. It is the start of a perilous journey which will after many bizarre adventures bring him back to the city he is fleeing from.

Stevenson's abrupt demise from a brain haemorrhage in December 1894 prevented the completion of *St Ives*, whose final chapters were supplied by Arthur Quiller-Couch. Stevenson's text ends with an inebriated walk from Cramond to Edinburgh after a night of over-indulgence at 'a hostelry of no very promising appearance'. In 1990, persuaded by the late R J Storey whose research suggested that Stevenson had planned an ending rather different from the one Quiller-Couch supplied, I had a go myself at finishing Stevenson's narrative, which I brought to an end with St Ives successfully confronting his evil cousin on the shores of the Forth, and repairing thereafter to the comforts of Queensferry's Hawes Inn.

On a grey but mild October day I walk up Castlehill. Summer and the Festival are long over, but the street is still thronged with tourists. Cameras are clicking at a bagpiper in full tartan gear and a little further on a young girl is playing the cello. On the opposite pavement a man with a blue face and draped with fur is attracting attention but I don't stop to examine who or what he represents. From the castle esplanade I take the steep path that leads down to Princes Street Gardens. A few people are toiling upwards. Climbing towards me is a young woman of colour wearing massive green headphones and carrying a coffee. Here the path zigzags down a grassy slope which in the spring is thick with daffodils, but the dark unforgiving rock looms at my left hand. On the right Ramsay Garden offers a colourful and cheerful contrast. The original house was the home of the poet and song-collector Allan Ramsay, who died in 1758, but in the late 19th century the site was developed into a collection of apartments by Patrick Geddes, whose career began in biology and ended in sociology, taking in pioneering town planning along the way. Geddes was highly conscious of Edinburgh's divisions, and wrote of the 'practical indifference to deplorable conditions which strikes every Continental visitor, even every American tourist, with an outspoken astonishment far from flattering to Edinburgh'.

Ramsay Garden, however, *is* flattering to Edinburgh. It is a vivid conglomeration of architectural styles which, perhaps improbably, seem to harmonise organically with its neighbours. Allan Ramsay could probably see from his windows the snow on the Pentland Hills, which triggered his poem 'To the phiz, an ode', which celebrates, among other things, the art of keeping warm in a Scottish winter. Fling coals on the fire, he advises, and 'get in the tappit hen', the name for the usually pewter jug that held claret.

> Good claret best keeps out the cauld,
> And drives away the winter soon.
> It makes a man baith gash and bauld,
> And heaves his saul beyond the moon.

Down below his house, in the northeast corner of the west Gardens, the poet himself is celebrated in marble.

But today it isn't cold and the wind is quiet. I walk down the hill, pass the ruins of the 14th-century Wellhouse Tower and cross the railway, pausing on the footbridge almost instinctively, as it was a favourite vantage point when I, and then my children, were young. If you approach Edinburgh by train from the west you become aware of the ominous closeness of the castle rock. There's the Ross bandstand, where my grandmother sometimes took me as a child to watch Scottish country dancing, and the elaborate and ornate Ross fountain, originally commissioned for the 1862 International Exhibition. It was purchased by Daniel Ross, an Edinburgh gunsmith (then as now weapons manufacture was lucrative) and presented to the city. Not everyone was impressed. According to Dean Ramsay, a prominent Episcopal clergyman (no relation of Allan) whose own memorial stands close by, the fountain's sculptures were 'grossly indecent and disgusting; insulting and offensive to the moral feelings of the community and disgraceful to the city'. When I passed the fountain a while back two photographers, one with a tripod, were intent on taking pictures. It has now been restored, repainted in colours that can't be missed, and given a new pumping system.

I pass the play area, busy with small people climbing and swinging. Looming behind it are the rear ends of two churches, the Presbyterian St Cuthbert's and the Episcopalian St John's – Dean Ramsay's church. The former stands on the site of a church dating from the eighth or ninth century.

Its parish included the castle – its graveyard is the burial place of many soldiers as well as notable citizens and sojourners: John Napier, inventor of logarithms, artists Henry Raeburn and Alexander Nasmyth, author Thomas De Quincy and George Meikle Kemp who designed the Scott Monument, among many others. But perhaps a more resonant attraction for many is the connection with Agatha Christie, whose second marriage, to Max Mallowan, took place in St Cuthbert's in September 1930.

The graveyard's proximity to the castle brought a certain amount of collateral damage. When Cromwell occupied Edinburgh he used the building as a barracks which made it a target of attack from the uncaptured castle. A later building was added to and extended, until finally it was considered beyond repair and in the 1890s was rebuilt to a design by Hippolyte Blanc. Its interior is unusually ornate for a Presbyterian Church. Among other features is a window made by the Tiffany Glass Company showing David and Goliath. The metaphorical suggestion was perhaps not intended.

St John's is much later in origin, designed by William Burn and built between 1815 and 1818 – 'a remarkably convincing Gothic exercise for its time', according to the authors of the Edinburgh volume of *The Buildings of Scotland* (1984). Its interior is impressive, with splendidly vivid stained glass windows from the locally based studio of Ballantyne and Allan added in the middle of the century. The building of the church responded to the growing numbers of Episcopalians at the time, but was perhaps also conceived as an assertion of Episcopalianism in a predominantly Presbyterian Scotland. The cost of £18,000 was raised from donations and an issue of shares which brought investors a three per cent dividend. The money was recovered through seat rents. This was an accepted way of financing church buildings, and those who contributed could expect not only their three per cent but an acknowledgement of status as they took their places of a Sunday.

Now St John's stands, an emphatic termination to the west end of Princes Street and rather overshadowing its Presbyterian neighbour. For many years it has hosted the ecumenical Edinburgh Peace and Justice Centre, a fair trade shop, a café and a bookshop. Featured against its Princes Street wall is a changing procession of murals highlighting issues of concern. 'What is Europe good for?' asked one, and 'Some pigs are more equal than others'. Another featured a small red-clad figure in front of a row of tanks. It is dated 2008, 20 years after the tragedy of Tiananmen Square. Today's mural draws attention to those seeking refuge in Europe from North Africa and the Middle East.

Congregations in the 19th century were competitive. Did the 19th-century congregation of St John's exchange greetings with those attending services in the church next door? I like to imagine the citizens of Edinburgh in their Sunday clothes making their segregated journeys to worship, from the New Town, or down Lothian Road, or from the west where the city was expanding past Haymarket and Roseburn to the village of Corstorphine. I like to think that they acknowledged each other politely if not with friendliness. Now the two churches are united, along with St Andrew's and St George's in George Street, as Edinburgh City Centre Churches Together.

I leave Princes Street Gardens from the west gate. At the corner there is a cluster of slender birch trees, their leaves beginning to turn yellow, and a sprinkling of pale purple autumn crocuses. In the southwest corner of the Gardens more birches were planted as a memorial to Robert Louis Stevenson. Here near the gate there is also a pile of empty McEwan's Export cans on an otherwise unoccupied bench.

RL Stevenson memorial, Princes Street Gardens. Rachel Calder.

I walk up Lothian Road. The red sandstone Caledonian Hotel is a reminder that there was once a railway station at the west end of Princes Street – the Caley was built as a railway hotel at the turn of the 19th century, on top of a rebuilt railway station, the original dating from 1848. Lothian Road was a favourite haunt of Stevenson, who was a small child when St John's Church was receiving its new stained glass windows. (Stevenson's parents, staunch Presbyterians, probably never set foot in St John's.) In a letter written from the other side of the Atlantic RLS evokes the youthful excitement of what was then an insalubrious thoroughfare: 'the Lothian Road was grand fun too; I could take an afternoon of it with great delight'. This was a couple of decades before the Usher Hall introduced a rather more elevated tone and a century before the building of hotels and banks and insurance offices partially changed the street's character. But there is still something louche about Lothian Road, not dispelled by the rather sterile Festival Square and the new commercial buildings around and behind it, existing, in Ian Rankin's words, 'only to serve themselves' and 'as if humans had been dropped from the planning equation'. I have often found it menacing and have dodged gangs of youth noisy with what seems a marauding aggression. At other times it is bleak, with wind-blown litter drifting in the gutters and expensive cars parked on double yellow lines.

I turn away from Lothian Road to walk along King's Stables Road at the back of the castle. Once 'the jousting-ground of jealous nobles', it is now a sombre, cavernous street, with the castle towering oppressively on the left and a multi-storey car park incongruously on the right. If on the north side the castle is tamed by the carefully tended gardens with its flowers and memorials, on this south side the castle on its rock is uncompromising and sometimes ominous. This is where St Ives made his descent. Even when the sun is shining, there is a darkness, and the bridge which carries Castle Terrace above King's Stables Road further darkens the street. You wouldn't choose to walk along King's Stables Road unless it's the quickest route to where you want to go. I want to go to the Grassmarket, which is where it takes me.

I re-enter the old burgh limits, but not by the old route in from the west. That would have taken me through the West Port at the southwest corner, the gate through which *The Heart of Midlothian*'s Reuben Butler is attempting to leave when he is hijacked by the Porteous protesters. I am back at the scene of executions. But the Grassmarket now is quite a jolly area. It is lined with places to eat and drink, and sometimes there is an outdoor market, reviving its old function. And there is Dance Base, Scotland's national centre for dance, a lovely building combining, in a design by Malcolm Fraser, the old and the new. You have to go inside to appreciate its sympathetic blend of built and natural features.

A little further on from Dance Base is Castle Wynd. Back in the early 1960s there was a decaying building near the corner in which my brother Alan had a ground floor flat and studio. It was dark and damp and mysterious, and long since demolished. That was where he developed and printed the pictures in this book. The climb up Castle Wynd has lost some of its forbidding character but nostalgia lingers mingled with sadness, as

Castle Wynd. Alan Daiches. Courtesy National Library of Scotland.

Alan died in 2006 and I miss him greatly. His pictures bring back the time when I was making my first adult explorations of the city. Today, I don't sense Norman MacCaig's 'dangerous shadows... heavy with centuries' as I once did, but nevertheless I am feeling rather sombre as I make my way up to Johnston Terrace and on to Castlehill. I have come full circle. Edinburgh offers many possibilities of making circles in time and space.

An Old Town close. Alan Daiches. Courtesy National Library of Scotland.

3

That ridged and chimneyed bulk of blackness

*That ridged and chimneyed bulk of blackness, with splendour bursting*
*out of every pore, is the wonderful Old Town.*
Alexander Smith, *A Summer in Skye*, 1865

*Listen hard enough, you'll hear the double-handed hack of claymores*
Ron Butlin, 'Afternoon in a café on the Royal Mile'

WHEN THE TOLBOOTH was constructed the town of Edinburgh was crowded but thriving. A late 16th-century description pictures a 'high-crested' city 'adorned with many noblemen's towers'. From the palace of Holyrood in the east 'the city rises higher and higher towards the west, and consists especially of one broad and very fair street'. It adds that the 'side streets and allies' are 'of poor building and inhabited with very poor people'. The poor, however, and the realities of crowded living, were not confined to the wynds and closes.

When English writer Daniel Defoe visited Edinburgh early in the 18th century, he commented that there was no other city in the world where 'so many people live in so little room'. The tall tenements that lined the High Street were crammed with humanity, and the High Street itself was no longer, if it ever had been, a 'broad and very fair street'. It was narrow and filthy, with the tall buildings robbing it of light and trapping the stench of the middens piled outside front doors. There were many who admired Edinburgh's lofty situation and numerous handsome buildings, but the most consistent theme of comment from those who visited the city was the smell. It is hard to believe that any city in the centuries before modern sanitation was particularly sweet-smelling, but Edinburgh seemed to have a quality all its own. 'I never came to my own lodgings in Edinburgh,' said one 17th-century traveller, 'or went out, but I was constrained to hold my nose.'

It was partly the city's situation that was responsible. Clustered on its narrow rocky spine it could not expand northwards: the precipitate drop and the North Loch prevented it. To the east was the King's Park and Arthur's Seat. Only to the south, and then a creep westwards round the back of the castle, did the city slowly extend. Because there was little room for expansion the buildings grew upwards, and the concentration of humanity became denser. The richer you were the further you wanted to be from the stench and jostle of the street, yet too high and the labour of carrying water – in limited supply – and fuel up multiple stairs became arduous. So the wealthier residents tended to occupy the centre of the tenements, with tradesmen and craftsmen at street level and the very poor at the very top. But wherever you were, you could hardly be unaware of the beggars outside your window, street sellers, unruly prentice boys, perhaps, causing some disturbance, the clatter of horses' hoofs on the cobbles, or feuding families paying off old scores in the darkness of the wynds. The elegance of its finer buildings was constantly under threat.

There were efforts at improvement. Mary, Queen of Scots, and later her son, James made attempts to clean up the town, to combat filth of both a physical and moral nature. A string of edicts was issued, aimed against 'whoremasters, harlots, fornicators, vicious persons and idolators'. In spite of an order of 1562 recommending ducking in the Nor'Loch as punishment for such heated offences, this did not seem to have a cooling effect, for later that same year the Town Council was complaining that 'the abhominabill viceis of adulterie and fornifications daylie increscit within this burgh for laik of punishment'. Attempts to legislate against these and other leisure activities were, not surprisingly, unsuccessful. Twenty-five years later the Council was still trying, this time hoping to banish from the town minstrels, pipers, fiddlers and singers of 'filthy songs'.

This may look like a rearguard action against a continual orgy of fiddling and fornication, but there were some real improvements. By the end of the 16th century Edinburgh had several newly founded schools as well as the university, and until James VI's departure in 1603 the court was a hub of sophisticated music and poetry. When the court moved south, it took much of this cultural richness with it, and it would be more than a century before Edinburgh was re-established as a centre of learning and the arts. But before he left, James continued his mother's attempts to clean up the city, with a particular interest in the elimination of witchcraft. His enthusiastic encouragement, backed by the clergy, led to numerous self-confessed witches – confessions extracted often with the help of torture – being burned alive on Castlehill. It must have added another note to the stench of the city. The practice persisted until the 1670s.

In spite of a promise to return to Scotland every three years, James came back only once. The distance, of course, was great, in miles, time and culture. It may seem that four centuries later the distance has not greatly contracted; perhaps in some ways it has increased. On my occasional visits to London I feel very much a stranger, although I lived there for five years in the 1960s. The transplant of the heart of Scotland's cultural life left Edinburgh diminished, and the efforts to improve the town's aspect and amenities could not compensate. The new parliament building, completed in 1640, was part of that effort, although not a Town Council initiative. Intended to house both parliament and the law courts, it almost immediately ran out of space. It was added to and reorganised numerous times over the next two centuries as needs evolved and activity increased.

The statue of Charles II in Parliament Square is a reminder of the Stewart connection. In 1633, Charles was crowned in Edinburgh but thereafter, like his father, took little interest in Scotland. The splendid mounted figure is a few metres from where he was crowned in St Giles, and a few metres from the spot where the Earl of Argyll, who had set the crown on Charles's head, was executed. The statue was erected in 1685, the year that Charles died. It is described as life-sized, but on its raised plinth it looks massive and heroic, presumably the intended impression. But its site invites speculation. With the cathedral bulking huge on one side and the parliament building on the other, the monarch, in spite of his bold and elevated stance, seems challenged by both church and state. John Knox is buried nearby. Charles II, as Flora Grierson commented, 'tramples the grave of John Knox', but in many respects Knox survives more durably than the king.

Around the corner from Charles II is the Mercat Cross, a late 19th century reworking and repositioning of the original market cross where tradesmen and weel kent figures regularly congregated to do business and exchange views. (The earlier site is nearby, marked by an octagon set into the pavement.) Tobias Smollett in his novel *Humphrey Clinker* (1771) describes the men of business 'and even the genteel company' standing about the cross 'in crowds every day, from one to two in the afternoon in the open street'. But in former years it had been the scene of punishment and execution. In 1584 a baker's apprentice called Robert Henderson was accused of setting fire to his father's house and burnt alive at the Mercat Cross. He was one of many to suffer a hideous demise on that spot.

Close to the Mercat Cross, appropriately though I suspect not much noticed, is the figure of firemaster James Braidwood, a sculpture by Kenneth Mackay. At the age of 24 Braidwood became Edinburgh's Master of Fire Engines, and shortly after had to deal with a major conflagration, the High Street's 'great fire' of 1824. This led him to pioneer the training of fire fighters and develop Edinburgh's first professional fire service. In

1833 he moved to London, to become Master of the London Fire Engine Establishment. His warning that a warehouse near London Bridge was a fire hazard was ignored. As he predicted, there was a fire, which burned for two weeks and caused a huge amount of damage. While fighting it, he was killed by a collapsing wall. Braidwood is commemorated in London as well as in Edinburgh.

Improvements to the city continued through the 17th century. There was considerable rebuilding in the High Street, which brought the disappearance of most of the buildings' timber fronts, which were both obstructive and a fire risk. In the Lawnmarket, a few minutes stroll from Charles II, is a house, built before work on the new parliament buildings was begun, which is a reminder of Edinburgh's role as a centre of trade and commerce. The merchant Thomas Gledstanes was a burgess of Edinburgh, a role that conferred considerable status, privilege and power. He traded in an eclectic range of goods: prunes, iron, pots, honey and vinegar are among the commodities listed in the Leith Customs Books. In 1617 he and his wife Bessie Cunningham commissioned the building of a new house in the Lawnmarket, and over the next couple of decades added to and improved it. Although Thomas's enterprises did not always run smoothly – in 1627 he lost a cargo to pirates and financial pressures forced him to borrow money and sell some of his land – he clearly did not stint on the furbishment of his house, now restored to its 17th-century character by the National Trust for Scotland. Step inside, and there's a suggestion of both comfort and elegance, but also of refuge. On the second floor there is a ceiling painted in rich, warm colours which reinforces a sense of distance from the unsavoury world of commercial transaction and crowded humanity. What the restored interior can't convey is the turmoil of the street outside, the sounds and smells, the sense that the life on which the Gledstanes' fortunes depended teemed on the doorstep. The tourists who now crowd the pavement outside Gladstone's Land, as the house is called, are far too clean to serve as reminders of the 17th century.

And then in 1674 the city acquired a piped water supply. The water was brought from Comiston, to the southwest of the city, piped to a reservoir on Castlehill, and from there to five public wells. It was still hard work for those who lived maybe ten storeys from street level to supply themselves with water, and it was understandable that it was used somewhat sparingly. There were efforts to clean up the streets, and some public street lighting

Gladstonesland. Rachel Calder.

was introduced. In spite of these improvements, in the early 18th century Edinburgh was still a city of 'stench and nastiness'.

Here is Daniel Defoe again. At the time of his visit in 1706 he had published satirical pamphlets which had got him into trouble, but was not yet known as the author of *Robinson Crusoe* (1719). He found Edinburgh's citizens living under considerable inconvenience:

> The city suffers infinite Disadvantages, and lies under such scandalous Inconveniences as are, by its Enemies, made a subject of scorn and reproach; as if People were not as willing to live sweet and clean as other Nations, but delighted in stench and nastiness: whereas, were any other people to live under... a rocky and mountainous situation, throng'd buildings, from seven to 12 story high, a Scarcity of Water, and that little they had difficult to be had, and to the uppermost lodgings far to fetch: we should find a London, or a Bristol as dirty as Edinburgh, and perhaps less able to make their Dwellings tolerable.

Defoe suggests that people crammed into tall buildings crammed onto a narrow spine of rock have little chance of living 'sweet and clean'. More than half a century later poet Robert Fergusson found Edinburgh's High Street not much changed. In his poem 'Auld Reekie' he celebrates the city's vigour and spirit, in which 'stench and nastiness' are an inseparable part. He describes the flirtations of housemaids, the arguments of neighbours at their front doors, shoppers braving the filthy gutters and fending off the smells with Gillespie's Snuff (we'll meet Gillespie again), the underworld of thieves and prostitutes, and Sundays when people 'change their faces wi' their clo'es'. And most of all, perhaps, he highlights the resort to alcohol when evening ended the day's work.

> Now some to porter, some to Punch,
> Some to their Wife, and some their Wench,
> Retire, while noisy Ten-hour Drum
> Gars a' your Trades gae dandring home.
> Now many a club, jocose and free,
> Gie a' to Merriment and Glee,
> Wi' Sang and Glass, they fley the Pow'r
> O' Care that wad harass the Hour:
> For Wine and Bacchus still bear down
> Our thrawart Fortunes wildest frown:
> It maks you stark, and bauld and brave,
> Ev'n when descending to the Grave.

Alcohol, and particularly claret, fuelled Edinburgh's professional life, and not just in the evenings. 'To get drunk in a tavern,' wrote Cockburn, 'seemed to be considered as a natural, if not an intended consequence of going to one.' Alcohol was the accepted accompaniment to business as well as pleasure, and much of Edinburgh's business was conducted in the numerous taverns as space was at a premium. The streets also saw much commerce. Merchants and customers haggled in the markets and the Luckenbooths, the stalls set up in the St Giles area selling a wide variety of goods. Making money was a public activity.

A favourite haunt of lawyers and literary types was Luckie Middlemist's oyster cellar in the Cowgate, a 'steaming, crowded, low-roofed room poorly illuminated by a scattering of tallow candles,' as imagined by James

Old Town tenements. Alan Daiches. Courtesy National Library of Scotland.

Robertson in his novel *Joseph Knight* (2003). Robertson brings together three historically prominent lawyers, John Maclaurin of Dreghorn, James Boswell, best known for his travels with and biography of Samuel Johnson, and Allan Maconochie, who would later become professor of law at the university and Lord Meadowbank. The year is 1773, the year of Boswell's 'Highland adventure' with Dr Johnson. Boswell, accustomed to London society, is not entirely comfortable in these 'uncouth' surroundings, yet loves 'the charged atmosphere that might explode at any moment'. Maclaurin quotes Fergusson, with enthusiastic approval.

Robert Fergusson himself had an early descent to the grave. He died in 1774 at the age of 24, after a period of incarceration in Edinburgh's Bedlam, the city's madhouse situated at the west end of what is now Chambers Street. It was an ending that was hardly 'bauld and brave'. His was a brilliance that ended in darkness, and he is one of a large cast of characters that throws into relief Edinburgh's contradictions. The 'jocose and free' relaxation offered by the taverns was only a step away from the gutter, or worse. Fergusson's expression of the complex intertwined layers of mid-18th-century Edinburgh life had a profound influence on Robert Burns, who arrived in the city for the first time in 1786, and on Robert Louis Stevenson of a later generation. The compounded influence of these three writers can be detected in most fictional representations of the city in the 20th and 21st centuries. When Norman MacCaig wrote of Edinburgh's High Street that 'old history greets you with a Bedlam stare' he clearly had Fergusson in mind. More recently, one writer who strikingly explores the tangled relationship between the layered respectability and criminality of the city is Ian Rankin. His Detective Inspector John Rebus has at least one foot in the gutter, and, though born and raised in Fife, owes his creation to Edinburgh and the writers who mined its contradictions before Rankin explored its underworld.

It is February, and Diana, my friend of six decades, is spending a few days with me in South Queensferry. We take the train from Dalmeny into Waverley Station. Diana arrived by train the day before, travelling from Cornwall, with 29 stops and one change, at Edinburgh's Haymarket Station. An epic journey, from England's southern tip – and beyond that from Vancouver – to Scotland's capital. We pause in Waverley's roofed concourse. I still have the vestige of a memory of awe when I first arrived in Edinburgh at the age of four. I had travelled on the train from London, and to London by sea from Washington, D.C.

It's good to see that the station's debt to Walter Scott is acknowledged, at least for now, with his words featured at strategic points. Not many people pause to read them, but perhaps that doesn't matter. They are at least a reminder that Scott is more than his monument in Princes Street. He is books, he is words, he is an incomparable chronicling of Scotland's past. Edinburgh has done much in recent years to celebrate the city's extraordinary literary achievement. When the Victorians instigated the Scott monument they no doubt felt that there was no need to encourage readers to engage with the master's work. But now it is necessary; all power to Edinburgh UNESCO City of Literature.

I want to introduce Diana to the Scottish Parliament. We take the escalator to the station's upper level and leave at the Market Street exit. We turn towards Jeffrey Street. It is a dreary stretch, with a backyard feeling, but we're soon on the High Street, the Royal Mile, and walking down the Canongate towards Holyrood. 'A queerlike canyon is the Canongate,' wrote Sydney Goodsir Smith,

> That murmurs yet wi the names
> O' lang deid bards

And at every hand we pass reminders of Edinburgh as a city of writers. There is the Storytelling Centre, hard against John Knox's house (in which he stayed only briefly). They share an entrance and a shop. I like the conjunction – Knox had a powerful story to tell. On the south side of the Royal Mile is Tweeddale Court, the first home of the Scottish Poetry Library. Tweeddale House started life as the 16th-century home of Neil Laing and his wife Elizabeth Danielstoune. It fell into disrepair, but was reconstructed by John and Robert Adam in the middle of the 18th century. Then in 1791 it became the head office of the British Linen Bank. Was it here that *Kidnapped*'s David Balfour collected his inheritance? He wanders down the High Street, quite overwhelmed by the tall buildings, 'the narrow arched entries that continually vomited passengers, the wares of the merchants in their windows, the hubbub and endless stir, the foul smells and the fine clothes' until 'the hand of Providence brought me in my drifting to the very doors of the British Linen Company's bank'. The bank in turn became Oliver & Boyd, printers and publishers, and is now the home of Canongate

Publishing and the Saltire Society. For a while the City of Literature had an office in the basement. I wonder if the custodians of Scottish culture and of Edinburgh's literary past and present relish the connection with banking.

The Scottish Poetry Library rapidly outgrew its cramped but congenial quarters in Tweeddale Court, and after 15 years it was able to move down the High Street to a new building in Crichton's Close, designed by Malcolm Fraser. And on the other side of the High Street there is poet Robert Fergusson striding vigorously in bronze away from his grave in Canongate Kirkyard. He was never going to stay put, as James Robertson suggests:

> Ye're stridin doon the Canongate, brent new
> And lookin like ye've never been awa.

We've met Robert Fergusson already. You can't reimagine Edinburgh's Old Town before the New without his aid.

Diana and I continue our walk, brisk-ish but not striding. This is the Canongate, once a street of mansions occupied by aristocracy and people of influence, 'eminent men' in the words of Robert Chambers. The Canongate tollbooth, which now houses The People's Story exhibition, is a reminder that the Canongate was once a separate burgh. The houses had elegant gardens stretching down to the Cowgate, but at the time of Chambers' writing – his *Traditions of Edinburgh* was first published in 1824 – the Canongate was 'wretchedly squalid', the street 'encumbered' by 'herds of the idle and the wretched'. Today there is no one obviously idle or wretched, although we are accosted by a youngish man who complains that we are not walking single file along the uncrowded pavement.

Ahead of us is Holyroodhouse, the palace at the foot of the Royal Mile and still a royal residence although over the centuries it has been the victim of both neglect and attack. Holyrood began as the site of an abbey, founded by David I in the 12th century. The story is that while hunting in what was then the royal forest of Drumsheugh he was thrown from his horse and attacked by a 'muckle white hart'. He was saved by the miraculous appearance of a crucifix – the holy rood – in his hands and endowed the monastery in gratitude.

Gradually the place evolved as a royal residence, more comfortable than the castle but also more exposed, as it lay outwith the city walls. Successive Jameses added rooms and embellishments, but, particularly during the

English invasions of 1544 and 1547, Holyrood was severely damaged. The remnants of the abbey survive. Mary, Queen of Scot's father James V added a new façade and grander apartments, and Mary herself repaired the buildings and made Holyrood her main Scottish residence. It was, famously, the scene of the murder of her favourite David Rizzio. Susan Ferrier in her novel *Marriage* (1818) has her heroine submit to 'the picturesque pageantry' of Edinburgh and Holyrood. Shown the floor purported to be still stained with Rizzio's blood, 'she readily yielded her assent to the asseverations of her guide, as to its being the *bona fide* blood of David Rizzio, which for nearly three hundred years had resisted all human efforts to efface it'.

But Mary's son James VI abandoned Holyrood, Edinburgh and Scotland, and the palace fell into decay. It was rebuilt in 1665 by Sir William Bruce for the viceroy of Scotland, the Duke of Lauderdale, and brought to life briefly when Charles Edward Stewart occupied it during his weeks in Edinburgh. It was a false dawn. Tobias Smollett in *Humphry Clinker* describes Holyrood as 'an elegant piece of architecture, but sunk in an obscure, and, as I take it, unwholesome bottom, where one would imagine it had been placed on purpose to be concealed'. When John Wesley visited in 1827 he found that the 'stately rooms are dirty as stables; the colours of the tapestry are quite faded; several of the pictures are cut and defaced'. Stevenson half a century later saw Holyrood standing 'grey and silent in a workmen's quarter and among breweries and gasworks'. John Geddie at the end of the century is similarly unimpressed. 'It is very like a building for some natural establishment, a hospital for soldiers or sailors,' he wrote. 'On two sides of it the squalour and the noisy industries of a poor quarter of the city press close up against the walls'. He does point out that on the other side 'are free air and the everlasting hills'. Chiang Yee remarked on the 'gloomy atmosphere' of Holyrood. But Stevenson reminds us that 'wars have been plotted, dancing has lasted deep into the night, murder has been done in its chambers'. The squalour has gone, but there is still a touch of gloom, and a dreariness about the east end of the Royal Mile which the new Scottish Parliament doesn't entirely dispel.

Diana and I skirt the flank of the Parliament and pause over the quotations featured on samples of Scottish stone: marble from Iona and Glen Tilt, sandstone from Shetland, Aberdour and Dumfries and Galloway, granite from Aberdeenshire, Lewissian gneiss, Easedale slate. Diana is impressed, and points out that there is plenty of space for more, although

Scottish Parliament. Rachel Calder.

there are only two samples that have no text. I hope they are being reserved for the words of women. Of the 26 quotations only one comes from a woman's pen, unless – not impossible? –some of the psalms were written by a woman.

The cumulative effect of the words and the stones they are written on resonates with a sense of place, of Scotland from Shetland to Galloway and of Edinburgh in particular. 'Who possesses this landscape?' asks Norman MacCaig, but then concludes that it is a false question, for:

> This landscape is
> masterless
> and intractable in any terms
> that are human

James Robertson, in *Voyage of Intent* (2005), the collection of poems and essays he wrote during his period as the Scottish Parliament's first writer in residence, wrote:

> The Parliament will grow from Arthur's Seat,
> A bridge between the city and the rock,
> A mirror of the land it represents.

Edinburgh is a city of hills and declivities, of sudden heights and abrupt descents. 'Most of her roads rush headlong downhill like salmon rivers,' wrote James Bone in 1926. Bridges are a crucial feature of what holds the city together, and the intimacy with rocks is everywhere. Enric Miralles, the building's architect, wanted the parliament to grow out of the land. It also grows out of the nation's history. It is built of granite, oak and steel, three iconic materials which themselves are the foundations of many different stories of Scotland's past. There is still plenty granite and oak trees are common. Steel is another story, which may have entered its closing chapter.

At the foot of the Canongate, with the entrance to Holyrood Palace in front of us, we turn the corner, and Diana exclaims again, this time at the proximity of Salisbury Crags, sharply outlined against a blue sky and seeming just a stone's throw from parliament, with Arthur's Seat beyond. And then we discover that today the building is closed. Parliament is in recess. We cannot wander in, as I had assured her we could. A year earlier I, my partner, my eight-year-old grandson and the dog, had climbed Arthur's Seat on a day of sunshine and wild wind. After our descent, in need of shelter and refreshment, we presented ourselves at the parliament's door (the dog abandoned, resigned in the car). No one protested at our muddy boots, scruffy jeans and windblown hair, and we sat in the café enjoying coffee and buns. Kristian, my grandson, lives near Cardiff. They have a fine and welcoming assembly building there, the Senedd, close to the water but a long way from hills.

But on this day disappointment for me and Diana. We walk far enough on to look back at the building. The scale has always seemed to me just right, commanding enough to take its place in the landscape yet not dwarfing its immediate neighbours. It's a richly textured building, reflecting both the city and the nation, with a hint of defiance, a hint of contention, a hint of fitfulness, of Hugh MacDiarmid's 'mad god's dream' and 'passionate imaginings'. MacDiarmid's words describing Edinburgh are there on the wall. And with that assemblage of words and landscape there is a real sense that the parliament building is a place for all of Scotland's people. It is an appropriate riposte to Holyroodhouse, which has always seemed to me without distinctive character. For James Robertson, the parliament is 'a fleet of boats against the sky', 'a bold flotilla... all cabins, crow-stepped fo'c'sles, sterns and prows', and he imagines the members of the Scottish Parliament within, dreaming in their 'port-holed pods', 'charting new routes for health or schools or work'. Is there anyone at home today? Does the work of government continue as the nation's representatives gaze out at the crags sharp against the bright sky?

We turn and stroll back to the High Street, and Diana comments that the space between parliament and Holyrood Park is perfect for demonstrations. We're old hands at demos, Diana and I. We once spent a night in a London jail for our pains, sleeping on a concrete floor in an overcrowded cell. In the morning we were each handed a mug of tea and a ham sandwich.

We retrace our steps up the Canongate and reach the rather grim entrance to Moray House, a 17th-century building much added to, and since 1835, a teachers' training college now part of the University of Edinburgh. Like so much of this part of Edinburgh, it is a strange mix of the domestic and the institutional, the stone evocative of past activity but the kind of life it once contained long gone. Robert Fergusson, still striding, again reminds us of what has been lost.

Canongate Kirk is a handsome building with a large circular window and two arched windows looking out over the High Street. It opened for business in 1691, when it became the parish church for the burgh of Canongate after the local community no longer had access to the former parish church in Holyrood Abbey. In 1687 James VII had ordered that the Abbey nave be converted into a chapel for the Order of the Thistle. The exclusion may have been resented at the time, but the result was a fine church which was perhaps hedging its bets in terms of future forms of worship. The authors of the Edinburgh volume of *The Buildings of Scotland* speculate that as 'the chancel and transept make no sense in the context of reformed worship' that perhaps the layout was 'a deliberate attempt to build a church adaptable for Roman Catholic practice'. That would have pleased James VII. The Stewart monarchs' continuing resistance to the reformed church would have a profound impact on events in Scotland in the coming century. Among the many monuments in the kirkyard is Fergusson's gravestone, not set up at the time of his miserable death in 1774 in the Edinburgh Bedlam, but added by Robert Burns 15 years later and presenting this inscription:

> No sculptur'd Marble here nor pompous lay
> No storied Urn nor animated Bust
> This simple Stone directs Pale Scotia's way
> To pour her sorrows o'er her poet's Dust.

Burns made it clear that it was Fergusson's poetry that gave him the confidence to continue with his own. He also wrote less conventional and more heartfelt lines condemning neglect of the poet's legacy:

> Curse an ungrateful man that can be pleased
> And yet can starve the author of the pleasure!
> O thou my elder brother in misfortune,
> By far my elder brother in the muses,
> With tears I pity thy unhappy fate!
> Why is the bard unpitied by the world,
> Yet has so keen a relish of its pleasures?

A hundred years after the birth of Fergusson a third poetic Robert was born in Edinburgh. Robert Louis Stevenson acknowledged his debt to the first two Roberts and was scathing at the way adulation of Burns had suppressed 'all mention of the lad who handed to him the poetic impulse'. Stevenson felt a close affinity with Fergusson, 'so clever a boy, so wild, of such a mixed strain, so unfortunate, born in the same town with me... so like myself'. Towards the end of his life, Stevenson wrote from Samoa to his friend Charles Baxter in Edinburgh, suggesting that the neglected monument to Fergusson might be improved. It was duly accomplished, with words added from RLS. 'This stone, originally erected by Robert Burns, has been repaired at the charges of Robert Louis Stevenson and is by him rededicated to the memory of Robert Fergusson as the gift of one Edinburgh lad to another.' The bronze Fergusson is walking away from this triple monument, but a pause in the kirkyard is a reminder of three towering literary figures whose words still convey the vigorous beat of Edinburgh's pulse, a beat echoed in a melancholy tone by the 20th-century poet Robert Garioch reflecting on death.

> Canongate kirkyaird in the falling year
> is auld and grey, the wee roseirs are bare

He stands

> bareheidit in the haar,
> murnin a man that gaed back til the pool
> twa-hunner years afore our time.

In *The Prime of Miss Jean Brodie* (1961), Miss Brodie takes her girls on a walk 'through the old parts of Edinburgh'. It is the 1930s, and the 'reeking network of slums... a misty region of crime and desperation' was unknown territory to the respectable schoolgirls. For one of them, Sandy, it was her 'first experience of a foreign country'. There are women in shawls, children without shoes, and boys who 'shouted after Miss Brodie's violet-clad company, with words the girls had not heard before, but rightly understood to be obscene'. Sandy reflects on Edinburgh's double life. Miss Brodie herself is, it seems, a descendent of Deacon Brodie, who combined daytime respectability as a tradesman and night time lawbreaking. Brody, central character in the television series *Homeland*, also leads a double life. And did Kate Atkinson, the creator of Jackson Brodie, the detective who appears in several of her novels, intend a reference to the deacon?

Eric Linklater also writes of the Old Town in the 1930s. The High Street houses seem 'fiercer than shop-keeping bricks and mortar, and those who inhabit them, breathing the spirit of their greatness, have more vitality than their respectable neighbours'. Miss Brodie, keen in her own contradictory way to cut through preconceptions though wrapped in preconception herself, might have agreed. Linklater goes on to compare the Old Town tenements with an aristocracy:

> debauched and ruined... sprawling in rags and dirt where once it flaunted itself in threadbare finery and three-piled pride, and lived in the high perfume of insolence and treachery and blood.

And Norman MacCaig on a November night sees the darkness swirling with tenements, while

> brown air fumes at the shop windows,
> Tries the doors, and sidles past.

Diana and I need a pause for refreshment, so go into the Storytelling Centre for coffee and apricot cake. The Centre's shared premises with John Knox's House is perhaps another tribute to doubleness – Knox would have taken a poor view of some of the stories told there. The launch in March 2016 of the University of Edinburgh's 'Year of Dangerous Women' would have brought thunderous fulminations – Knox had much to say about women he believed dangerous. Yet he himself was an influential story teller. Tucked away behind the Centre, through the narrow entry of Trunk's Close, is the home of the Scottish Book Trust, a charity that promotes reading and writing and a powerhouse of encouragement, advice and support for literary activity. I have spent a lot of time there.

We continue on our literary way, making for Blackwell's, the bookshop that many remember as Thin's. I was very young when I heard of it first – it was a favourite haunt of my parents when they were students. Diana comments on the shabbiness of South Bridge. Has it gone downhill? But I have no memory of it being without an aspect of decay and litter drifting in the street. In Ian Rankin's *The Falls* (2001) his character Jean Burchill walks down the Bridges, 'all cheap clothes shops and take aways, with queues of buses and lorries waiting to crawl through the traffic lights at the Tron Kirk'. There are beggars in doorways 'staring at the passing parade of feet.' The 19 original arches of South Bridge – now only the arch crossing the Cowgate remains open – were constructed to cross the chasm below. Looking down now there is little of interest to see, traffic but few pedestrians, more than a century ago Stevenson commented that to look down from South Bridge into the Cowgate 'full of crying hawkers, is to view one rank of society from another in the twinkling of an eye'. That elevation, built in the 1780s, is for Stevenson more of a division than a link.

A dozen years or so earlier Alexander Smith had made a similar comment. The inhabitants of the Cowgate, he wrote, 'are morally and geographically the lower orders. They keep to their own quarters, and seldom come up to the light of day. Many an Edinburgh man has never set foot in the street; the condition of the inhabitants is as little known to respectable Edinburgh as are the habits of moles, earthworms, and the mining population.' Stevenson, though, was fascinated by the life of 'the lower orders', and made a point of trying to connect with them. In the 1840s and '50s Thomas Guthrie was at work founding ragged schools for poor children. 'Circumstances make people what they are much more than many suppose,' he wrote. 'There is not a wretched child in this town but if my children had been born and bred up in its unhappy circumstances they might have been as bad.' A painting by James Edgar in the Scottish National Portrait Gallery shows barefoot children gazing hopefully up at the top-hatted Guthrie, whose left hand rests on an urchin's head.

At around the time Stevenson was making his youthful explorations,

Isabella Bird was engaged in reporting on Edinburgh's slums. The title of her publication, *Notes on Old Edinburgh* (1868), suggests something innocently picturesque. The contents are quite the reverse. What she found as she penetrated the High Street closes were 'strata of misery and moral degradation under the shadow of St Giles's crown and within sight of Knox's house, more concentrated and unbroken than are to be met with elsewhere'. She encountered families crowded into dark, filthy, stinking holes, often sharing space with the sick and the dying.

> It was not possible to believe that the most grinding greed could extort money from human beings for the tenancy of such dens as those to which this passage led. They were lairs into which a starving dog might creep to die, but nothing more.

Bird called for the provision of 'houses to dwell in, not dens to rot and perish in, morally and physically. Blissful ignorance of the abyss of preventable misery which exists in Edinburgh is impossible now.' Her words have a 21st-century relevance.

> It is one thing to hear unpleasant facts stated by unwelcome speakers, or to meet with them fossilised in statistical tables, but altogether another to confront them in beings clothed in kindred flesh and blood, in men, women, and children claiming a common Fatherhood, and asserting their right to be heard. These our brethren, haggard, hopeless, hardened, vicious, on whose faces sin has graved deeper lines than either sorrow or poverty; this old age which is not venerable, this infancy which is not loveable, these childish faces, or faces which should have been childish, peering from amidst elvish locks, and telling of a precocious familiarity with sin, these glowering upon us from the tottering West Bow, with its patched and dirty windows, from the still picturesque Lawnmarket, from the many-storeyed houses of the High Street, these are spectres not easily to be laid to rest, and 'polite society', which has become perfect in the polite art of indifference, must encounter them, sooner or later, in one way or another.

More than half a century later Alastair Alpin MacGregor is still finding the Cowgate dangerous territory, 'a quarter into which, unarmed or unguarded, only the most intrepid ventured'. Its inhabitants are 'a sorry representation of human kind, scrambling into, and oozing out of, public-houses, lodging-houses, or missions, sinning and sorrowing through most of their earthly sojourn'. Muriel Spark in *Curriculum Vitae* (1992) reflects on the poverty and the 'social nervousness' she was aware of growing up in Edinburgh in the 1930s, dole queues, ill-nourished barefoot children contrasting with equally evident privilege. More recent writers, Ian Rankin and Quentin Jardine among them, remind us that sin and sorrow in Edinburgh are not hard to seek.

We buy books in Blackwell's, just around the corner from Rutherford's, a favourite haunt of Stevenson's, and make our way back to the High Street and up to Lady Stair's Close and Makars' Court, where stone underfoot rings with the words of many of Scotland's most memorable writers. They complement and amplify the words we have been reading on the walls of the Scottish Parliament. Here is Fergusson again:

> Auld Reikie, wale o ilka town
> That Scotland kens beneath the moon

And Stevenson:

> … there are no stars so lovely as Edinburgh street-lamps. When I forget thee, Auld Reekie, may my right hand forget its cunning!

And Nigel Tranter, whose historical fiction has introduced so many readers to Scotland's past:

> You intend to bide here? To be sure. Can you think of anywhere better?

Read them all and you absorb a portrait of Scotland, in the rich and vibrant colours of Gaelic, Scots and English.

My father's words are also there: 'Bridge-building is my vocation.' I like the fact that he was building intellectual bridges in a city of stone bridges, and that he is remembered at the doorstep of the Writers' Museum, which occupies Lady Stair's House. It houses material relating to Burns, Scott and Stevenson, all writers he advocated and explained at a time when particularly the latter two were often overlooked. William Power in his book *Literature and Oat-*

*meal* (1935) suggested that the Royal Mile could become a 'living museum' inhabited by writers and artists, although it seems unlikely that they would have taken kindly to being on display. Certainly, the Writers' Museum is predominantly concerned with what has gone before, though it does feature temporary exhibitions on current writers and writing.

Lady Stair's House dates from the 17th century, and though an appropriate home for these three great writers it is not ideal as a museum. The house was originally built for Sir William Gray of Pittendrum, an Edinburgh merchant, but takes its name from Elizabeth, Dowager Countess of Stair who acquired the house some years after the death of her husband in 1707. Her husband, Sir John Dalrymple, 1st Earl of Stair, was Lord Advocate and Secretary of

The Writers' Museum. Rachel Calder.

State, but is most remembered for his role in engineering the notorious Massacre of Glencoe of 1692. This proved only a temporary blot on his political career, and in 1703 he was created earl.

Although the Earl of Stair never lived in the house there is inevitably an association with the bloody incident, in which the Macdonalds of Glencoe, considered by government a troublesome clan, welcomed Campbell soldiers into their homes, only to be slaughtered by their guests. One way or another, in Edinburgh's High Street you're never far from blood; our three writers could not escape the echoes of violence. Stair itself is in Ayrshire, not far from Mauchline and Tarbolton, familiar to Burns. When you enter Lady Stair's House you climb a narrow spiral stair that at once suggests an opening to the past. Its transformation into a museum has not altered its character, which means there are problems of accessibility. These will never be solved. In 1895 the house was bought by the Earl of Rosebery, descended from the original owner, who renovated it and in 1907 gifted it to the city for use as a museum. Its use cannot be changed and the building cannot be radically altered.

However, its use can be extended. Since 2005, Scottish PEN, the Scottish centre of the writers' organisation PEN International, has had a tiny office in the building. I am very familiar with it as I have spent many hours working there. The small space pulses with Scotland's literary present, while within reach lies Scotland's literary past.

4

A very battlefield of old creeds and factions

John Knox, Assembly Hall courtyard. Rachel Calder.

*A very battlefield of old creeds and factions, strewn and heaped with the*
*corpses of those who… hated each other 'to the death'.*
John Geddie, *Romantic Edinburgh*

*the clamour of competing bells*
Alasdair Alpin MacGregor, *Auld Reekie*

AT THE TOP of Candlemaker Row, which curves steeply down to the Grassmarket, is a statue of a small dog. The statue, which originally included a drinking fountain for people as well as dogs, was erected in 1873 at the instigation and expense of Lady Angela Burdett-Coutts, the wealthy and philanthropic granddaughter of Thomas Coutts the banker. Thomas Coutts was the son of John Coutts, an Edinburgh merchant who in 1742 was elected lord provost of the city. This image of a Skye terrier, the creation of sculptor William Brodie, is probably the most photographed statue in Edinburgh. It is rare to pass it without getting in the way of an eager tourist with a camera.

The original terrier is buried in Greyfriars Kirkyard, close to the grave of his master John Gray, a farmer or a night watchman, or possibly a farmer who became a night watchman, who died in 1858. His dog Bobby kept faithful watch by his grave for 14 years, until his death in 1872. When the city made it obligatory for dogs to be licensed, the lord provost, William Chambers – Chambers Street is a few steps away – paid for Bobby's licence and provided him with a collar, which is now displayed in the Museum of Edinburgh. Greyfriars Bobby has become an icon of 'affectionate fidelity', as the statue's inscription says, celebrated in story and film. My own dog is somewhat bemused when I ask her to sit beside Bobby for a photo opportunity. I suspect her own fidelity would not last beyond the first passer-by who offered her a biscuit.

A few yards from Bobby is the gateway into Greyfriars Kirkyard. It may be a dog who draws visitors through the gate, but perhaps if they linger long enough the word 'fidelity' will come to have a different connotation. Not far from the graves of man and dog is the table tombstone of Boswell of Auchinleck, a convenient surface for the signing of the National Covenant in 1638, an act of protest against Charles I's attempts to impose royal authority on church and state in Scotland. The men of standing and influence assembled at Greyfriars Kirk were the first to put their names to the Covenant, but copies were carried all over the country to collect support for an insurgency that initiated decades of conflict. Fidelity to the cause of a Presbyterian Scotland, with church governance independent of the monarch, drove thousands to death in battle or execution, or into exile.

Calvinism had come to Scotland in the middle of the 16th century, brought from its home in Geneva by John Knox. Knox was a man of extraordinary determination and courage – 'the bravest of all Scotchmen' according to Thomas Carlyle – influenced by the radical reformer George Wishart, who in 1546 was convicted of heresy and burned at the stake in St Andrews. When, after years of exile including two years as a prisoner on a French gal-

Greyfriar's Bobby and the author's Labrador. Rachel Calder.

ley, Knox returned to Scotland in 1559 as minister of St Giles he quickly established a reputation as a powerful orator. With the Scottish Parliament's adoption of the reformed religion in 1560 a new kind of struggle entered Edinburgh's history. Religious strife would bring yet more violence to the city's streets.

The building known as John Knox's house commands a corner of the High Street, though he was probably there only briefly. A plaque in Warriston's Close further up the High Street tells us that he lived in the close from 1560 to 1566. He must have been a kenspeckle figure as he made his way the short distance to St Giles. His grave is beside St Giles, close to Charles II on his fine horse. I have an ambivalent relationship with cathedrals and all large spaces devoted to religious worship. Some I can admire, but I don't care for them very much. The very intention of creating a structure so far beyond a human scale makes me uncomfortable. Yet cities must have their imposing places of worship, and St Giles, cheek by jowl with the old Scottish parliament building and once with the Tolbooth, is impressive, not so much for its architecture as for its immersion in the past. Its interior, cleaned up and restored in recent years, is now lighter and brighter than the murky depths I remember from the past.

A bit of murk probably enhanced the impact of Knox's words powering from the pulpit. 'I assure you the voice of this one man, John Knox, is able in one hour to put more life in us than five hundred trumpets continually blustering in our ears.' This was Thomas Randolph, England's ambassador to Scotland, writing in 1561. Even as an old man, too weak to ascend the pulpit without help, Knox somehow summoned such vigour that, according to a contemporary observer, 'he was like to ding that pulpit in blads and flee out of it'. Trumpets, a shattered pulpit, a fierce, grey-bearded, keen-eyed figure towering over the congregation: Knox's legacy has cast a long shadow. Stevenson described him as having 'a grim reliance in himself, or rather in his mission', and that grimness colours all subsequent views of Calvinism. Muriel Spark in *The Prime of Miss Jean Brodie* described St Giles and the Tolbooth as 'emblems of a dark and terrible salvation which make the fires of the damned seem very merry to the imagination by contrast'. A choice between darkness and fire rather than darkness and light, and there were plenty who willingly leapt into the fires of the damned, as well as those who resolutely endured the fires of salvation. Spark's Sandy is frightened by the 'outsides of old Edinburgh churches, they were of such dark stone, like presences among the colour of the Castle rock, and were built so warningly with their upraised fingers'.

The High Kirk of Edinburgh (not formally a cathedral as the Church of Scotland has no bishops) has withstood much battering and reconfiguring. Twelfth-century in origin, when David I established a parish church for Edinburgh, it was set alight in 1385 by the troops of Richard II of England, and thereafter rebuilt and somewhat haphazardly augmented over the centuries. It gained its distinctive stone crown in 1495. By the end of the following century the church had been partitioned to accommodate different congregations and forms of Presbyterian worship. The destruction of the Tolbooth and adjacent Luckenbooths revealed the building to be in a state of deterioration and the architect William Burn was appointed to restore it. A second phase of restoration came later in the century when the

High Kirk of St Giles. Rachel Calder.

lord provost William Chambers, the same who provided Greyfriars Bobby with his licence and collar, initiated major restoration. The first service held in the restored kirk was his funeral.

The partitions were removed, opening up the interior, and the building was cleaned. For the first time windows were furnished with stained glass, not generally approved by Presbyterians. One of the windows features a depiction of Knox preaching. He is also present as a statue, the work of Pittendrigh MacGillivray in 1904. There are memorials to others, to James Graham, Marquis of Montrose and to his foe Archibald Campbell, Earl of Argyll, whose heads were displayed nearby, and rather more pacifically to Robert Burns, honoured with a stained glass window, and Robert Louis Stevenson, who is commemorated with a bronze relief by the American sculptor Augustus Saint-Gaudens. Stevenson, who was often ill, is in his bed, writing.

St Giles has a distinctive tower, but it is not a tall building and sits rather squatly a third of the way down the Royal Mile. Even today, with its crammed proximity to the Tolbooth and parliament long gone, it seems not to occupy its own space. Further up the hill is the 'stunningly sited'

Victorian Gothic Tolbooth Church, designed by James Gillespie Graham and AWN Pugin. Originally it served as both a place of worship and the meeting hall of the General Assembly of the Church of Scotland, but now it is the location of the Edinburgh International Festival Hub, with booking office, performance space and a restaurant. It's a comfortable and, outwith festival time, a quiet place to sit on a sofa with a cup of tea.

Protestantism became the established religion of Scotland as it did of England. Yet there remained strong leanings towards the Church of Rome, which later Stewart kings reinforced. The Calvinists, especially John Knox, did not care for Mary, Queen of Scots, with her dubious French and Catholic connections. Her return in 1560 to Scotland from France, where she spent most of her childhood, did nothing to dampen the Stewart legacy of power struggle, now intensified by religious contention. Knox had little time for Catholics or women or monarchs so there was scant chance Mary would receive his approval. After James VI left Edinburgh for London, Protestants, themselves often disagreeing about the form the new religion should take, were especially sensitive about interference from outwith Scotland.

James's son Charles was much less in touch than his father with Scottish feelings and aspirations. When he attempted to introduce a new service book to the Scottish church there was outrage. The 18th-century historian William Maitland described the mood:

> King Charles I, being resolved to put in execution his darling scheme, of having all his people of the same religion, ordered a liturgy, or service book, with one of canons, to be prepared, for the use of the Scottish Church, which being accordingly performed, his Majesty, without further ceremony, issued a proclamation for the due observance of them throughout Scotland. This being impolitickly done, without the Privity of the Secret Council, or general approbation of the clergy; they were regarded as foreign impositions,

When the new service book first appeared in St Giles in the hands of James Hannay, Dean of Edinburgh, uproar ensued. This was the occasion when Jenny Geddes was said to have launched a stool at him. Whatever really happened, the threat was such that the Dean had to beat a hasty retreat through a back way to escape the congregation's wrath. But 'impolitick' government from London did not go away.

This was just the first of the riots that broke out in Edinburgh against the attempted imposition of a form of service distasteful to Presbyterians. Scots clergy and many others made their position clear with the signing of the National Covenant. Ready to do battle for their beliefs, the Covenanters assembled an army under General Alexander Leslie. Initial success came with the capture of Edinburgh castle and the defeat of a Royalist army near Newcastle.

Charles I was soon to have problems nearer home. In 1642, with the outbreak of Civil War, he faced a more formidable opponent in the shape of Oliver Cromwell. His troubles multiplied when the following year the Scottish Covenanters joined forces with the English Parliamentary army, and with the Solemn League and Covenant pledged a commitment to uphold the reformed church in Scotland, England and Ireland. General Leslie's Scottish troops were crucial in the defeat of the Royalists at Marston Moor in 1644. But military success did not answer the concerns of many Covenanters at Cromwell's refusal to impose Presbyterianism nationwide. The execution of Charles in 1649 brought the end of Covenanting support for Cromwell, who promptly turned his attention to the uncooperative Scots.

In the meantime, while battles were being fought in the south, Edinburgh had a more urgent problem to deal with. Plague arrived on the city's streets. All who could, fled the city. Parliament moved to Stirling, the university to Linlithgow, and prisoners in the Tolbooth and the castle were set free. The sick were herded out of the city into shanty towns on Burgh Muir (now the Meadows) and the King's Park, and those guilty of concealing the disease could be punished by hanging or drowning. In Leith, two thirds of the population died.

Then, in 1650, Cromwell entered Edinburgh, having defeated a Covenanting army at Dunbar. He stayed at Moray House in the High Street, laid siege to the castle and did considerable damage to city churches and to Holyrood Palace, where much of the building was destroyed by fire. There followed several years of English occupation, with troops garrisoned around the country. Scotland was pacified and Edinburgh uneasily peaceful. But Cromwell's death in 1658 and the restoration of the monarchy brought a resurgence of Covenanting zeal. Although Charles II's kingship was welcomed and wine flowed in the city's fountains, the conflict between government and Covenanters became more brutal. The appointment in 1661 of James Sharp, minister at Crail in Fife, as Archbishop of St Andrews,

Greyfriars kirkyard. Rachel Calder.

confirmed Charles's antagonism towards Presbyterians.

It was now unlawful for Covenanters to meet for worship. They did so in secret, in lonely country places with their weapons at hand in case of attack. Many were arrested and brought to Edinburgh for trial. Their fierce belief and fanatical courage brought suspicion and fear. They were imprisoned and tortured, some were executed, others transported to the West Indies. By their supporters – and there were many in Edinburgh, though they tended to be quietly discreet – they were considered saints and martyrs.

Edinburgh's citizens had experienced so much turmoil and destruction that there was a reluctance to provoke open conflict, but in 1666 the city was yet again under threat. A Covenanting army had gathered and was marching towards Edinburgh. It was a small and ill-equipped group of men that was stopped in its tracks by government forces led by General Tam Dalyell, who had supported Charles II in exile and campaigned in Russia. At Rullion Green in the Pentlands the ragtag Covenanters were overwhelmingly defeated by Dalyell's troops and many made prisoner. Around 30 of them, who refused to take the oath of allegiance, were hanged in the Grassmarket. The first work of Stevenson's to be published was his teenage account of the Pentland Rising (1866). John Galt in his novel *Ringan Gilhaize* (1823) describes the experiences of Covenanters captured at Rullion Green.

> On reaching Edinburgh I was placed in the Tolbooth, where many other sufferers from the cause of the Gospel were then lying. It was a foul and unwholesome den: many of the guiltless inmates were so wasted that they were rather like frightful effigies of death than living men. Their skins were yellow, and their hands were roped and warpt with veins and sinews in a manner very awful to see. Their eyes were vivid with a strong distemperature...

Sometimes it appears that all Scotland's roads lead to the Heart of Midlothian.

The defeat at Rullion Green must have seemed like the last whimper of a lost cause. But 13 years later it all flared up again, with the murder of Archbishop Sharp of St Andrews, dragged from his carriage on lonely Magus Moor in Fife and hacked to death in front of his daughter. The government responded by hunting down even more ruthlessly those who continued to cling to the Covenant, and sent John Graham of Claverhouse, celebrated later as 'Bonnie Dundee', to sniff out the open air conventicles, combing the moors and hills of the southwest astride his handsome black horse. Claverhouse was defeated at Drumclog, a bleak stretch of Lanarkshire moorland, by a scratch Covenanting army equipped largely with pitchforks and other makeshift weapons. But final defeat came for the Covenant with the battle of Bothwell Brig in June 1679. Again, prisoners were brought back to Edinburgh where they were kept, 1,200 of them, crammed within the confines of Grefriars Kirkyard. According to Robert Chambers, they were 'kept in this frightful bivouac for five months' under 'circumstances of privation barely credible'. Their sustenance was 4ozs of bread a day. Two hundred and fifty of them who refused to end their rebellion were transported to Barbados, or would have been if their ship had not gone down in a storm off Orkney. Covenanters perished on land also, for this was the 'Killing Time', the mopping-up period of savage reprisal through the countryside in an effort to end for good this politically threatening and particularly unrelenting current of belief.

The Covenanting battles were not fought on the streets of Edinburgh, but inevitably the city saw and felt the repercussions and consequences. Now on a summer's day the grassy slope of the graveyard at Greyfriars is a pleasant spot, sheltered from city traffic by high stone walls and often scattered with lunchtime picnickers. When I worked at the museum, just across the road, I often came here with a sandwich. In the museum you can linger over a display on the Covenanters and reflect on a brutal past and its close connection with the kirk and kirkyard a few yards away. But most of those who frequent the kirkyard, or who go perhaps to a Festival concert in the kirk, probably don't pause to consider the fidelity and cruelty that surrounds them. They are unlikely to give much thought to the 1,200 prisoners confined in a small section of the grassy slope, many of them wounded or sick, just a few yards away from where the National Covenant was first signed. They probably don't stroll down to the bottom of the slope where the Martyrs' Monument bids passers-by to halt and

> heed what thou dost see
> This tomb doth shew for what some men did die.

And the inscription ends:

> They did endure the wrath of enemies
> Reproaches torments deaths and injuries
> But yet they're these who from such troubles came
> And now triumph in glory with the LAMB

From Greyfriars it's a short walk down Candlemaker Row to the Grassmarket where there is a second memorial, to mark where the Covenanters were executed. You can't, in your daily life, bear the weight of history but from time to time it is good to acknowledge it.

In Scott's *The Heart of Midlothian* it is Edinburgh's Grassmarket that introduces us to the city, an open space flanked by tall but mean houses, though 'not without some features of grandeur, being overhung by the southern side of the huge rock on which the castle stands, and by the moss-grown battlements and turreted walls of that ancient fortress'. Why the Grassmarket? Because it is the place of public execution, and Scott deliberately plants in the reader a powerful sense of what that means. In the shadow of the castle, a dominating emblem of power and impregnability, a huge black gallows is erected. Most of the people who live in that shadow are ordinary folk leading modest if not impoverished lives. The convicted person is paraded through the streets 'dressed in his grave clothes... looking like a moving and walking corpse, while yet an inhabitant of this world'. Spectators will mass to witness the event and, Scott says, learn the lesson that is the only justification for public execution. But for sympathisers who witnessed the hanging of Covenanters it may have strengthened their conviction in the triumph of martyrdom. There are uncomfortable contemporary echoes.

The Grassmarket is a place of violence, but also of vitality. It signals the ultimate in punitive action, but it was also a space where Edinburgh's people, of all classes, gathered. Public execution needed an audience, and if on the High Street it was hard to avoid the gristly remnants of the dead displayed at the Tolbooth, in the Grassmarket there was much more room for spectators. The theatre of execution is an example to the living, and a reminder of their own precarious lives. The events of the Porteous riots of 1736, and perhaps also those of the previous century, were also reminders of the power of the people. It is a theme that runs through Edinburgh's history, perhaps the more emphatic for the fact that the city's configuration compressed the mob. A few hundred people in a narrow street can appear very threatening.

For Flora Grierson, the Grassmarket in the 1920s was 'one of the loveliest things in Edinburgh, with the mellow quiet aspect of a district that has seen much and endured much'. Today it is still a place of congregation, but the attractions have radically changed. The castle on its rock still towers above this space which was once, as the name suggests, a market where horses and cattle were sold as well as grain and straw. It is still, from time to time, a space for markets of a very different kind, selling clothes and craftwork. By the middle of the 19th century, the original market activity was beginning to shift and in 1911 disappeared entirely. This part of Edinburgh had declined, along with the Cowgate and much of the Old Town, and like them had become a notorious slum. In the 1950s and '60s when I first knew it, it was an area that caused some alarm, a place of decomposing buildings and men and women huddled over bottles and cans. The Salvation Army Women's Hostel at the foot of the West Bow and the work of the Grassmarket Mission attracted the destitute.

Today the Grassmarket is promoted as a location of vibrant commerce, a tourist attraction with a string of hotels, pubs and eateries, where you can absorb simultaneously the old and the new. Have a drink in the White Hart Inn, where Robert Burns stayed in 1791, followed by Dorothy and William Wordsworth a few years later. Dorothy's verdict was that it was 'not noisy, and tolerably cheap'.

In April 1916 a German Zeppelin made a raid on Leith and Edinburgh, dropping bombs that, *The Scotsman* reported, did 'considerable damage to working class dwellings' around the Grassmarket – the castle was the target – and caused several deaths. As the Zeppelin approached the city's trams were stopped and street lights extinguished:

> The loud detonations awakened the inhabitants, many of whom went into the streets. An empty tramcar was blown to fragments and a tramway inspector was killed... A well-known magistrate, the leader of the local Labour Party, was killed in the street.

Charles II was a Catholic in secret. James, his brother, who succeeded him in 1685, was openly Catholic. Scottish Presbyterians were not happy. In 1688, Protestant William of Orange and his wife Mary, daughter of James VII, ousted Catholic James. William wasn't much interested in Scotland but there remained north of the border strong support for the Stewart monarchy, which erupted in rebellion. It began with John Graham of Claverhouse, Viscount Dundee, who had so vigorously persecuted the Covenanters. On 18 March 1689 he made a dramatic exit from Edinburgh's West Port in a bold abandonment of the city, at the head of 50 dragoons. Walter Scott celebrated the event with a rousing song:

> Come fill up my cup, come fill up my can,
> Come saddle your horses, and call up your men;
> Come open the West Port, and let me gang free,
> And it's room for the bonnets of Bonny Dundee!

The ghosts of the martyred dead must have been stirred to fury by the clattering hooves of Dundee and his men.

> Dundee he is mounted, he rides up the street,
> The bells are rung backward, the drums they are beat

Dundee rides through the Grassmarket crammed with 'sour-faced Whigs' and away from the city to the north.

> There was spite in each look, there was fear in each e'e,
> As they watched for the bonnets of Bonny Dundee.

Before he rode out of Edinburgh Dundee tried to persuade the Duke of Gordon, in control of the castle, to join him. He climbed the castle rock for a secret meeting. But Gordon, though a Stewart supporter, declined. The castle was besieged by Cameronian troops, named for Richard Cameron, a particularly zealous and militant Covenanting preacher who had been hunted to his death eight years earlier. His head and hands were displayed on Edinburgh's Netherbow Port.

Bonny Dundee headed north, gathered an army of Stewart-supporting Highlanders, and in August 1689 confronted government troops at the Pass of Killiecrankie, near Dunkeld. Dundee was victorious, but he himself was killed, and his troops, pursuing their fleeing adversaries into Dunkeld, found themselves trapped and ambushed by waiting Cameronians. The threat from those labelled as Jacobites was felt in Edinburgh, but the remnant of the Highland army was finally defeated at the Haughs of Cromdale near Grantown-on-Spey. The first chapter of the attempt to restore the Stewarts to the throne was over.

In the following century religious contention was largely a battle of words rather than swords, with one major exception. The 1689 Jacobite eruption was followed by others, fuelled by a desire to have a Stewart and a Catholic on the throne. Open warfare came to Edinburgh in 1745 although there was no great damage. There were clashes and cannon were fired, but the bloodiest encounters happened elsewhere. Catholicism, outlawed in 1560 with the coming of the Reformation, had long survived underground but the failure of the Jacobite risings drove it further to the margins.

There is a formidable bronze statue of John Knox in the quadrangle of the Assembly Hall in Mound Place. Built originally as a place of worship and theological college for the Free Church, it was completed in 1850, seven years after the Disruption of the Church of Scotland brought the Free Church into existence. Knox, the work of sculptor John Hutchison, didn't make an appearance until 1895. By that time there were Free Churches all over Edinburgh. There had been Presbyterian splits and schisms before

1843, but this was the moment when around two hundred ministers and elders rebelled against what they considered a dilution of church democracy. On 18 May, they voted with their feet, abandoning the General Assembly of the Church of Scotland meeting in the Church of St Andrew and St George in George Street and walking down the hill to Canonmills, where in the Tanfield Hall (previously the home of the Oil Gas Company whose chairman was Sir Walter Scott, and across the road from where Robert Louis Stevenson was born seven years later) they convened for the first gathering of the Free Church under the auspices of Thomas Chalmers. About a third of Church of Scotland ministers signed an Act of Separation. Ahead of them was the formidable task of building again from nothing – new churches, new congregations, new sources of funding for ministers, their families and their homes. The spiritual resources were abundant. The physical and financial resources required much dedication and hard work.

Knox's presence outside the Assembly Hall indicates that the Free Church saw itself as part of his legacy. The Free Church rebels were also inheritors of Covenanting conviction. But Knox is closed in. He is not looking out from the top of the Mound across the city, overseeing the route that the Disrupters took down from the New Town to Canonmills. He is facing stone walls and an often empty courtyard. On a visit to New College, which occupies part of the quadrangle, I pause to regard his stern presence. I am on my way to meet Hannah Holtschneider who is working on a biography of my grandfather, Salis Daiches, who was for nearly 30 years Edinburgh's rabbi. I never met him, but his photograph suggests a sternness in him also, though tempered by a thoughtful dignity. He knew, of course, that he was preaching in the territory of John Knox. But it was also the territory of the Enlightenment. He had written his doctoral thesis on David Hume, and part of the attraction of Edinburgh was that it was Hume's city. He believed that Edinburgh's Jewish community should be distinct but participatory, that it had a responsibility to make a contribution to the religious, social and cultural life of the city and the nation. He worked hard to achieve this.

Through the 19th century the city's population was expanding exponentially and there was money for building to meet the demand for housing. There was also a demand for churches. All the major Scottish denominations were making their mark in stone, and it's interesting to see how the saints are distributed. St Cuthbert is shared by the Church of

Scotland and the Roman Catholic Church, St Columba by them and also the Episcopal Church and the Free Church. There are not as many churches of St Andrew as one might expect, while St Ninian and St Margaret seem to be the provinces of the Catholics and the Episcopalians. A walk from my home in South Queensferry (population about 11,000 and growing, and now within the bounds of the City of Edinburgh) can take me past some representative landmarks of Scottish church history. If I walk down the hill towards the High Street I pass the 17th-century Vennel Kirk, now a private house. Alongside is the kirkyard, the gate locked to ensure that a casual wanderer among the graves isn't injured by an ancient toppling tombstone. Further on, at the west end of Queensferry's High Street, the Episcopalian Priory Church, its origins dating from the 14th century when a Carmelite Friary was established, is now a pleasing venue for meetings, concerts and events as well as worship. I turn up the Loan and pass on either side two Victorian churches, on the left the Church of Scotland parish church and on the right St Margaret's Roman Catholic church. It was St Margaret who put Queensferry on the map. The 19th century saw an influx of Irish families to the area, providing labour for the building of canals and railways, the nearby shale mines and the construction of the Forth Bridge. They settled in Edinburgh too, and swelled the congregations of the Catholic churches.

I have never heard church bells in Queensferry, so there is no echo of Alasdair Alpin MacGregor's 'clamour of competing bells' announcing 'a score of incongruous orthodoxies'. And the Victorian Sunday is long gone. Queensferry's churchgoers compete for parking space with shoppers in a nearby supermarket. Stevenson in California remembered the city 'where the bells clash of a Sunday, and the wind squalls, and the salt showers fly and beat', and Hugh MacDiarmid's 'Sabbath Morning' is even more uncompromising:

> Stagnant and foul with the rigid peace
> Of an all-tolerating frigid soul

Was a 'rigid peace' worse than open warfare? I doubt if MacDiarmid's belligerence would have taken him to the battlefield.

The bells Chiang Yee heard on an Edinburgh Sunday did not suggest competition. From Salisbury Crags he listened to the chimes ring out from one church to another.

At first I could distinguish a single tune quivering through the mist with notes so clear and pure they seemed to cleanse my heart and shake old dusty thoughts out of my mind. More chimes floated up, each distinct and yet blending with the rest to produce an extraordinary harmony. I held my breath with a happy feeling of expansion and clarity until the peals ended in a soothing trail of sound.

An extraordinary harmony. Bells, like any kind of music, are liberated from particular attachments to designations of faith. Chiang Yee reflected that perhaps the bells were improved by hearing them at a distance with the chimes 'washed by the morning mist', rather than in the street 'cramped by walls and tarnished with urban reek'. It is likely that the Old Town's cramped walls and urban reek intensified the religious strife that simmered and on occasion erupted in the streets.

Today, dozens of Edinburgh's churches have been transformed into commercial premises, places of entertainment, bars and restaurants. The Church Hill Theatre in Morningside was once the Morningside Free Church. Filmhouse on Lothian Road and The Queen's Hall in Newington both started their lives as churches. St George's in York Place and St Thomas's in Rutland Place are now casinos. The Queen's Gallery at Holyrood was once the Holyrood Free Church. Edinburgh Sundays are not what they were. I am neither a Christian nor a churchgoer, but I have some sympathy with those who mourn the passing of the Sabbath as a day of difference. My mother reminisced about Edinburgh Sundays when she escaped boredom by knitting, but even that she had to hide from her own mother. It seems her father was rather more forgiving – I never knew either of my maternal grandparents. I wouldn't want a return to a ban on knitting, but the clamour of bells, harmonious or otherwise, is surely preferable to the clamour of tills.

Central
Controlled
ZONE

Mon - Sat
8.30 am - 6.30 pm

5

Grandeur and gloom

Piper on the Royal Mile. Rachel Calder.

*...an appearance of grandeur and gloom, rendered more terrific when*
*Waverley reflected on the cause by which it was produced, and that each*
*explosion might ring some brave man's knell.*
Sir Walter Scott, *Waverley*

*S iomadh àrmunn, làsdail, treubhach*
*An Dùn Eideann*
*There's many a valiant, daring hero*
*In Edinburgh*
Alasdair mac Mhaighstir Alasdair

EDINBURGH IS NO stranger to financial crisis. The worst, and probably that with the most far-reaching effects, was the failure of a scheme to establish a trading colony on the Darien isthmus of the Panama coast. At the time of the Northern Rock collapse in 2007 I found myself sitting on a bus beside an elderly woman in a state of great distress. She was on her way to the George Street branch of Northern Rock to withdraw all her money. I tried to imagine what it would have been like for Edinburgh's citizens when the news came that the Company of Scotland had lost everything, that the Darien scheme which had attracted enthusiastic investment from citizens with little cash to spare as well as from the wealthy, had ended in death, devastation and surrender.

In the months that led up to the departure of five ships from Leith on 12 July 1698 there had been rising excitement. A trading colony was to be founded that would enable Scotland to trade independently of England with America, Africa and the East. A land route would be carved out to link east and west coasts of the American continent which would give the Scots an advantage over those who had to battle round Cape Horn to reach the Pacific Ocean. The ships sailed with 1,200 potential settlers on board and carrying a cargo of rings, combs and bibles which they hoped to trade with the natives of Central America.

This was a time when Scotland was debarred from England's expanding colonial trade. It was also a time of growing poverty in Scotland. The poor and dispossessed wandered the streets of Edinburgh. 'Thousands of our people,' said Fletcher of Saltoun, 'afford us the melancholy prospect of dying by shoals in our streets and have left behind them reigning contagion which hath swept away multitudes more and God knows where it might end.' Edinburgh's merchants believed that the way to revive a depressed economy was through foreign trade. The Company of Scotland was founded in 1695. £500,000 was raised to finance the Darien venture. It's been estimated that this could have been as much as half of all the money circulating in Scotland.

By the time the five ships reached Darien, in early November, they had lost 40 of their potential settlers through disease. In the sticky heat of the jungle they labored to build their settlement, which they called New Edinburgh. But the heat, the lack of appropriate equipment, and the rotting food took their toll. 'Our bodies pined away and grew so emaciated with such rations and hated work that we were like so many skeletons.' Then the Spanish moved in, claiming Darien as their territory. The Scots looked to the English colony of Jamaica for help, but in 1699 a royal proclamation ordered that the Scots should be refused assistance. By this time, anyway, 300 of them were dead.

A second expedition, unaware of what was happening, arrived a year later to find New Edinburgh deserted. 'Expecting to meet our friends and countrymen we found nothing but a vast, howling wilderness, the colony deserted and gone, their huts all burnt, their fort most part ruined.' Hundreds died of fever. The survivors surrendered to the Spanish. None of the four ships that were allowed to set sail for home reached Scotland. In all, about 2,000 lost their lives and £500,000 were gone. Many Edinburgh citizens were financially ruined.

Edinburgh was appalled and seethed with indignation against the English. When news of a Scottish victory over the Spanish arrived, the city, in spite of the fact that the victory came too late to be of any help, erupted in a frenetic celebration that ended in a riot. In their anger against the English, the mob shattered windows and released Tolbooth prisoners accused of political offences – a kind of dress rehearsal for the Porteous riots a few decades later. When the leaders of this disorder were rounded up and sentenced to the pillory, it is said that those convicted were brought flowers and wine by the people of Edinburgh.

In the National Museum you can see an extraordinary iron chest with a formidably complicated system of locks which was intended to keep Darien cash safe. It stands open and empty. By the time King William died in 1702 there was not much love for the English. Poverty and unrest were increasing. Edinburgh rumbled with discontent. The English government began to feel that the only way to quieten Scotland would be to bring about a political union with England, and thus to strengthen the union of the crowns. Perhaps it had been a mistake to allow the Scots 100 years of their own parliament.

There were to be five years of debate and argument in Edinburgh before union was achieved, five years during which the issue was discussed and wrangled over on street corners, in taverns, in drawing rooms, as well as in Parliament House. For many, union was the ultimate sell-out, the end of Scottish political and cultural independence. But others saw it as the beginning of economic expansion and prosperity: now they would be able to share in England's commercial success and imperial booty. Some of the arguments and ideas expressed during these years have a very contemporary flavor. Fletcher of Saltoun, for example, argued for regional government, claiming that it would bring not only stability but a greater 'variety of entertainment' to the whole country.

> I am of the opinion, that if instead of one, we had 12 cities in these kingdoms possessed of equal advantages, so many centres of men, riches, and power, would be much more advantageous than one… That London should draw the riches and government of three kingdoms to the south-east corner of this island is, in some degree as unnatural, as for one city to possess the riches and government of the world.

Fletcher was one of the most striking voices in the parliamentary debate, although his argument did not prevail then. Today it is being revisited.

While the Scottish Parliament debated, Edinburgh folk expressed their views in no uncertain terms. Daniel Defoe, quietly watching events and reporting back to the English government on how Edinburgh was reacting to the idea of union, described one of the many incidents.

> The rabble attended at the door; and by shouting and noise, having increased their number to several thousands they began with Sir Patrick Johnson, who was one of the treaters and the year before had been Lord Provost. First they assaulted his lodgings with stones and sticks, and curses not a few; but his windows being too high, they came up the stairs to his door, and fell to work at it with great hammers, and had

they broke it open in their first fury, he had, without doubt, been torn in pieces without mercy; and this only because he was a treater in the Commission to England, for before that no man was so well beloved as he over the whole city.

Not only in Edinburgh but all over Scotland anger fuelled the possibility of rebellion as the Treaty of Union drew closer to becoming law. It was feared that there would be an uprising and an attack on the city. English troops were poised on the Border at Berwick in case of trouble. When the articles of the treaty became known a mob gathered outside Parliament House who greeted the engineers of the treaty 'with hootings and execrations', and those who opposed it with 'the loudest acclamations'. But on 1 May 1707 the Act of Union came into force. It was celebrated in London with due splendor and solemnity. 'That whole day was spent in feasting, ringing of bells, and illuminations, and gave reason to believe that at no time Scotsmen were more acceptable to the English than on that day,' wrote John Clerk of Penicuik, one of the architects of the Treaty. In Edinburgh the bells of St Giles rang out a rather different tune: 'How can I be sad on my wedding day?' For many Scots the Act of Union was seen as an end rather than a beginning. 'Now there's an end of an auld sang,' said Scotland's last Lord Chancellor as he put his signature to the act. For the next few decades whenever things seemed not to be going right, the Union would be blamed. It's a habit that has persisted.

With the removal of government came the removal of those who believed it important to be close to the source of government. Edinburgh became a duller place. 'From the Union up to the middle of the century,' wrote Robert Chambers, 'the existence of the city seems to have been a perfect blank. An air of gloom and depression pervaded the city.' Edinburgh had lost more than its place as the focus of political activity. It was, in the words of architectural historian Charles McKean, 'no longer the location of stirring scenes which had kept its plainstanes slippery with blood and wine over the previous two centuries'. Good riddance, some might say. But that sense of loss was profound, although there would be more blood and plenty more wine to come.

At the time of the Union, Edinburgh was a city of about 40,000 people, much the largest city in Scotland. Most of the population lived within the Old Town. Glasgow had a population of 13,000. In the decades after the Union, Glasgow grew with dramatic speed, in both population and wealth.

The city thrived on the tobacco and sugar trade with the West Indies and the American colonies, now open to Scotland legally though there had been an illegal trade before the Union. The direct benefits to Edinburgh were not so obvious, at least not immediately, and a sense of grievance simmered for a long time. The turbulence of the past may have dissipated, and it was clear that the Act of Union marked a new direction, but regret and resentment at the way the change had been imposed lingered. Edinburgh, wrote 20th-century novelist Eric Linklater, was 'in stubborn denial of its altered state'. Yet there were those poised to take advantage of the opportunities that opened up, and by the end of the century Edinburgh was making a mark on the world unprecedented in her history.

But first there was a brief return to the edgy contention that had once seemed integral to Edinburgh life. In some quarters disaffection after the Union was channelled into the continuing dream that the Stewarts might yet be restored to the throne. On 15 September 1745, an army composed largely of Highlanders, under the leadership of Charles Edward Stewart, grandson of James VII of Scotland and II of England, was approaching Edinburgh from the west. The following day they reached Corstorphine, a village three miles out of the town. Edinburgh was about to be occupied, for the last time, by an army hostile to the government. Thirty years earlier another army, also raised to restore a Stewart king to the throne, had threatened the city. A Jacobite army crossed the Forth in fishing boats and was only just driven off by the Duke of Argyll and 3,000 men. This army continued south into England, but could not raise the hoped-for support and was defeated at Preston. On the same day, 14 November 1715, a second Jacobite army under the Earl of Mar, was defeated by Argyll at Sheriffmuir near Stirling.

In spite of the 1715 defeat and the measures taken to suppress the Highlanders, Jacobitism remained strong, and although the men who gathered around Charles Edward when he raised his standard at Glenfinnan on the west coast were few and ill-equipped, the advance of a Highland army on Scotland's capital brought panic. The two regiments of dragoons protecting the city retreated with undignified haste from the village of Coltbridge on the Water of Leith, just to the north of today's Corstorphine Road, and in full view of the city, sped along the Long Dykes – now Princes Street – and headed for the safety of government troops to the southeast. The manoeuvre became known as 'the canter of Coltbridge' and did not bode well for the defence of the city.

Volunteers were raised to assist the defence, summoned by a fire bell to assemble in the Lawnmarket. It was a scene of confused excitement. Amidst cheering and the clashing of swords, 'a universal consternation seized the minds of the people of every rank, age, sex, and party', according to one witness.

> The relations of volunteers crowded about them... The men reasoned, and endeavoured to dissuade their friends: the women expostulated, complained, and, weeping, embraced their sons and brothers.

As a child I was enamoured of the Jacobites. My hero was DK Broster's creation Ewen Cameron. I read *The Flight of the Heron* (1925) when I was nine years old. Ewen enters Edinburgh, 'that stately city', with the Jacobite army after a period of 'ludicrous indecision and terrors' on the part of the city fathers who attempted to negotiate with Charles Edward. The Jacobite capture of the city was something of an anticlimax, with no call on the volunteers to face the invading army. Cameron of Lochiel, a key supporter of Charles Edward, and his men slipped through the Netherbow Port as it was opened to let a carriage through. The Jacobites possessed the town but not the castle, which remained in government hands and from time to time let loose largely ineffective cannon fire from the ramparts.

Lord Elcho, a leading Jacobite, described Charles Edward's approach, 'met by vast Multitudes of people, who by their repeated Shouts & huzzas, express'd a great deal of joy to see the Prince'. He entered the town from Duddingston to the east and rode his horse through the King's Park, 'full of people... impatient to see this extraordinary person', to Holyrood, where he set up his headquarters. John Home, among the crowd, recorded that Jacobite supporters were 'charmed with his appearance':

> They compared him to Robert the Bruce, whom he resembled (they said) in his figure as in his fortune. The Whigs looked on him with other eyes. They acknowledged that he was a goodly person; but they observed, that even in that triumphant hour, when he was about to enter the palace of his fathers, the air of his countenance was languid and melancholy.

Melancholy or not, the prince was determined to put on a good show and demonstrate both military and social leadership. The palace of his fathers hummed with activity. There were plans to be made, alliances to be forged and followers to be entertained.

> At the other end of the town Holyrood House was lit up, for there was dancing to-night in the long gallery… Whatever the future might hold, [Charles Edward] was here as by a miracle in the palace of his ancestors, having defeated in a quarter of an hour the general who had slipped out of his path in August and returned by sea to the drubbing which awaited him among the morasses and the corn stubble of Prestonpans.

This is DK Broster again, who owed much to an earlier fictional description of Charles Edward's occupation of Edinburgh in Walter Scott's *Waverley*. I read *Waverley* when I was a little older. It did nothing to dispel my fascination with the Jacobites. Edward Waverley approaches Edinburgh from the west, under escort from Stirling. As they draw near they see 'Edinburgh stretching along the ridgy hill which slopes eastward from the Castle' and hear the sound of cannon, firing 'at intervals upon such parties of Highlanders as exposed themselves'.

> The morning being calm and fair, the effect of this dropping fire was to invest the Castle in wreaths of smoke, the edges of which dissipated slowly in the air, while the central veil was darkened ever and anon by fresh clouds poured forth from the battlements; the whole giving… an appearance of grandeur and gloom, rendered more terrific when Waverley reflected on the cause by which it was produced, and that each explosion might ring some brave man's knell.

The allegiance of Waverley to the Jacobite cause, an Englishman inadvertently caught up in the rising, is sealed when he meets Charles Edward at Holyrood. Scott portrays the prince as graciously manipulative. A few days later the Jacobite troops are assembling in the King's Park before marching to confront government forces led by General Cope. On his way to join the troops Waverley climbs 'a small craggy eminence, called St Leonard's Hill' and looks down at the scene spread out below Arthur's Seat and Salisbury Crags.

The rocks, which formed the back-ground of the scene, and the very sky itself, rung with the clang of bagpipers, summoning forth, each with his appropriate pibroch, his chieftain and clan. The mountaineers...with the hum and bustle of a confused and irregular multitude, like bees alarmed and arming in their hives, seemed to possess all the pliability of movement fitted to execute military manoeuvres. Their motions appeared spontaneous and confused, but the result was order and regularity; so that a general must have praised the conclusion, though a martinet might have ridiculed the method by which it was attained.

For the citizens of Edinburgh the spectacle of Highland clans, armed though many were with only makeshift weapons, gathering virtually on their doorsteps must have seemed both alarming and alien. The city was accustomed to violence, but this scene of 'picturesque wildness' was something different. And when the Jacobite army returned victorious, having defeated General Cope at Prestonpans, the uneasiness increased. There were plenty of Jacobite sympathisers in Edinburgh, including people with influence and authority, among them the Lord Provost Archibald Stewart. And others, regardless of political leanings, were dazzled by the handsome young prince and Holyroodhouse brought to life again. But there was tension and many were afraid. At the west end of the mile the castle remained defiant, continuing a sporadic bombardment. ''Tis not safe

Holyrood Park and Holyrood Palace. Rachel Calder.

being in Lawn or Grassmarkets,' wrote an observer.

Looking down from St Leonard's Hill today, you will see a large car park, cars and cyclists on the road, runners, walkers and dogs on the paths leading to the Crags and Arthur's Seat. But – especially if you've read *Waverley* – it's not too hard to visualise the massing tartan-clad troops, the officers on their horses galloping back and forth, bonnets sporting white cockades, and to hear the cacophony of the bagpipes' competing pibrochs. On 1 November, the troops massed again to begin their march south, destination London and the throne. Edinburgh was relieved to see them go. Apart from other impositions and inconveniences, Charles Edward had raised a tax on its citizens. Most of the city's populace now felt they could breathe more freely.

By the time the Jacobites reached Derby the colour and confidence of their Edinburgh sojourn had dissipated. There had been many deserters, men who could not bear to be so great a distance from their own country, and the anticipated new recruits did not materialise. Equipment and provisions were scanty. 'They were in general a crew of shabby, lousy, pitiful-look'd fellows, mixed up with old men and boys dressed in dirty plaids and as dirty shoes, without breeches, some without shoes,' commented a resident of Derby. Between them and London were two large armies, one commanded by the Duke of Cumberland, George II's son, the other under General Wade, who had already left his mark in the Highlands by building roads and bridges to facilitate the movement of troops. The roads had made the Jacobites' march to Edinburgh that much easier.

Early in December the decision was made, after much argument, to turn back. John Buchan in his novel *Midwinter* (1923) describes the retreating army, 'furtive banditti slinking through the mud like riff-raff of a fair'. They paused in Glasgow long enough to demand supplies from its citizens to feed and clothe the near destitute soldiers. Through the winter months, via a momentary victory at Falkirk, they edged northwards, ill-clad, ill-equipped, ill-fed. On 16 April the 5,000 that remained were on Culloden Moor near Inverness, awaiting the onslaught of the Duke of Cumberland and his troops.

The defeat of the Jacobites and the savage reprisals carried out by 'Butcher' Cumberland had few direct repercussions in the capital. Edinburgh was largely unscathed by the rising. Charles Edward had brought a colourful if nervous interlude, but news of his defeat was greeted with rejoicing and celebration. Bonfires burned and toasts were drunk in the streets. Captured Jacobite flags were paraded along the High Street and burned at the Mercat

Royal Scots Greys memorial, Princes Street. Rachel Calder.

Cross. The Duke of Cumberland, praised for his 'wise conduct... and heroic example', was awarded the freedom of the city and presented with a gold box engraved with the city arms. Life was uncomfortable for noted Jacobites for a while, and they were well advised to keep a low profile. When Scott's Edward Waverley returns to Edinburgh after the Jacobites' defeat he has to skulk in the dusk, 'shunning observation'. There were some convictions, some fines and imprisonment, and many felt it wise to remove themselves from Scotland altogether. But the brutal scenes of vindictive punishment were enacted elsewhere, in the Highlands themselves, in London and in Carlisle, where there were executions. The head of Waverley's Jacobite friend and comrade, Ian MacIvor, ends up on Carlisle's Scotch gate, the gate that faced to the north. Edward nervously looks up as he leaves the city, but his friend is not there – Edward is returning to his uncle's estate in the south. And although he will be back in Scotland and will marry a Scottish bride, his future lies in England.

The streets of Edinburgh would never again see hostile troops or be battered by cannon fire. But they would see troops parading on their way to war, and parading again on their return. My mother, ten years old at the time, remembered returning First World War troops greeted by cheering crowds. Like hundreds of others, my mother Isobel, Billie as she was always called, waved a union flag. Her mother stood silent beside her, until she said, 'All the cheering in the world won't bring Harry back.' Harry was her only son, Billie's older brother, who died at the age of 19 when his plane was shot down. He had lied about his age to join the Gordon Highlanders and volunteered for transfer to the Royal Flying Corps.

In August 1962 I was staying with my family in a borrowed flat in Ramsay Garden. Every morning we were woken by the clatter of hooves on Castlehill. It was Gurkha cavalry practising for the Edinburgh Tattoo. The Tattoo, first brought to the castle esplanade in 1949, is an annual display of military music and prowess, as well as dance and athletic performance. My children loved it. It makes the most of the castle's dramatic setting, and can hardly fail to stir the most cynical hearts. It mines the resonance of Scotland's and Edinburgh's past, celebratory and upbeat, without lingering on the darkness beyond the spotlights and the fireworks. The crowds who cheered the tartans and bagpipes of Charlie's army were probably not very different from the packed audiences who join in 'Auld lang syne' at the end of each Tattoo performance, many with a tear in their eye.

On a wet, blustery November evening more than half a century after the Gurkha manoeuvres on Castlehill, my partner Arthur and I are at Edinburgh's Traverse Theatre to see a play called *Hector* by David Gooderson. My daughter Gowan is acting all the female roles. The play concerns Sir Hector Macdonald, 'Fighting Mac', a Black Isle crofter's son who rose from the ranks to distinguish himself at the battle of Omdurman in the Sudan in 1898, where his extraordinary bravery rescued the British army from disaster, and during the Boer War as commander of the Highland Brigade. After Omdurman, he was guest of honour at a City of Edinburgh Council lunch. Later posted to Ceylon, he failed to fit in with the colonial establishment who colluded to brand him as a homosexual. In 1903, faced with court martial, he committed suicide in a Paris hotel room. His body was shipped back from France incognito, and buried in Edinburgh's Dean Cemetery. In the days following his funeral thousands visited his grave. Damned by a self-seeking, vindictive establishment, he remained a hero in the eyes of ordinary Scots. In his home territory there are two imposing memorials to Fighting Mac or *Eachan nan Iath*, Hector of the Battles, in Dingwall

Hector Macdonald memorial, Dean
Cemetery. Rachel Calder.

and in Mulbuie, his birthplace. A government commission found no evidence to support the allegations, and referred to the 'irreproachable character of so brave, so fearless, so glorious and unparalleled a hero'. It went on to state the belief that 'the inhuman and cruel suggestions of crime were prompted through vulgar feelings of spite and jealousy in his rising to such high rank of distinction in the British Army'. Sir Hector's sword and medals are held by the National Museum. They reflect military courage and success, and the pomp and ceremony that Macdonald himself had little time for. They don't suggest the darker side, the torment of a man driven to suicide and the terrible damage to its own people caused by a nation's colonial ambition.

There are military memorials all over Edinburgh, 'uncomfortable reminders' Alexander McCall Smith writes in *The Careful Use of Compliments* (2007), 'of how things in the past were otherwise than one might wish they had been': war memorials of course with their chilling lists of the dead in two world wars, regimental memorials, and commemorations of particular individuals. Wellington commands the east end of Princes Street, and if you walk west you'll pass a dragoon of the Royal Scots Greys. But you'll have to go further to find Sir Hector, across the Dean Bridge, past Buckingham Terrace where I lived for five years, past the Baptist Church where my daughters went to Brownies, and across the road to the Dean Cemetery.

In 1669, the Duke of Lauderdale, Viceroy of Scotland, processed up the Royal Mile to open Parliament attended by a grand and dazzling parade of nobility, heralds and servants, 'a very glorious sight... The heralds of arms and other officers... were wonderfully gay and finely habited, and the servants that attended were clad in the richest liveries... all the nobles appeared in the greatest pomp and gallantry'. This was the annual Riding of Parliament, a demonstration of power at a time when Scots were still shedding each other's blood.

Three hundred and forty years later there was another procession, on the day of the opening of the restored Scottish Parliament, 1 July 2009. Queen Elizabeth, wearing a splendid purple feathered hat, drove in an open carriage with Prince Philip and Prince Charles, from Holyrood to the Assembly Hall on the Mound, where the Parliament was to be temporarily housed until the new building, at the time an empty site, was ready. They were escorted by a detachment of the Household Cavalry. Like thousands of others, I was in the crowd, standing at the corner of the Mound and George IV Bridge. Processing on foot from Parliament Square were MSPs and other dignitaries, schoolchildren and bands, a jolly and somewhat shambling parade with bystanders shouting out encouragement and the procession responding in kind. There were pipe bands, of course. There was a 21-gun salute fired from the castle – I'm sure no one gave a thought to the bombardment that had come from the castle ramparts in 1745. It combined, said one commentator, the grandeur of a state occasion with the informality of a family party. And the figure who drew it all together, when speeches were made inside the Assembly Hall, was Donald Dewar, who managed to sidestep the pomp and speak with a dignified lack of ceremony, formally addressing the monarch but speaking to the people of Scotland with friendly integrity. It was, he said, 'a moment anchored in history'. Anchored in history, yes, but a significant, and democratic, departure from the past.

Royal Botanic Garden. Rachel Calder.

5

Learned, practical and useful

*She is learned, she is practical, and she is useful.*
Sir Arthur Conan Doyle

*A literary mart, famous with strangers, and the pride of its own citizens.*
Lord Cockburn

THE EDINBURGH THAT the departing Jacobite army left in the autumn of 1745 was still essentially a medieval city. There were some fine houses and gardens, but life continued to be dense, crowded and insalubrious. There was a change, however, a growing spirit of revival and an urge to rebuild. The Jacobite threat had passed and the Hanoverian monarchs were firmly on the throne. It was time not only to accept change but to make it happen.

When I lived in Buckingham Terrace, built in the 1860s north of the Dean Bridge, I and my three children would often walk down the hill to Comely Bank and Inverleith Park and on to the Royal Botanic Garden. I didn't then know much about its origins, but we liked to wander through the glasshouses and visit the Gallery of Modern Art, which was at that time located in Inverleith House. Inverleith House was built in 1774 for James Rocheid, owner of the Inverleith estate. The children liked the gallery. There was something about its scale and layout that was inviting. It was light and bright and not overwhelming. Our visits would usually end with some refreshment in the café before the long slog back up the hill to home.

By the time Edinburgh said goodbye to the tartan army, the seeds of what would become the Botanic Garden had long since been planted. Around 75 years earlier two Edinburgh physicians, Dr Robert Sibbald and Dr Andrew Balfour, had established near Holyroodhouse a Physick Garden for medicinal plants. Like many physicians at the time, they combined their medical activities with a keen interest in flora and fauna. Sibbald was author of the first natural history survey of Scotland, *Scotia Illustrata* (1684), in which he summed up his collecting aspirations:

I resolved to make it part of my studie to know what animals, vegetables, minerals, metals and substances cast up by the sea, were found in this country that might be of use in medicine or other artes useful to human lyfe, and I began to be curious in searching after them and collecting them, which I continued to do ever since.

A few years later the Physick Garden was moved to a site next to Trinity Hospital, later demolished – amidst much outcry – to make way for Waverley Station. In 1763 there was another move, to a five-acre site at Leith Walk, but half a century later this site was also outgrown, as it gradually became a repository for plants collected from far beyond Scotland. During the 19th century, Scottish botanical collectors were in the Americas, the Far East and many parts of Europe collecting material that found a home in Edinburgh – and in botanic gardens around Britain, most notably at Kew. In 1822, 15 acres of the Rocheids' Inverleith estate were acquired, and the former farmland was transformed into the nucleus of the current Royal Botanic Garden. Over the years the site has grown vastly, and now occupies an extensive 100 acres. Glasshouses were built, the new Palm House completed in 1858. It was designed by Robert Matheson, who also had a role in the construction of the new museum in Chambers Street, which started going up in 1861.

When Chiang Yee from China visited the Garden he was particularly struck by the number of plants and shrubs that originated in Asia. It was spring and the rhododendrons were out. He stops in fine rain beside the Garden's little lake to admire a rhodie with brilliant orange blooms. There are birds and dragonflies, and trees beside the water with leaves just coming out. 'Most attractive of all was a weeping willow with all its slender yellow branches drooping round it like silken tassels.' He wanders peacefully in the rain, admiring the flowering trees and shrubs, absorbing the colours which 'made me feel so cheerful that I wanted to dance instead of walking slowly'. He resists the urge, but the combination of peace and cheerful energy that he records on the page captures the

Royal Botanic Garden. Rachel Calder.

experience of sharing space with planned and ordered nature: 'this human-ising scientific place' in the words of poet Duncan Glen. It reflects a need, the need to identify and explain and control, which was at the heart of the Scottish Enlightenment.

Another favourite destination with my children in the 1970s, and another Enlightenment legacy, was the Royal Scottish Museum in Chambers Street. Sibbald and Balfour had a role in its origins also. Their efforts provided the founding collections of a museum at the university. When Daniel Defoe visited the museum early in the 18th century, an off-duty distraction from spying on the activities of Edinburgh's citizens, he was impressed. It was, he wrote, 'a curious and noble museum... a vast treasure of curiosities of Art and Nature, domestic and foreign from almost all Parts of the World'. The university's Natural History Museum would become the nucleus of a splendid new museum built next door to Playfair's Old College.

'Curious and noble': curiosity, intellectual aspiration and the practical application of knowledge would soon become the hallmarks of a new Edinburgh. It was as if there were a collective resolve to move beyond the upheavals of the first half of the 18th century and ensure that the city would no longer be identified as the seat of riot and rebellion. In 1780 the Reverend John Walker took up the chair of natural history at the university, and from that would stem a focus of enquiry that became world-renowned. In that same year the Society of Antiquaries was founded, signaling a burgeoning interest in the past. William Robertson had published his *History of Scotland* 21 years earlier. 'This is the historical age and we are the historical people,' David Hume, brilliant and controversial philosopher, had written. He died in Edinburgh in 1776 but his luminescence continued. Edinburgh was on the map as a place of 'genius and learning', a place where not only were great things achieved by many individuals but where the exchange and cross-fertilisation of ideas transformed a sense of human potential.

The men of genius and learning included lawyers and philosophers, medical men and geologists, writers and painters and architects. The lands and closes of the Old Town buzzed with argument and debate. Hume, cheerful and convivial although as a young man he had had periods of depression, lived for a while in the Lawnmarket. He would die in the New Town. That transition is in itself an emblem of what became known as the Scottish Enlightenment. Its roots were in the Old Town, before the Union, before the entry of a Jacobite army, and by the time of Hume's death it

Adam Smith. Rachel Calder.

was in full flower. And it wasn't an inward, ivory tower project. It was blossoming on Edinburgh's streets and in Edinburgh's taverns as well as in drawing rooms and lecture halls. It was having material consequences in art and industry and education.

Clubs and societies were focal points of exchange, and dozens sprang up at this time. Economist and philosopher Adam Smith, author of *The Wealth of Nations* (1766), with Hume and the younger Allan Ramsay formed the Select Society in 1754, only one of many clubs where well-lubricated discussion took place. It's not hard to imagine these hugely influential men picking their way home through the murky streets after rather too much claret, dodging the contents of chamber pots, making their way up a dark and stinking stair to their cramped Old Town quarters, where their children might be sleeping in makeshift beds in the parlour for lack of space for bedrooms. This is the Edinburgh of Robert Fergusson, whose favourite tavern was Luckie Middlemass's in the Cowgate, where he drank gin and ate oysters. It is the Edinburgh Scott was born into. It is the Edinburgh Robert Burns visited in 1786, ten years after Fergusson's death in the same year as Hume died. Did Fergusson and Hume ever meet? Scott met Burns when still a teenager.

The congestion of the Old Town, the forced proximity of living, the fact that lack of space drove social, commercial and intellectual interaction into public spaces, accelerated the spread of ideas. In this confined space ideas travelled readily. Insalubrious surroundings proved fertile ground for intellectual exchange. High thinking manured by robust reality. And the Old Town offered other kinds of proximity. Geologist James Hutton could look out of his window onto Salisbury Crags and Arthur's Seat and muse on the evidence revealed by their formation. University professors, such as Joseph Black, professor of medicine and chemistry, lived a short walk from the lecture rooms and laboratories where they taught and experimented. The notion of a division between intellectual activity and quotidian materiality could only come with the creation of a spacious environment with room not just for uncongested living but for uncongested elegance. There is a kind of irony in the fact that the intellectual ferment fostered in the crowded Old Town was by the 1780s finding sandstone expression in what Stevenson called the 'draughty parallelograms' of the New. But free-ranging ideas and high aspirations didn't need high ceilings. It is another strand of Edinburgh duality. Hume and Fergusson may never have met, but their coterminous end is a reminder of their connection.

Since 1995 a bronze statue of David Hume by Sandy Stoddart has graced the corner of the High Street and Bank Street. Appropriate as it is that he should be located in the Old Town, his appearance is nevertheless somewhat incongruous. There is nothing to suggest the environment in which his ideas took shape. In life a ruddy-complexioned, portly gentleman – see Raeburn's portrait in the Scottish National Portrait Gallery – here he has athletic limbs clothed in a toga-like garment hardly suitable for the wynds and closes and taverns where he was a familiar figure. He looks solemn and thoughtful, as maybe a philosopher should: perhaps bronze is not conducive to the joviality and irreverence which we know was part of his personality.

Hume expressed a wish that after his death a monument should be built 'with an inscription containing only my Name and the Year of my Birth and Death, leaving it to Posterity to add the rest'. How would he have reacted to his own larger-than-life presence on the High Street? I suspect he would have been as dismissive as he was of the prospect of life after death. He was buried in the Old Calton burial ground, and there is a monument to mark

Deacon Brodie's tavern. Rachel Calder.

his grave, a tower designed by Robert Adam, the architect who has left his mark on many parts of the city. Hume's confident atheism caused such hostility that after his burial his tomb had to be guarded against attack.

Across the street from Hume in bronze is Deacon Brodie's tavern, which unashamedly commemorates the life and death of the man who has become an emblem of Edinburgh's duality. William Brodie was a respected cabinet maker who became Deacon of the Guild of Wrights. He turned to burglary to help finance his gambling habit and the two families he maintained with two different women. This doubled double life came to an end when he robbed the Excise Office in the Canongate and was informed on by his accomplices – double-crossed. Although he escaped to Holland, he was apprehended in Amsterdam and brought back for trial. He was hanged in the Lawnmarket in 1788 in front of a large crowd, on a gibbet that he himself had improved – 'a kin' o' ghoulish joke', wrote Sydney Goodsir Smith. According to Robert Chambers, 'he exhibited a sort of levity… looking gaily around and finally went out of the world with his hand stuck carelessly into the open front of his vest'.

The tavern's sign shows Brodie holding up a bunch of keys, and keys were the key to his initial success. His trade gave him access to wealthy homes and premises, and the opportunity to copy their keys, which he then used to enter the premises at night and at leisure. Brodie's keys and lantern are now held by the National Museum. A cabinet made by him furnished the Heriot Row home where Robert Louis Stevenson grew up. It was perhaps inevitable that Brodie's doubleness deeply imprinted Stevenson and found expression both in a play about the man and more famously in *Strange Case of Dr Jekyll and Mr Hyde* (1886).

The Deacon was a much younger man than Hume, but it is very possible that the philosopher and the thief passed each other in the Lawnmarket. And just as Hume represents the achievement and influence of Edinburgh's Golden Age, so Deacon Brodie permeates a perception of the city as the locus of duplicity and deception, a theme that Alexander McCall Smith gently explores in his series of novels featuring philosopher Isobel Dalhousie.

A little further down the High Street from David Hume is Adam Smith, author of *The Wealth of Nations*, gazing down towards Holyrood, and beyond that to a ribbon of blue – on a good day – that is the Firth of Forth. Perhaps his gaze is directed to Kirkcaldy, his Fife birthplace. Smith may also have encountered the Deacon. Hume didn't live long enough to see Brodie hanged, but Adam Smith did.

By the 1780s the exodus to the New Town was well under way. Ideas nurtured in the Old Town were transplanted to the ordered modernity of the New. But when Burns arrived in Edinburgh in 1786 the focus of creative energy was still the Old Town, and although the contrast with his native rural Ayrshire must have been striking, the sophistication of Edinburgh's upper crust was never more than a step away from urban foulness, which was likely more noxious than the rural variety. The first phase of Edinburgh's Golden Age was already passing when Burns rode into town. Hume was gone. Lord Kames, lawyer and philosopher known for the coarseness of his language and the elegance of his wit, was gone. Adam Smith, James Hutton and historian William Robertson were elderly. The brief, hectic, brilliant life of Robert Fergusson was over. But the raw, robust vigour he immortalised in his poetry hadn't faded, and was a source of inspiration for Burns, who arrived in Edinburgh as a published poet and was greeted with enthusiasm by the city's cultural and social elite. Like Fergusson, Burns wrote affectionately and acutely of human behaviour, of the passions and weaknesses of ordinary life.

Burns, an outsider wary of patronising attentions, is a link between the first phase of Edinburgh's Golden Age, the period of social, philosophical and scientific enquiry, and the second, the time of the great writers – Burns himself, Henry Mackenzie, Henry Cockburn, and the giant, Sir Walter Scott – and a burgeoning of literary magazines. The original *Edinburgh Review* began life in 1755 and didn't last long, in spite of its unionist proclivities and its aim to promote 'the progress of knowledge'. A second attempt in 1773 lasted a little longer, but it was mark three, founded in 1802 with lawyer Francis Jeffrey as its first editor, that made a real impact. Jeffrey would later become eminent as a judge, as an MP and as Lord Advocate. Jeffrey at this time stayed in Buccleuch Place near the university, where he edited the magazine which in five years reached a circulation of 7,000. By the 1820s each monthly issue was selling 14,000 copies. Its political stance was 'aggressively Whig'. Historian Michael Fry describes it as 'the most famous periodical in the world' and 'the ancestor of modern serious journalism'. It published substantial articles on political and cultural issues and criticism of contemporary literature. Henry Cockburn was a keen supporter. The magazine, he wrote, represented 'an entire and instant change', and he went on, 'The learning of the new journal, its writing, its independence, were all new.' Although some of its literary judgments were dubious – Jeffrey scorned the generation of poets that were coming to the fore, Wordsworth, Coleridge, Byron, and did not care for Scott. But nevertheless the magazine's approach, pro-English and conventionally progressive, clearly struck a chord.

Some 15 years later came *Blackwood's Magazine*, founded by William Blackwood, a bookseller on South Bridge. Edited by John Wilson, who wrote as 'Christopher North', and JG Lockhart, it arrived on the scene with deliberate provocation. There was explosive literary criticism – Coleridge and Leigh Hunt were targets – and in particular a satire on Edinburgh literary life in the guise of the spoof 'Chaldee manuscript'. According to James Ferrier, historian and philosopher, the piece 'fell on Edinburgh like a thunderbolt'. There followed a satirical series, the 'Noctes Ambrosianae' (after Ambrose's Tavern in Picardy Place where the *Blackwood's* gang liked to drink), full of scathing and often scurrilous ridicule, targeting mainly Whig opinion and personalities. As the century progressed, *Blackwood's* would publish many of Britain's foremost authors, and was a lifeline for some, like Margaret Oliphant, who were struggling to earn a living from their work. If the Whiggish *Edinburgh Review* saw a Scottish future subsumed by England, the Tory *Blackwood's* asserted and celebrated a Scottish identity.

At the height of the Enlightenment, Edinburgh was described by Dunbartonshire-born Tobias Smollett as 'a hotbed of genius'. In the next century it would become a hotbed of printing and publishing. Scotland's first printing press was set up in 1507 in the Cowgate by Walter Chepman and Andrew Myllar, under a patent granted by James IV. They are remembered on the front of the Central Library in George IV Bridge, and a plaque at the bottom of Blackfriars Street tells us that on 4 April 1508 Chepman and Myllar completed the printing of *The Complaint of the Black Knight*. More than 200 years later, Allan Ramsay, wigmaker and poet from Leadhills in Lanarkshire, where his father was manager of Lord Hopetoun's mines, set up as a printer and bookseller at the sign of the Mercury, opposite Niddry's Wynd. In 1725 he opened what was possibly Britain's first circulating library. In the early 18th century Edinburgh's publishing was largely, according to Robert Chambers, the printing of 'newspapers and of school-books, of the fantastic effusions of Presbyterian clergymen, and the law papers of the Court of Session, joined to the patent Bible printing', which gave 'scanty employment to four printing-offices'. By 1779 there were 27 printers in Edinburgh. This expansion was not just due to the publishing of social, historical and philosophical work generated by the Enlightenment, but also to the opportunities opened by the fact that the English law of copyright did not apply in Scotland. Scottish booksellers were free to reprint cheap editions of English authors and, in some cases, cheekily sell them from premises opened in London.

Printing, publishing and bookselling were commonly all under the same roof. William Creech, who began a career in publishing and bookselling with Alexander Kincaid, was from 1773 running his own business from premises at the east end of the Luckenbooths, further down the High Street from what had been Ramsay's shop. He became friendly with many prominent literati of the time, Lord Kames, Hugh Blair, professor of rhetoric and belles lettres, Henry Mackenzie, author of *The Man of Feeling* (1771) and Dugald Stewart, professor of moral philosophy. He also published the Edinburgh Edition of Burns's poems. Burns described him as 'a strange multiform character', a mix of vanity, selfishness and 'great goodness of heart'. The printer of the Edinburgh Edition was antiquarian William

Smellie. Burns would visit the composing room while his poems were being typeset, William's son Alexander remembered: 'Burns would walk up and down the room three or four times, cracking a whip that he carried, to the no small surprise of the men.' Smellie, antiquarian and naturalist as well as printer, had founded the Crochallan Fencibles, a club frequented by Burns which met in a tavern in Anchor Close, near Smellie's printing office.

Smellie was editor of the original *Encyclopedia Britannica* (1771), and was another multiform personality celebrated by Burns:

> A head for thought profound and clear unmatch'd;
> Yet, tho' his caustic wit was biting rude,
> His heart was warm, benevolent and good.

The intimate relationship between author, publisher and printer was an important part of Edinburgh's intellectual and creative environment, but it was never quite the same after the descent to the New Town.

James and John Ballantyne, printers and newspaper publishers from Kelso, came to Edinburgh in 1803 to set up business just off the Canongate. They later moved to larger premises to the north, between the Canongate and Leith Wynd. The Ballantynes had printed Scott's *Minstrelsy of the Scottish Border* and his narrative poem *The Lay of the Last Minstrel*, and it was Scott who urged the brothers to relocate to Edinburgh. He himself put substantial amounts of money into the business. The Ballantynes published Scott's *The Lady of the Lake* in 1810, which proved a great success but brought a false sense of security. When seven years later they were running into difficulties they were bailed out by Archibald Constable. This was not enough to save the firm from collapse in 1826, partly the consequence of the wider financial situation but exacerbated by the fact that Scott himself was channelling profits into the building of Abbotsford. The Ballantyne press which printed some of the Waverley novels has come to rest in the Writers' Museum in Lady Stair's Close.

Edinburgh printing and publishing, however, continued to flourish and expand. William and Robert Chambers, like the Ballantynes from the Borders, started out selling books from a stall in Leith Walk and developed into publishers based in Hanover Street. Chambers Street and a statue in front of the National Museum are reminders of William's role as Lord Provost and his contribution to cleaning up parts of the Old Town and repairing St Giles. Robert Chambers' *The Traditions of Edinburgh* (1824) is a treasure trove for anyone interested in the city's past. Adam Black also made the move from bookseller to publisher, with a business based on North Bridge.

When Harriet Beecher Stowe visited Edinburgh in 1854 she was probably thinking of Scott when she wrote 'Edinburgh has had an effect on the literary history of the world for the last 50 years, that cannot be forgotten by anyone approaching her'. But without the energy and enterprise of the city's printers and publishers that history would have been much diminished. In the middle of the 19th century many London-published books were printed in Edinburgh. George Eliot was published by Blackwoods, the proofs of her novels speeding back and forth between London and Edinburgh. By this time the Scottish literary output had passed its heyday (RL Stevenson, whose writing career was beginning in the 1870s, was published in London) but there was plenty of energy left in Edinburgh publishing. The firm of Thomas Nelson began as a bookseller in West Bow before in 1843 establishing a print works at Hope Park. In 1878 the works were destroyed by fire and the city allowed them temporary accommodation in the Meadows. The stone pillars at the east end of Melville Drive are in acknowledgement of this. The firm moved on to large premises on Dalkeith Road. Although Nelson's first publishing endeavours concentrated on religious and educational books, they widened their interests and were the original publishers of Arthur Conan Doyle. John Buchan was a partner in the firm.

When I was at Cambridge University in the 1960s I edited a student magazine. The chief pleasure of this activity was visiting the printer and discussing layout enveloped by the pounding of the press and the smell of paper and printer's ink. You won't find any of that in Edinburgh's High Street now, but once it must have been difficult to walk through the Old Town and not be aware of the production of the printed word – newspapers, pamphlets, legal papers, text books, journals, novels, poetry. There are no bookshops in the High Street now, but a diversion into Tweeddale Court takes you to Canongate Publishing and the premises that were once Oliver & Boyd. There's still a sign as a reminder. Thomas Oliver was a printer, George Boyd a bookbinder, and they established premises in Tweeddale Court in 1820. The firm flourished as printers and publishers for more than 140 years.

So there's printer's ink running down the High Street as well as blood, and the clank and pound of presses as well as the clash of claymores. Among the ghosts lurking in the wynds and closes there are surely compositors peering at the handwriting of some of the world's greatest writers and deftly sifting their cases of type. Perhaps we need a counterpart to Fergusson striding down the Canongate and Hume thoughtfully contemplating the congested traffic flow at the top of the Mound to commemorate the trade that they both depended on.

In 1785, nine years after the protests against Hume's atheism, the geologist James Hutton, 'that true son of fire' (in Edwin Morgan's words), was presenting a theory of the formation of the earth which would, at least by implication, challenge Christian orthodoxy. In that year he gave two papers to the Royal Society of Edinburgh which argued that rocks were formed from molten matter from the earth's interior, and that this was a continuing process. Morgan's poem, 'Theory of the earth', continues:

> What but imagination could have read
> granite boulders back to their molten roots?
> And how far back was back, and how far on
> would basalt still be basalt, iron iron?

He draws a parallel between Hutton and Burns, geologist and poet, the latter pledging love till 'aw the seas gang dry', something that perhaps Hutton

Salisbury Crags. Rachel Calder.

could imagine, Scotland's coast dissolving 'in crinkled sand and pungent mist'.

Hutton's *Theory of the Earth* was published in 1795. He died in 1799, a year after Burns. Although *Theory of the Earth* became accepted as a basic principle in geology there was heated controversy, with supporters of a rival theory put forward by the German geologist Abraham Werner fiercely contesting Hutton. Werner maintained that rocks and minerals had been formed from layers of sediment deposited by oceans that had originally covered the whole of the earth.

The debate over the rival theories raged, with Edinburgh at the centre of the storm. Many of the city's leading intellectuals, including Scott, entered the fray, which illustrates how the natural sciences at that time were not the domain of specialists. John Gibson Lockhart, Scott's son-in-law, commented with evident glee: 'Though I don't care for geology, I do like to see the fellows fight.' An ardent supporter of Werner was Robert Jamieson, who in 1804 became professor of natural history at the university and presided over the museum. Jamieson was not content with argument. When the Royal Society passed on Hutton's geological collection to the museum, Jameson not only ignored it, but attempted to deny known Huttonians access to geological specimens.

The Royal Society of Edinburgh was founded in 1783, for the 'advancement of Learning and useful Knowledge… suited to the state of that part of our realm which is called Scotland'. Unlike the London Royal Society, which focused on science, the RSE was from the outset more broadly based, concerned with the arts as well as science, and with the process of education. It reflected the close intellectual and personal relationships which were at the heart of Edinburgh's Enlightenment. 'The nature of Enlightenment scholarship,' wrote Charles Waterston, '…required one branch of learning to be informed and counterbalanced by another.' The RSE became the locus for presenting research and testing theories, which often resulted in robust debate. Like the Society of Antiquaries, founded three years earlier, it was a vehicle for formalising and propagating the advances in knowledge which fuelled new ideas.

On a grey summer Sunday Arthur and I, and the dog, follow the Braid Burn past Hermitage of Braid, with Blackford Hill rising on our left and the Braid Hills on our right. Like the castle rock and Arthur's Seat, Blackford Hill is a volcanic stump, another reminder of the ancient earth activity which shaped the contours of the city. The path is busy with the usual joggers, walkers and dogs. In her novel *The Road to Hell* (2012) Gillian Galbraith describes just this walk, through 'a miniature Highland glen within the Lowland city'. But there is something ominous and sinister about this glen. Her walker experiences a rising terror as she hears 'a strange scrabbling sound, as if something, or someone, was clawing its way through the undergrowth'. This pleasing oasis in the midst of the city is about to become a crime scene.

Today there is nothing to disturb the peace of Sunday recreation. We pass the outcrop of dark, smooth and furrowed rock that attracted the attention of the Swiss geologist Louis Aggasiz some half a century after Hutton's *Theory of the Earth* appeared. Agassiz's interpretation of the rock's smooth surface and its striations was that they were the result of the movement of ice. With this he initiated the glacial theory in Scotland. By the time of Agassiz's visit, Edinburgh was well-established as a centre of geological study, helped by the fact that local quarrying to provide stone for the expanding city revealed much of geological interest. On an earlier visit Agassiz himself helped to identify some of the uncovered fossil remains. In 1833 fossil fish had been found in a limestone quarry at Burdiehouse, then a rural area to the east of the Pentland Hills, causing great excitement among Edinburgh geologists. Their location in Devonian and Carboniferous rock between three hundred and four hundred million years old indicated that vertebrates existed on earth many millions of years before the biblical version of their creation.

Agassiz, described as a 'brilliant intellect, a man of outstanding ambition and enthusiasm with a charming manner and seemingly boundless energy and endless resources', stirred the enthusiasm of Edinburgh geologists and stimulated the collection of geological material. This in turn benefited the university's Natural History Museum. It also spurred a campaign to establish a geological museum, which in turn led to the growing demand that Edinburgh should have a new museum containing a wide range of natural history specimens and artefacts, ancient and contemporary, from throughout the world. It was envisaged as a key educational institution, open to the wider public.

In 1840, the year of Agassiz's second visit, Hugh Miller, a former stone mason from Cromarty, made his home in Edinburgh. He came to take up the position of first editor of *The Witness*, the newspaper published by the

Evangelical Party of the Church of Scotland, which grew into a movement that eventually divided the church. But Miller had another identity, as a self-taught geologist who had developed his own interpretations. He had spent many years collecting fossils.

> Hugh Miller, without chart or compass, was navigating the creeks and bays of Cromarty, gathering and laying up creatures of new and strange mould, or gazing with blank wonderment on forms of which no one could tell him the names, or furnish him a key to unravel the mystery of the rocks in which they were entombed.

These were the words of Dr John Anderson, a Fife minister who had himself discovered fossil fish at Dura Den near Dairsie.

Miller and his family stayed first in a tenement in St Patrick Square, south of the High Street, before moving to Sylvan Place, part of a recent development in the area that was known as Sciennes, a name derived from a 16th-century convent dedicated to St Catherine of Sienna. The convent was a casualty first of English attack in 1544, then of the Reformation. A few remnants survive in a St Catherine's Place garden, not far from Miller's home.

He may have reflected on this, and perhaps on the vestiges of Jewish graves nearby, on his daily walk across the Meadows to *The Witness* office in the High Street. The walk was almost rural. In Sciennes there was no primary school and no Hospital for Sick Children (now no longer a hospital), both of which came later in the century. The development of the Grange estate to the south was yet to come, and on the north side there was no Royal Infirmary (now also moved and replaced by the Quarter Mile assemblage of shops and restaurants) and no McEwan Hall. It would be more than a century before the university displaced much of George Square, although Playfair's new building was conspicuous to the east.

Miller first came to Edinburgh in 1824, arriving from Cromarty by sea. The Leith smack on which he sailed approached Leith harbour through mist. He was full of anticipation, having read Ramsay and Fergusson and Scott – 'I was not yet too old to feel as if I were approaching a great magical city' he wrote in *My Schools and Schoolmasters* (1854). While waiting for the tide to allow the boat into the harbour he had time to gaze at an Edinburgh fitfully appearing through the mist.

At one time a flat reach of the New Town came full into view, along which, in the general dimness, the multitudinous chimneys stood up like stacks of corn in a field newly reaped; at another, the Castle loomed out dark in the cloud; then, as if suspended over the earth, the rugged summit of Arthur's Seat came strongly out, while its base still remained invisible...

He had come to work at his trade as stonemason, but had time to walk, in the city and its environs, and to observe. When he made his home in Edinburgh 16 years later he continued his habit of walking. Geologist Archibald Geikie described him:

Among the picturesque figures that walked the streets of Edinburgh in the middle of the [19th] century, one that often caught the notice of the passer-by was that of a man of good height and broad shoulders, clad in a suit of rough tweed, with a shepherd's plaid across his chest and a stout stick in his hand. His shock of sandy-coloured hair escaped from under a soft felt-hat; his blue eyes, either fixed on the ground or gazing dreamily ahead, seemed to take no heed of their surroundings...

Geikie added that the name Hugh Miller 'had not only grown to be a household word in Edinburgh and over the whole of Scotland, but had now become familiar wherever the English language was spoken, even to the furthest wilds of Canada and the United States'.

Yet in Victorian Edinburgh Miller, household word or not, was an outsider, like James Hogg before him who similarly was identified by his shepherd's plaid. Hogg, who aspired to be part of the *Edinburgh Review*'s literary set, was mocked by the literary establishment. Miller was not concerned with any sort of establishment and certainly had no wish to belong to the New Town elite. His religious, social and scientific beliefs were uncompromising, but hard to reconcile. In 1854, he and his family made their home in Portobello, by that time a pleasant residential area. It was there, on Christmas Eve 1856, that Miller, after a night of torment, shot himself with the pistol he always carried with him. Five days later he was buried in the Grange Cemetery, with some 4,000 mourners joining the funeral procession and shops along the route closed. A post-mortem revealed evidence of brain disease. He is another in Edinburgh's cast of troubled characters. One of the narrow streets of the Stockbridge Colonies, built in the 1860s, is named for him. My friend and former colleague, the late Liz Robertson, used to live there.

New Town. Alan Daiches. Courtesy National Library of Scotland.

Spaciousness, order and good sense

*Everything in it breathes spaciousness, order and good sense.*
Edwin Muir, *Scottish Journey*

*Mun cuairt, coire thaighean drùidhteach*
*comharra aois glòir-mhiannich*
*All round, a cauldron of imposing houses,*
*sign of an ambitious age*
Meg Bateman, 'Gàrradh Moray Place, an Dùn Eideann'
('Moray Place Gardens, Edinburgh')

THE FIRST EDINBURGH street I got to know was Heriot Row, in the heart of the New Town. I arrived there with my family in a taxi from Waverley Station. It was the summer of 1946 and I was four years old. My earliest impressions of Edinburgh were of broad streets and tall grey terraces of houses quite unlike the house I lived in at the time. The bulky statues at the George Street junctions made a particular impression on me, although George IV and William Pitt and William Chalmers of course meant nothing to me. We had come from Washington, D.C., by ship across the Atlantic to Southampton and by train via London. London was a place of dust and bombsites. Memories blend of course, and I can't distinguish four-year-old perceptions from later childhood memories, but compared with what I'd glimpsed of London, Edinburgh seemed clean and commodious. The New Town streets were quiet. There were very few cars, but there were still horse-drawn coal carts and brewers' drays, and trams.

My grandmother lived in her Heriot Row flat for around half a century. At the time she moved in, in the year following the death of my grandfather and not long before our 1946 visit, number ten was newly converted. Her flat was on the first floor, a handsome drawing room, two bedrooms, one large, one small, and a small kitchen. There were two large walk-in cupboards full of intriguing stuff. Over the years I would come to know the flat very well.

Heriot Row wasn't part of the initial plan for the New Town. James Craig's scheme of 1766 allowed for three parallel streets to the north of the Nor' Loch, the first following the line of the Lang Dykes and looking to the castle, and the third looking north: Princes Street, George Street and Queen Street, with connecting streets running north to south, and with squares at either end diplomatically named for St Andrew and St George. St Andrew survived. St George retained a church, but his square was given to Charlotte, the wife of George III who had come to the throne in 1760. A difficult choice between the patron saint of England and the queen – but Charlotte is the only woman to be acknowledged in the naming of the New Town's streets and squares. The two main north-south connecting streets were named Hanover and Frederick – George III's uncle and son were both Frederick.

The New Town is a paean to the Union and the House of Hanover. It is the latter that dominates. The two narrow intermediary streets of Rose and Thistle were not intended for the Edinburgh elite, and Thistle Street in particular is easily overlooked. The plan and the naming of streets were a statement of intent. The city had outgrown its squalid, crowded ridge. Its spirit of enquiry and creativity turned its eyes to the north. There, below the castle and beyond the festering Nor' Loch, a 'noxious lake', was space, space that would accommodate a new Edinburgh and a new outlook.

The first challenge was making a connection between old and new. Drainage of the 'noxious lake' began in 1759; the whole process took 60 years. The foundation stone of the North Bridge was laid in 1763 by Lord Provost George Drummond who had been instrumental in getting plans for the city's expansion under way. North Bridge was completed in 1772, though there had been a disaster in its making. In 1769 it collapsed, killed five people, and William Mylne, the bridge builder, had himself to finance the rebuilding, which left him penniless. He had little option but to head for the colonies, which he did, spending a number of years engaged in subsistence farming in Georgia. (The rebuilt bridge was rebuilt a second time in the 1890s.) The slow process of creating the Mound began in 1781 when the first of 2,000,000 cartloads of earth displaced by building work was dumped to create a sloping connection between the two Edinburghs.

At the time these first steps towards transformation took place there were about 70,000 people living in Edinburgh. It was, according to Robert Chambers, 'a picturesque, odorous, inconvenient, old-fashioned town'. And he went on, 'It had no court, no factories, no commerce; but there was a nest of lawyers… and a considerable number of Scotch gentry'. This wasn't entirely accurate as without commerce and manufacture (though mostly situated outwith the city boundaries) the Old Town – and the nest of lawyers – would have struggled.

Craig's plan provided a formal pattern of streets and squares with the Nor' Loch transformed into a canal running through a park planted with trees. There were terraces of houses, churches, assembly rooms, galleries and other amenities. Although the plan wasn't followed precisely, its general principles and many of its specific details became reality, though the canal never materialised.

The project attracted some notable architects. Robert Adam, the Kirkcaldy-born architect who had already made his mark in London and elsewhere in England, designed Charlotte Square at the west end and Register House at the east. But the building that faces what was once St George's Church in Charlotte Square is in St Andrew Square, and is now the headquarters of the Royal Bank of Scotland. It was designed by William Chambers as a freestanding house for Sir Laurence Dundas who amassed a fortune as commissary general and contractor to the army and was much involved in industrial developments on the shores of the Forth. A church, a bank and a storehouse of archives – apt punctuation points for a reimagined city where religion, money and history shaped so much of its character. Almost opposite Register House was the Theatre Royal taking its place in Shakespeare Square in 1769, which later became the site of the General Post Office built in the 1860s. The building is now occupied by Amazon's Scottish headquarters and Creative Scotland, a link between the commercial and the cultural which probably doesn't impinge on the working lives of those who occupy the premises.

In *Guy Mannering* (1815), set towards the end of the 18th century when the building of the New Town was just beginning, Scott writes that 'the great bulk of the better classes, and particularly those connected with the law, still lived in flats or dungeons of the Old Town' and it is in the Old Town that his hero encounters the legal fraternity. 'The desire of room, of air, and of decent accommodation had not yet made very much progress in the capital of Scotland.' And lawyers, according to Scott who was of course a lawyer himself, were particularly reluctant to embrace change: 'the custom of mixing work and revelry with serious business was still maintained by those senior counsellors, who loved the old road'. Colonel Mannering makes his way, with a guide, along the High Street, which clangs 'with the voices of oyster-women and the bells of pie-men'. He is unaccustomed to crowded streets, the noise, the 'sounds of trade, of revelry and of license'. The colonel is seeking the lawyer Mr Pleydell, whom he eventually tracks down

Old Town doorway. Alan Daiches. Courtesy National Library of Scotland.

indulging in his customary Saturday night entertainment, which involved a great deal of claret in insalubrious surroundings. Mannering is baffled that 'a gentleman of liberal profession, and good society, should choose such a scene for social indulgence'. The place, in a dark alley and up a dark stair, is 'paltry and half ruinous', with a window that admits little light and 'a

Heriot Row. Rachel Calder.

villainous compound of smells'. But all this would be left behind by the gentlemen 'of liberal profession'.

Wealthier residents of the Old Town could hardly wait for the chance to buy a neo-classical terrace house, spacious and convenient, with modern plumbing and streets broad enough for carriages. Both houses and streets were rapidly constructed, with local quarries providing the stone for housing and paving. And the New Town spread, continuing down the northward slope to Heriot Row, Northumberland Street, the impressive Great King Street ('of truly Roman frozen grandeur', according to Charles McKean), the more modest Cumberland Street. To the west a series of circles broke the regularity of the grid: Randolph Crescent, Ainslie Place, Moray Place. The curves were deliberate. When in 1822 William Burn developed a plan for the Moray estate he said that he was 'most anxious to produce something that shall be extremely productive of advantageous speculation and totally different from the monotony of our present streets and squares'. To the east the curve of Abercromby Place relieves the parallels while down the hill towards Stockbridge, Royal Circus seems to herald the less regular development of the Raeburn estate.

Lord Cockburn joined the exodus, taking a house in Charlotte Square, but had many reservations.

> Our escape from the Old Town gave us an unfortunate propensity to avoid whatever had distinguished the place we had fled from. Hence we were led into the blunder of long straight lines of streets, divided to an inch, and all to the same exact duplicate of its neighbour, with a dexterous avoidance, as if from horror, of every ornament or excrescence by which the slightest break might vary the surface.

He added that people went to Abercromby Place to 'stare at the curved street'. The Old Town, with its crooked closes and abrupt angles was not a place of curves; an elegant curve was indeed a novelty.

Over several decades the people of Edinburgh witnessed the disappearance of the country that rolled north to the shores of the Forth. Cockburn lamented as some of his favourite haunts were built over. In 1802 the Bellevue estate was sold. 'The whole place waved with wood,' he wrote, but the trees were going to go. He would no longer see them 'gilded by the evening sun' or hear 'the tumult of the blackbirds and thrushes sending their notes into all the adjoining houses in the blue of a summer morning'. Part of the attraction of the first phase of the New Town was the proximity of a rural domain and the unbroken prospect 'over the Forth to the north-western mountains'. Later developments curtailed the views and drastically eroded the possibilities of rural enjoyment. Cockburn recognised that some trees would have to go, but felt that many could have been spared 'to the comfort and adornment of future buildings'.

> I remember people shuddering when they heard the axes busy in the woods of Bellevue, and furious when they saw the bare ground. But the axes as usual triumphed; and all that art and nature had done to prepare the place for foliaged compartments of town architecture... was carefully obliterated; so that at last the whole spot was made as bare and as dull as if the designer of the New Town himself had presided over the operation.

The axes triumphed and the New Town advanced. Henry Mackenzie remembered shooting snipe in what became Heriot Row. For many, the New

Town was architectural perfection, an example of the favoured neo-classical style in all its calm, controlled stateliness. As the carriages bowled along the wide streets and the glasses and tea cups clinked in the high-ceilinged drawing rooms, most of Edinburgh's more sophisticated townspeople congratulated themselves on their city's achievement. The Old Town may have been picturesque, but spacious dignity was finer, and certainly more comfortable and salubrious.

But Cockburn wasn't alone in his criticism of the New Town. Half a century after Bellevue succumbed to the axe John Ruskin, whose father came from Edinburgh, visited the city to deliver a series of lectures. He was invited as one of the foremost commentators on art and design. His verdict on the New Town was uncompromising:

> Walk around your Edinburgh buildings, and look at the height of your eye, what will you get from them? Nothing but square-cut stone, square-cut stone – a wilderness of square-cut stone for ever and for ever; so that your houses look like prisons, and truly are so; for the worst feature of Greek architecture is, indeed, not its costliness, but its tyranny. Those square stones are not prisons of the body, but graves of the soul.

He echoed Cockburn's distress at the straight lines of streets and the avoidance of ornament. 'What a site did nature give us for our New Town!' Cockburn had lamented. 'Yet what insignificance in its plan! What poverty in all its details!'

Meg Bateman's '*Gàrradh Moray Place, an Dùn Eideann*' ('Moray Place Gardens, Edinburgh'), quoted at the start of this chapter, finds the Georgian facades, the 'cauldron of imposing houses', oppressive:

> òrduighean choibh clasaigeach
> nach aithnich laigse san duine.
>
> orders of classical columns
> that do not countenance human frailty.

The stretch of land above the Water of Leith, where Cockburn remembered hearing corncrakes, has become a territory where the architecture seems to demand certain attitudes, certain assumptions of entitlement, certain lifestyles. And yet, when I think of my grandmother's modest existence in her high-ceilinged first-floor (the drawing room floor) flat in Heriot Row, the widow of a rabbi, I am reminded that the imposing houses could accommodate different lives.

For Henry Mackenzie the New Town's houses were 'calculated for show, not convenience', and for Stevenson the prison was perhaps less the architecture than the life and attitudes it enclosed, though the two are closely related. In spite of the brooding presence of John Knox in the Old Town, and the proximity of the Covenanting martyrs, it's hard to associate the rigid confines of Presbyterianism with the Old Town as pictured by Fergusson or even Scott. And it's hard to imagine the New Town providing fertile territory for either writer, although Scott joined the descent and after his marriage in 1797 made his home in Castle Street. His son-in-law John Gibson Lockhart's first impression of the new development came in 1819 from the top of Calton Hill. It sent him into 'a sort of stupor of admiration':

> The broad glare of Prince's Street, that most superb of terraces – all beaming in the open yellow light of the sun – steeples and towers, and cupolas scattered bright beneath our feet – and, as far as the eye could reach, the whole pomp and richness of distant commotion – the heart of the city.

This, Lockhart implies, is what a city should be, striking but ordered buildings flanked by the 'distant commotion' of the city's working heartbeat. At the same time, he wrote with approval of the modest social life of Scott and his circle:

> the evening hours passed in a round of innocent gaiety, all the arrangements being conducted in a simple and inexpensive fashion, suitable to young people whose days were mostly laborious, and very few of their purses heavy.

A far cry from lawyer Pleydell's Saturday nights.

When in 1839 Hugh Miller came to Edinburgh from Cromarty he too was impressed. He found Edinburgh 'a picturesque city of the grey, time-faded past, drawn out side by side, as if for purposes of comparison, with a gay, fresh-tinted city of the present, rich in all the elegance and amenities'.

For him town and country were not in 'uncompromising opposition' but co-existed 'as if they had resolved in showing how congruously, and how to their mutual advantage, they could unite and agree'. But Miller had not known the trees and blackbirds and thrushes before they disappeared.

Most who made the transition from old to new recognised that something was lost. Whether that something was to be regretted was another matter. Life no longer spilled out onto the streets. The legal elite no longer rubbed shoulders with hawkers and fishwives. The taverns ceased to be places of intellectual exchange and the conclusion of business deals. The New Town was planned to create a separation between the domestic and the commercial, between respectability and the services on which respectability depended. The New Town, in Cockburn's words, 'altered the style of living, obliterated local arrangements, and destroyed a thousand associations'. The New Town 'obliterated our old peculiarities'. And it wasn't just that life in the New Town was different; life in the Old was changed irrevocably.

As the aristocrats and professionals made the descent into Georgian terraces, businesses moved with the exodus. Blackwood's bookshop relocated from South Bridge to Picardy Place. The luckenbooths disappeared with the demolition of the Tolbooth, but the New Town's new residents needed shops. Princes Street, devised as residential, became a street of retail. For Flora Grierson, writing in the 1920s, this did not destroy the appeal of this unique thoroughfare:

> Princes Street by night is a poem... the long ribbon lying in the blue of a northern evening against the black shadow of the old town, the misty hollow of the gardens, the high line of shops.

And today it's not so easy to recapture that sense of separation from the crude realities of commerce and working life. George Street and Queen Street have long since ceased to be mainly residential. Few original New Town houses remain intact. They've been converted into flats, like my grandmother's, or offices. In the 1970s I knew a family who lived in George Street in an upper flat, but even then almost all the street level premises were businesses of some kind. Now it is a street of designer shops and bars and restaurants. Those who today live in the New Town may be distant from deprivation but are never far away from commercial transactions and the incessant onslaught of consumerism.

Rose Street North Lane. Alan Daiches. Courtesy National Library of Scotland.

In the 19th century the price the New Town paid for exclusivity was to have an underworld a short step away. The area east of Leith Walk became notorious for narrow, fetid streets and illegal taverns and brothels. From time to time there were police raids. To the west there was Lothian Road. Along the broad streets of the New Town, gentlemen emerged from their Georgian front doors to attend their places of occupation, in the law, or medicine, at the university, or, like Stevenson's father Thomas, in civil engineering. To reach them, most of these professional men had to ascend to the Old Town, where the law courts, the university and the Royal Infirmary were located. They could not fail to be aware of ragged, barefoot children playing and scrapping at the mouths of dark closes, of women soliciting, of the destitute inclined to spend their last pennies on a tot of gin. And when they left their places of work and descended again to their neat rows and squares, the castle and the crooked outline of the Old Town looked down on them, an unceasing reminder that however firmly their doors were closed, barbarity and squalor remained an integral part of the city's past and present life.

The New Town and the legacy of the Enlightenment heightened the contrast but they couldn't obliterate the relationship. Nothing illustrated this so emphatically as the notorious case of William Burke and William Hare. The two Ulstermen came to Scotland to work, like many of their countrymen, on the Union Canal, which opened in 1822. They graduated to more lucrative activity when they responded to the needs of those who conducted classes in anatomy. The teaching of medicine in Edinburgh was highly regarded. The second half of the 17th century saw the university flourish as a pioneering centre of medical study and discovery, attracting students from all over the world. Its reputation continued into the next century, but the education of medical students depended on a supply of cadavers for dissection. Hanged criminals were one source of supply, but not sufficient to meet the need. The gap was filled by another form of criminality. The robbing of graves to supply cadavers for medical science became so common that many burial grounds had watchtowers to safeguard the newly interred, and coffins were sometimes enclosed in mortsafes to make them impossible to extract. You can see a mortsafe, a kind of iron cage intended to protect the coffin, in the National Museum. Stevenson's story *The Body Snatchers* is an account of a grave robbery that ends somewhat unexpectedly.

The two Williams didn't go to the trouble of digging up corpses. It was more efficient to provide their own, which they delivered to Dr Robert Knox, a former army surgeon who became a very popular teacher of anatomy in Edinburgh. From their base in the West Port it was not difficult for Burke and Hare to find likely targets, mainly waifs and strays whose disappearance was not likely to be noticed. When they were eventually apprehended they had been responsible for probably 17 murders. Hare escaped the gallows by turning king's evidence. Burke was hanged in 1829 in front of a large crowd. The mob then turned its fury on Robert Knox, who had made no enquiry as to the source of material for his well-attended and financially rewarding lectures. Knox had to leave Edinburgh and his reputation never recovered. 'No case ever struck the public heart or imagination with greater horror,' was Lord Cockburn's comment. He himself acted successfully in defence of Helen Macdougal, Burke's common-law wife. He believed Burke to be 'sensible' and 'respectable'. He was 'not at all ferocious in his general manner, sober, correct in all his other habits'.

Here in a single notorious tale of greed and iniquity is the intimacy between respectability and depravity, eminence and evil made manifest. Knox chose not to enquire as to how his cadavers were sourced, but it seems unlikely that, even though Burke and Hare smothered their victims to ensure no obvious signs of violence, he would have failed to spot evidence of unnatural demise. The streets where Burke and Hare tracked down their victims were no distance from Surgeon's Hall. Knox himself lived in Newington Place to the south so did not have to negotiate the unwholesome Old Town on his route between work and home, but he could not close his one good eye (the other was damaged) to its realities. Were some lives expendable? It was easier to assume so than to attempt to address the causes of destitution, easier perhaps to argue that expendable lives could become purposeful if they contributed to advances in medical science. Hare's skeleton is preserved in the university's medical school, an apt reminder of the fact that Edinburgh's renown as a seat of enlightenment went hand in hand with an ugly episode that is engrained in the city's contradictory character. A short walk from the order and elegance of the New Town was a dark territory of blurred boundaries between iniquity and progress.

Scott was very conscious of iniquity, and of its connection with the carefully contrived gentility he himself had embraced. He reflected on 'the simple and cosy retreats, where worth and talent and elegance to boot nestled, and which are now the resort of misery, filth, and vice.' Robert Louis Stevenson was acutely conscious of the same dichotomy, and as a young man sought out evidence of the subterranean life on which his own home was built. He haunted the city's underworld. 'I love night in the city,' he wrote, 'the lighted streets and the swinging gait of harlots'. He had a mission to observe and record beyond the comfort of Heriot Row, and he put the results to good use in the fiction he came to write later.

James McLevy, police detective operating in Edinburgh in the mid-19th century, commented that although the Old Town was a 'squalid theatre' and 'troubled with many miseries', it was 'the scene of more incidents, often humorous, nay romantic – if there can be a romance of low life – than can be found in the quiet saloons of the higher grades in the New Town'. In the New Town, he went on to say:

> you have nature over-laid with the art of concealment, the slave of decorum, in the other you have the old mother, free, fresh, and frisky – her true characters, rapid movements, quiet thoughts, intertwined plots, the jerks of passion, the humorous and the serious, the comedy and the melodrama of the tale of life.

Stevenson may have read these words, published in 1861. They may have encouraged his youthful excursions beyond the New Town's quiet salons into the melodrama of the Old. When he came to write he showed little interest in chronicling New Town life, except through experiences of childhood reflected in *A Child's Garden of Verses* (1885). And even there, many of the poems hinge on his grandfather's manse in rural Colinton, where a garden, a graveyard and the Water of Leith triggered adventure and spurred the imagination. (From 1874, the suburban railway line to Balerno passed close to the manse, and although Stevenson was fond of trains this inevitably altered the wilderness he evokes in his poems.)

It was in his Castle Street study that Walter Scott planned an extravaganza that had little to do with the Edinburgh of the New Town, still building, or the burgeoning industry on the edges of the city. It was 1822. George IV was to visit 'his ancient kingdom of Scotland' and it was Scott's belief that he 'must be received according to its ancient usages'. Exactly what those 'usages' were perhaps rested more in the realms of the imagination than in reality, but who more qualified than Scott to reimagine, and if necessary manipulate, history to present Scotland as a proudly distinctive player in a kingdom united under the House of Hanover?

To achieve this, Scott summoned the Highland clans to Scotland's capital (they didn't all respond) and instructed them in how to present themselves to their king. They were, of course, to wear the once-forbidden tartan and to be armed 'in the proper Highland fashion – steel wrought pistols, broadsword and dirk'. The descendants of those who once made a bid to remove George IV's grandfather from the throne were now considered tame enough to parade their identity and their weapons. And those with no claim to clan connections were also encouraged to wear tartan. The *Edinburgh Observer* commented, 'We are now all Jacobites, thorough-bred Jacobites, in acknowledging George IV.'

Preparations were elaborate. Huge crowds were expected and viewing stands and platforms constructed to accommodate them. When George finally arrived at Leith – after much prevarication – the rain was so heavy he was advised to delay disembarkation although crowds waited in the downpour. The next day he made his way from Leith to Holyrood in a procession escorted by Highlanders, bagpipes and the Scots Greys, and flanked by more Highlanders and the Royal Company of Archers. Mary Frances Grant described the crowd in Picardy Place, eagerly awaiting the procession:

> All the stages and platforms were crowded with people; the windows of each tall house full to the very top, the Calton Hill covered with tents and spectators; the streets crowded on each side, and a broad empty space lined with yeomanry left in the middle for the coming procession. Even the roofs of the houses were covered with people standing upright by the chimneys or clinging where they could; the doors and steps of the houses all full; boys seated on the top of the lamp-posts and hanging up the posts.

George did not stay at Holyrood but went on to be entertained by the Duke of Buccleuch at Dalkeith House some ten miles away. But that evening Edinburgh was lit up with candles placed in house windows, a bonfire on Arthur's Seat and iron baskets of burning coal on the castle. 'Every spot light as noon-day, each house illuminated with splendour,' wrote James Grant. Gas lighting had come to Edinburgh in January of that year but candlelight was more atmospheric.

The next day George IV famously made his appearance at a levée at Holyrood in Royal Stewart tartan and pink tights, which did nothing for his excess of flesh. Not everyone was impressed. 'The king did not seem to move a muscle,' wrote James Stuart of Dunearn, 'and we all asked ourselves when we came away, what had made us take so much trouble. He was dressed in tartan. Sir Walter had ridiculously made us appear a nation of Highlanders, and the bagpipe and the tartan was [sic] the order of the day'. Ridiculous, perhaps, but the confluence of tartan was indicative. It was more than a parade for the king's benefit, a demonstration of a heroically picturesque but safely defused and diffused past. With George's projection of himself in tartan he was signifying his Stewart ancestry and credentials. He was 'one of us', and the encouragement of all to collude in the presentation of 'a nation of Highlanders' was part of Scott's effort to convey both reconciliation and a historical identity which could be accommodated in a progressive present. Interestingly, George spent little time in the part of Edinburgh named for his family.

There was perhaps something else going on. Edinburgh, for a few days and in spite of the fact that the king did not actually spend many hours in the city, responded to his visit with extraordinary enthusiasm and was *en fête* in an unprecedented fashion. If not exactly a Saturnalia, it seemed to release something that Scotland generally, and Edinburgh in particular, needed. There were balls and assemblies and benign crowds on the streets. The declining muddle of the Old Town and the neat regularity of the New were transformed. It wouldn't happen again until a different kind of festival came to the city 125 years later.

The king departed from Dalkeith House in heavy rain on 29 August. His carriage briskly proceeded through Edinburgh to the sound of a salute fired from the castle. He drove through Lord Rosebery's estate at Dalmeny and on to Hopetoun House where he was received by Lord Hopetoun, bands and bugles, and another crowd of loyal onlookers. Among them were 'boy scholars from the parish school of Abercorn', where my own children went to school after we moved out of the city, though not in the same building. (The school was closed some years ago and the one-time schoolhouse and two classrooms now house an accountancy firm.) From Hopetoun it was a short drive to Port Edgar where the Royal Squadron awaited. Seven years later William Burke was hanged and William Hare was released from jail.

Eighteen twenty-two was the year in which Scott published both *The*

*Pirate* and *The Fortunes of Nigel*. He was still the anonymous 'author of *Waverley*', although the secret was not well kept. He was acknowledged as having the knowledge, the imagination and the authority to be allowed – encouraged – to invent and orchestrate Edinburgh's reception of the grandson of the king who had put an end to Stewart aspirations of gaining the throne of the United Kingdom. Dividing his time between Castle Street and Abbotsford, the first an emblem of ordered progress, the second a tribute to the past, he was a one-man literary powerhouse.

Today, the New Town itself has claim to be a literary powerhouse, if only for two weeks each year. Early in August the transformation of Charlotte Square is under way. It took much persuasion to allow giant marquees to be erected on the grass, under the stern gaze of Prince Albert, but now the Edinburgh International Book Festival is synonymous with Charlotte Square. It has resided there since its inception in 1983, and has greatly expanded since those early days. I used to watch on my daily journey to and from work as the book camp took shape. The big main marquee, the smaller marquees – more it seemed each year – the book tents and the wonderful spiegeltent. I can't remember the year in which the authors' yurt first appeared, but it is now a fixture, providing a comfortable refuge for participants and their guests. There have been years when the remaining grass has been churned into a sea of mud. The response has been to increase the extent of covered walkways. I have sat in the main tent while the wind howled and battered the canvas (though it's probably not canvas) while buses rumbled noisily round the square and sirens screamed. It's all part of the atmosphere.

For writers and readers it is hugely encouraging to have a gathering place that is all about books. It may also be about drinking wine, eating ice cream and celebrity spotting – but none of that would be happening without the books.

Charlotte Square. Rachel Calder.

I have attended the Book Festival in most capacities – as a member of many audiences, as an author, as a chair of events, and as a publisher. I have had only one bad experience, when the star author of an event I was chairing behaved with rude disregard for both organisers and audience. I have not read any of his books since.

The permanent headquarters of the Book Festival are now also in Charlotte Square, on the north side next door to Bute House, the official residence of Scotland's First Minister. On the other side of Bute House is the National Trust for Scotland's Georgian House. Scotland's first First Minister Donald Dewar was a dedicated reader. It must have been a joy to him to see books blossom each year at his front door. But the Square is not otherwise a bookish place, though for many years the Scottish Arts Council was located on its west side. Most of the buildings house businesses connected with finance. The austere facades and the grey stone mask the activities within. In the words of Ian Rankin: 'wealth was a very private thing in the city. It wasn't brash and colourful. It stayed behind its thick stone walls and was at peace.' Two hundred years earlier, in the Old Town, wealth was 'brash and colourful'.

Tucked away in Young Street, round the corner from Charlotte Square, is a place of literary pilgrimage. There you will find the cramped premises of Ian Rankin's Oxford Bar, where you might find the author himself but where you won't find Detective Inspector John Rebus although it is his favourite haunt.

Stevenson would have liked the Oxford Bar, a short walk from his family home, which is perhaps one reason why Rankin likes it. It is an anomaly in an age of the 21st-century wine bars and restaurants which liberally populate the New Town. For contrast with the haunt of Rebus, try out the nearby Panda & Sons, a bar which features a tartan-clad panda family and offers a range of whisky cocktails. Rankin has often acknowledged his debt to Stevenson, but even without that acknowledgement, his books echo Stevenson's fascination with the city's contrasts.

Oxford Bar. Rachel Calder.

Rebus himself doesn't live in the New Town, but it is characteristic that two things take him there – the criminal activities lurking behind those thick stone walls and the Oxford Bar. 'A pub like the Ox was about so much more than just the hooch. It was therapy and refuge, entertainment and art,' Rebus reflects in *The Hanging Garden* (1998).

Alexander McCall Smith's characters, in his many novels set in Edinburgh, are unlikely to be found in the Oxford Bar. Although plenty of his people behave badly, they move about a city that is likely to be comfortably familiar to many Edinburgh readers. 'One did not want too much excitement in a place like Edinburgh,' Isobel Dalhousie, central character of a series of novels, reflects. McCall Smith's people move through the New Town, Merchiston, Bruntsfield, the Grange, spend time in real cafés and shops, and meet some of the city's prominent individuals, but Isobel is aware that 'workaday' Edinburgh is mainly out of sight, 'the back greens, the closes, the streets where people led ordinary lives'. I like to imagine her enjoying a dram in the Oxford Bar while detective Inspector John Rebus disabuses her of the notion that 'if there was blood on Scottish pavements it was because of old wounds, not new'. I think she might be up for that and would find a way – philosopher as she is – of absorbing Edinburgh's underworld into her ethical landscape.

John Ruskin was severe on the subject of the New Town's uniformity, but if one is inclined to agree with his judgment it is worth reflecting on its most attractive feature. You are in the New Town never more than a few minutes' walk from trees and green space. Some of the gardens are private. As a child I played in Queen Street Gardens, as my grandmother had a key, but now I am not able to remind myself of what it was like to explore along the paths and under the trees or canter across the grass on an imaginary horse. There are smaller gardens in Ainslie Place and Moray Place. When my father and his second wife lived in Randolph Crescent they had access to the gardens at the back of their flat that stretched down to the Water of Leith. On the other side of the water are the Dean Gardens, and upriver Belgrave Crescent Gardens. When I and my family lived in Buckingham Terrace we paid an annual fee for a key to the latter, and my children often played there. At the bottom of the slope close to the water there was a picnic place, where Rachel, my eldest, once had a birthday party. We processed with the picnic, birthday cake included, round the corner, across the road, through the gate, along the tree-enclosed path. Down by the lively river we could have been in the heart of the Highlands. *Rus in urbe* indeed. No corncrakes or snipe, perhaps, but I did once spot a kingfisher on a branch above the water.

Today the less privileged can only peer through the iron railings of these guarded spaces. A few minutes from where I live now is a park, small but big enough for the dog's ball games and for children to ride their bikes and scooters and make dens in the shrubbery. There are roses and rhododendrons and hydrangeas, and benches. It is open to everyone, and although occasionally there is an abandoned beer can or crisp packet any suggestion that it might become the gated preserve of local residents willing to pay for the privilege would be outrageous.

Buckingham Terrace and the nearby streets on either side of Queensferry Road, the main artery out of Edinburgh to the northwest, are not the New Town. These are mid-Victorian terraces built in the 1860s. Most of them have very English names: Belgrave, Clarendon, Eton, Oxford as well as Buckingham. It is as if Edinburgh wanted to signal an alignment with England, to be identified as North Britain rather than as a separate Scottish nation. The New Town may have been a tribute to the Hanoverians, but the second and subsequent stages of its development included plenty of names that reflected a local identity: Moray, Ainslie, Heriot, Raeburn, Abercromby, Doune, Randolph, Drummond, that helped to balance the English character of Gloucester, Northumberland and – insulting to some – Cumberland.

On Saturday afternoons I and my children would walk across the Dean Bridge, along the three successive crescents of Randolph Crescent, Ainslie Place and Moray Place, and on to Heriot Row. There we would have tea with my grandmother and watch *Dr Who*, my son, the youngest, behind the sofa, replete with Jaffa cakes.

From Corstorphine Hill. Rachel Calder.

8

Nothing can abolish the hills

*Nothing can abolish the hills, unless it be a cataclysm of nature.*
RL Stevenson, *Edinburgh. Picturesque Notes*

*Arthur's Seat was perfect witchcraft.*
Washington Irving, *Correspondence*

IN THE LAST few years of my father's life I would visit him twice a week, driving from Queensferry to his flat in Belgrave Crescent, round the corner from the Dean Bridge and Buckingham Terrace. I often took the dog, and stopped on the way home for a walk on Corstorphine Hill. The hill is mostly wooded, but there are places where there is a grand view to the east and you see the coastline curving away to Berwick Law and the Bass Rock. And not so far away, the castle, the craggy roofline along the Old Town's spine, and Arthur's Seat. Our usual route took us from Clermiston Road up to the Rest and be Thankful, where Stevenson's David Balfour says farewell to Alan Breck.

We came the by-way over the hill of Corstorphine; and when we got near to the place called Rest-and-be-Thankful, and looked down on Corstorphine bogs and over to the city and the castle on the hill, we both stopped, for we both knew without a word said, that we had come to where our ways parted.

Down near the Corstorphine Road there is a statue by Sandy Stoddart commemorating the two heroes, both with stern rather than sad expressions, and David looking far too old.

At the foot of the hill to the east is Craigcrook Castle, a 16th-century tower house with many additions, including extensive reconstruction in the 1830s by William Playfair (as I write, soon to be commemorated in a new statue). At that time Lord Jeffrey, judge and editor of the *Edinburgh Review*, had taken on the lease, which had previously been held by Archibald Constable, the publisher. Craigcrook was then a rural retreat and Jeffrey was a generous host to gatherings of literary and legal friends and associates. Scott was there. 'A most beautiful place,' he wrote in his journal, 'tastefully planted with shrubs and trees and so sequestered that after turning into the little avenue all symptoms of the town is [sic] left behind you.' Cockburn remembered Craigcrook Saturdays with enthusiastic

Arthur's Seat. Rachel Calder.

affection: 'Escape from the court and the town, scenery, evergreens, bowls, talk, mirth, friendship, and wine inspire better luxury than that of the Castle of Indolence'.

In 1751, when *Kidnapped* is set, Corstorphine was still a small village. Its expansion mainly dates from the coming of the railway in 1901. Twelve years later the Zoological Society of Scotland acquired the Corstorphine Hill House estate, and a zoological park was laid out to plans by Patrick Geddes and FC Mears, which utilised existing quarries to make animal enclosures. I still walk occasionally on Corstorphine Hill as far as the outer perimeter of the zoo, and back by Clermiston Tower, built in 1871 to commemorate Walter Scott on the centenary of his birth. It can't rival the unmissable monument to Scott on Princes Street, completed some 25 years earlier. The Scott Monument, designed by George Meikle Kemp and built from sandstone from Binny in West Lothian, is a hymn to Scott and his fictional creations, inspired by Melrose Abbey and encrusted with Gothic detail. Originally intended for Charlotte Square, it stands over 200 feet high, 'a monstrous black stone spaceship' according to James Robertson, in East Princes Street Gardens, a lofty outlook between the castle and Calton

Scott Monument, Princes Street. Rachel Calder.

Hill. At the monument's centre sits Scott himself with his deerhound Maida, fashioned in marble by John Steel, while above him towers an extraordinary amalgamation of the historical and the products of his imagination. There are still plenty of 'towrists gowping up at Wattie Scott the Wizard o' Oz', Sydney Goodsir Smith with an irreverent swipe at Scott's reputation as 'the Wizard of the North'. Ascent of the monument up narrow spiral stairs should not be attempted by anyone inclined to vertigo or claustrophobia, although it brings you eyeball to eyeball with all kinds of creatures and the views from the top are splendid. The hills are the result of ancient volcanic activity, and chief amongst them is Arthur's Seat.

Many years ago on New Year's Day – it may have been 1976 or 77 – I and my family climbed Arthur's Seat with friends from Canada. There was snow on the ground, which made it all the more of an adventure, especially for the children. As we got to the top more snow began to fall and although scarcely half way through the afternoon the light was fading. We thought it wise not to linger on the summit. Rick from British Columbia decided that the straightforward way down to where we had left the two cars at Dunsapie Loch was not enough of a challenge, and to the children's alarm disappeared into the gloom in search of a more rigorous route. He's Canadian, we told them, suppressing our own anxiety. He's used to blizzards and mountains. We made our way down through the snow. There was no sign of Rick. Mountain rescue on Arthur's Seat seemed a bit extreme, but if it hadn't been long before the days of mobile phones we would have been tempted to call emergency services. We couldn't drive off without him, although our intrepid Canadian would probably have eventually found his way back to Buckingham Terrace. And then a shape appeared out of the thickening blizzard, smiling, brushing the snow off his jacket, bemused at our alarm. What was Arthur's Seat compared to the Canadian Rockies?

Not a mountain, perhaps, but Arthur's Seat has its own mystique. It is a place of mysterious appearances and disappearances, a place of myth and murder. On a sunny weekend it can be almost crowded and you'll hear many different languages spoken. There are serious walkers and people picking their way in unsuitable footwear along spiny paths. There are those who are there for the view, the air, the exercise, the geological evidence which was of such interest to 18th- and 19th-century geologists, or just to be able to say they climbed Edinburgh's most notable summit. Stewart Conn in his poem 'From Arthur's Seat' captures the juxtaposition of science and recreation.

Strange to contemplate this spot,
gouged cleanly out,
as going back millions of years;
its saucer fire and ice, volcanic
rock shaped by glaciers,
where now cameras click
and lovers stroll in pairs

In James Hogg's The Private Memoirs and Confessions of a Justified Sinner (1824) George Colwan climbs Arthur's Seat in the early morning. He looks out on a dazzling effect of sunlight, a brilliant but hazy rainbow. He sits down on a rock and enjoys

with a light and buoyant heart... the beauties of the morning'. But then he turns his head and sees 'delineated in the cloud, the shoulders, arms, and features of a human being of the most dreadful aspect... Its dark eyes gleamed on him through the mist, while every furrow of its hideous brow frowned deep as the ravines on the brow of the hill.

It is the face of his brother, with whom he is in bitter contention.

Its eyes were fixed on him, in the same manner as those of some carnivorous animal fixed on its prey; and yet there was fear and trembling, in those unearthly features, as plainly depicted as murderous malice.

What George Colwan sees is a Brocken spectre, the shadow of his brother hugely magnified by mist and diffraction of light. The hill has become a scene of menace and distortion.

Arthur's Seat was a place where outlaws might lurk. In Scott's *The Heart of Midlothian* Reuben Butler, deeply unsettled by the scenes he has witnessed in the Grassmarket, spends the rest of the night brooding on Salisbury Crags. He hears the bells of St Giles tolling each hour. When the sun rises he has an encounter with a young man 'with a certain audacity in look and manner, of that kind which is often assumed as a mask for confusion and apprehension'. After some hostile conversation during which the stranger announces, 'I am the devil!', Reuben is instructed to deliver a message to Jeanie Deans. She is to meet him 'at the Hunter's Bog tonight, as the moon rises behind St Anthony's Hill'. Jeanie, knowing that the man she is to meet is responsible for her sister Effie's predicament but knowing also that the rendezvous means entering 'a dreaded and ill-reputed district', a place of witches and demons, prepares herself with trepidation for her night walk.

The dim cliffs and scattered rocks, interspersed with green sward, through which she had to pass to the place of appointment, as they glimmered before her in a clear autumn night, recalled to her memory many a deed of violence… In earlier days they had been the haunt of robbers and assassins… The names of these criminals and their atrocities were still remembered in traditions of the scattered cottages and the neighbouring suburb.

With such thoughts 'of blood and horror' in her mind Jeanie makes her way to the rendezvous along a 'small scarce-tracked solitary path, every step of which conveyed her to a greater distance from help, and deeper into the ominous seclusion of these unhallowed precincts'. Her father's tales of encounters with the devil take hold of her imagination and she begins to think that that is what is in store for her. And indeed, when the stranger finally materialises he describes himself as 'predestined to evil here and hereafter'. He makes a desperate plea to Jeanie that she should lie to save her sister. But Jeanie refuses: 'I may not do evil, even that good may come of it'.

Arthur's Seat is an extinct volcano, one of the string of once volcanic peaks that have dictated the character of the city. That knowledge, and the crouching lion shape of the hill itself, suggest a latent violence. Benign as the grassy slopes seem in summer daylight, the scattered rocks and dark gullies suggest the ominous and unchancy. One day in 1836 some boys were out rabbit hunting on the slopes and stumbled on something very curious. Under slabs of slate they found 17 miniature coffins, each containing a little carved and clothed wooden figure. Eight of them survived and eventually in 1901 came to the National Museum. From the time of their discovery they gave rise to much speculation as to what they might represent. Was there some association with witchcraft, or were they surrogate burials for sailors who died at sea? Eventually a more convincing theory emerged. It was possible to date the coffins to around 1830, so they hadn't been long in their hiding place before they were discovered. The notorious William Burke was convicted of murder and executed in 1829. The victims of Burke and Hare numbered 17. Was it possible that the little figures in their coffins represented these victims and were buried on Arthur's Seat as a mark of respect and commemoration?

The fascination of the coffins was not lost on author Ian Rankin whose novel *The Falls* features a newly fashioned miniature coffin found near Edinburgh. Detective Inspector Rebus visits the National Museum to find out more about the originals. As they look at the coffins on display, surrounded by other reminders of mortality, he and the curator have a discussion about death. 'Aren't we all curious about the things we fear?' muses the curator. The mystery and the association with blood and malignancy prompt Rebus to remark of Edinburgh 'Some place this, eh?' There are plenty of other objects displayed in the Museum which signal the contradictions of Edinburgh and Scotland.

Nothing can abolish Edinburgh's hills, and you can't escape them. You cannot walk far in the city without a climb, whether a gentle slope or a flight of steps. The transition from New Town to Old Town is marked not just by the Mound or the less demanding rise of North Bridge, but by an array of challengingly steep closes and steps. Tourists toil slowly upwards. Cyclists swoop down the Mound at an alarming speed. I overtake youngsters on my way up to the Scottish PEN office in the Writers' Museum or my publisher on Castlehill, but then have to pause to catch my breath.

When Dorothy Wordsworth visited Edinburgh she climbed Arthur's Seat and found it 'as wild and solitary as any in the heart of the Highlands'. In his novel *Joseph Knight*, James Robertson has three 18th-century lawyers eschew the delights of a night's drinking to climb the hill. From the summit they look down on the Old Town and the beginnings of the New, and reflect on 'how huge the changes were that had already taken place, and how, in time, all the fields and gardens as far even as the village of Broughton might become paved over and built on'. Charles McKean watches a winter sunrise over Arthur's Seat:

> one of the great sights of the world; the black paganism of the castle to the west balanced against the serene classicism of Calton Hill to the east, silhouetted against a crimson sky. Ceaselessly, Edinburgh conveys the sensation of struggle between man and nature.

The castle itself epitomises that struggle, but every hill is a reminder. Calton Hill, almost part of Princes Street, is, in John Britton's words, a 'lofty, craggy, insulated eminence'. It may be planted with temples and memorials, but there remain hints of wildness, and the views, like those from the castle or Arthur's Seat, draw the eye out to the Firth of Forth and 'the dim shapes of islands and headlands, and of bays beyond dusky Leith, brick-coned Portobello, and the other near coast-towns' – David Masson writing of the 1860s. Or you might look in the other direction 'to where, over a maze of streets and chimney-stacks crowded under the very base of the hill, the sites of Burntisland, Aberdour, Inverkeithing, and the other coast-towns of Fife… seem so definite as to be within arm's hail or other friendly signal'.

Calton Hill was a favourite of Stevenson's. He liked to look across to the firth: 'Leith camps on the seaside with her forest of masts; Leith roads are full of ships at anchor; the sun picks out the white Pharos upon Inchkeith Island.' Closer at hand are 'ridge after ridge of chimney-stacks running downhill one behind another, and church spires rising bravely from the sea of roofs'. He watches figures at the windows, 'clambering chimney-sweeps', and then 'the wind takes a run and scatters the smoke; bells are heard far and near, faint and loud, to tell the hour'. The sights and sounds of the city are being observed from a 'pastoral hillside, among nibbling sheep and looked upon by monumental buildings'. Susan Ferrier's Mary, in her novel *Marriage*, is entranced by the view.

The blue water lay calm and motionless. The opposite shore glowed in a thousand varied hints of wood and plain, rock and mountains, cultured field and purple moor. Beneath, the old town reared its dark brow, and the new one stretched its golden lines.

The monuments are now as much a part of Calton Hill as the rocks and cairns are integral to Arthur's Seat. Dominated by the National Monument, the structures on the hill are an eclectic and somewhat random mix. Designed by Charles Cockerell and William Playfair, the National Monument was intended as a copy of the Parthenon, commemorating those who had died in the Napoleonic Wars. Both Scott and Cockburn were keen supporters of the idea and helped to raise funds for the monument's construction. Work began in 1826, but three years later the money ran out and it was never completed. Although disparaged as 'Edinburgh's folly' and 'Edinburgh's pride and poverty', there is something splendidly imposing about its 12 existing columns, built of stone quarried at Craigleith, and they have become a distinctive landmark. For those fit enough, the urge to clamber up onto the stone platform is irresistible. The view of the monument from Princes Street is as iconic as the castle.

Susan Ferrier's Mary has her inclinations to romance somewhat punctured by her acquaintance Bailie Broadfoot, who regrets that she is not seeing Leith glass manufacture in action – 'if the glass houses had been working, it would have looked as weel again', he says. To him 'the volcanic clouds of smoke from the glass houses… were far more interesting… than all the eruptions of Vesuvius or Etna'. Then he points out that the National Monument has been let to a pastry cook and you can now purchase 'pies and custards, and berries, and those sorts of things' but 'nothing of a spirituous nature'.

Another legacy of the Napoleonic Wars is the Nelson Monument, 'an edifice of such doubtful taste' wrote James Grant, 'that its demolition has been more than once advocated'. Work on this 30 metre tower was begun soon after the Battle of Trafalgar in 1805 but not finished until 1816. It was visible from the Forth, and a time ball at the top of the tower dropped at noon each day as a signal to ships. A few metres west of the Nelson Monument is the monument to Dugald Stewart, who was from 1785 to 1810 professor of moral philosophy at the University of Edinburgh and a key figure of the Enlightenment. But an odd choice, perhaps, out of all the Enlightenment thinkers who might have deserved a grand memorial. Yet Scott considered him 'most impressive and eloquent' and Cockburn, too, was much impressed by his lectures: 'His noble views, unfolded in glorious sentences, elevated me into a higher world.' You can climb the monument to a 'higher world' and 'noble views' of a different kind.

And then to complete the quartet of structures there is the City Observatory of 1824, another neo-classical Playfair design built to replace an older observatory which had never functioned adequately. The new building was instigated by the Astronomical Institution, founded in 1812. Ten years later the observatory was designated 'Royal' during George IV's visit to Edinburgh, and 12 years after that the first Astronomer Royal for Scotland, Professor Thomas Henderson, was appointed. The teaching of astronomy at the university had a long history, though it wasn't until 1886 that the first chair of astronomy was established. By 1895 the Calton Hill observatory was under-equipped and under-funded, with decline exacerbated by smoke from the railway below. A move was made to new, larger and better resourced premises on Blackford Hill, which has since then been at the forefront of astronomical research.

Down Calton Hill's southeast slope is the old Royal High School building, built in the 1820s to replace the original school in Infirmary Street and which for a while was mooted as a home for the new Scottish Parliament. In 1997, Scottish PEN hosted in the High School building the annual congress of International PEN, the worldwide writers' organisation. The building was hardly large enough to contain the gathering of writers from every continent and the words they generated, but its literary and enlightenment associations provided an appropriate ambience. Some of the delegates must surely have climbed to the top of the hill to reflect on those connections as well as admire the view.

The Royal High School is flanked by the Old Calton and New Calton Burying Grounds. In the former, opened in 1718 to receive tradesmen and merchants, you'll find headstones commemorating shoemakers, brewers,

Old Calton Burial Ground. Rachel Calder.

salters and upholsterers, as well as Robert Adam's monument to David Hume and the tall obelisk that commemorates five radicals who campaigned for parliamentary reform, only to be convicted in 1793 and '94 for sedition. Thomas Muir, William Skirving, Thomas Fysshe Palmer, Maurice Margarot and Joseph Gerrald were all found guilty and transported to Australia. The 1790s had seen considerable radical agitation and harsh sentences were expected, especially as the trials were presided over by Lord Justice Clerk Braxfield, notorious for an unrelenting ferocity towards criminals, who had sent Deacon Brodie to the gallows. He was probably the inspiration for Stevenson's creation, Lord Justice Clerk Adam Weir, in the unfinished *Weir of Hermiston* (1896).

Like Braxfield, Weir lives in George Square; like Braxfield, he was a 'mighty toper'; like Braxfield, he 'did not affect the virtue of impartiality... there was a man to be hanged, he would have said, and he was hanging him'. Cockburn described Braxfield as 'strong built and dark, with rough eyebrows, powerful eyes, threatening lips, and a low growling voice'. He spoke an 'exaggerated Scotch', and had no taste for 'refined enjoyment' and a 'contemptuous disdain of all natures less coarse than his own'. His conduct

147

as a judge, Cockburn unreservedly pronounced, was 'a disgrace to the age'. The most famous of the five radicals on trial, Thomas Muir, a lawyer from Glasgow, escaped from Australia and made his way to revolutionary France, where he died in 1799 (the same year as Braxfield). Words which he spoke at his trial are engraved on the monument:

I have devoted myself to the cause of The People. It is a good cause –
it shall ultimately prevail – it shall finally triumph.

William Skirving, born in Liberton, then a village near Edinburgh, also spoke memorably at his trial: 'I know that what has been done these two days will be Re-Judged.' These words are also there. Weakened by yellow fever, in 1796 Skirving died of dysentery in Australia. The memorial was erected in 1844, by which time at least some of what Muir and his associates had called for had been achieved with the Reform Act of 1832. When Lord Grey, the prime minister who steered the Reform Bill through parliament, visited Edinburgh he received a welcome that rivalled that of George IV 12 years before. But the radicals did not join in 'the homage of Scotland to its greatest political friend' (Lord Cockburn's words). The franchise had been only partially extended. There is in the burial ground another tribute to freedom fighting, in the shape of the memorial to the Scottish-American soldiers who fought in the American Civil War, over which presides a freed slave looking up in gratitude to the noble Abraham Lincoln.

The new cemetery, further along Regent Road, was created when the construction of Waterloo Place cut through part of the old. Some of the graves and monuments had to be relocated. A walk up Regent Road takes you there, past the grim 1930s edifice of St Andrew's House, once the home of the Scottish Office and where I had to go to sign the Official Secrets Act on my first day as an employee of the Royal Scottish Museum. On your left is what remains of Calton Jail and on your right you pass the monument to Robert Burns, oddly placed it seems now, as if he wasn't quite respectable enough to have a more central location. But the original aim was that it would catch the attention of travellers arriving by stagecoach from the south, the national poet welcoming visitors to the capital.

And so on Calton Hill a concentration of Edinburgh life and death, and Edinburgh aspirations and disappointments, protest and incarceration. War on land and sea, achievements in science, philosophy, literature and architecture, education, politics. A view to the Firth of Forth and the North Sea with all the associated suggestions of connections to northern Europe where so many Scots traded and studied, to France, the source of the claret that flowed so generously in Edinburgh, to Spain and Italy where Scottish soldiers fought (and all over Europe, too, of course), and west to the Americas. There were perhaps folk gathered on Calton Hill to watch the departure of the ill-fated expedition to Darien. Calton Hill is also the place of more ancient celebration, with an annual Beltane ceremony on 1 May, a revival of a Celtic ceremony marking the end of winter. It has the reputation also as a place to avoid at night. I have been there on a late summer evening, but never in the dark.

Edinburgh has long since spilled beyond the hills that once almost ringed it, but the hills remain as vital green spaces stalwart against the onslaught of housing and retail opportunities. To the south, beyond the 19th-century solidity of Newington and Morningside, is Blackford Hill and then the Braid Hills on the far side of the Braid Burn. On Blackford Hill there are the vestiges of a fort and the Royal Observatory. My father and his siblings used to play on Blackford Hill. Thanks to the generosity of a friend, I spent a couple of months living with her in Cobden Road, when I discovered Blackford Hill for myself. It's not a big hill – about 160 metres high – but there is still a sense of green airiness. You can rise above the stone-built villas and terraces and breathe.

Chiang Yee walked backwards up Blackford Hill as he wanted to keep his gaze on Arthur's Seat, in the hope that Blackford would prove the higher hill. Arthur's Seat 'seemed to keep pace with me, though at the same time it seemed that we were both standing still watching the houses and trees that smiled below us. Eventually both houses and trees vanished in the mist, while Arthur's Seat rose prominently in perfect outline in the distance.' Still walking backwards, he collides with a boy who is playing hide-and-seek with two others. They are vastly amused at Chiang Yee's misconception of height. Lingering on the summit he composed a poem, given in both Chinese and English in his *Silent Traveller in Edinburgh*.

> The steep rock squats like an elephant;
> But the Scots see it as a lion.
> How generously it floats in the air,
> Its ancient face full of valour and courtesy.

The houses are lost in the mist;
A lonely bird is playing in the wind.
Leisurely wandering with no single thought in my mind,
I stand to gaze round, regardless of time.

Chiang Yee was drawn to 'the massive yet graceful hill known as Arthur's Seat' and spent time on its slopes and on its summit, observing its changing moods and the 'variety of human life' to be found there, as well as absorbing it from many vantage points.

On the Braids, more extensive than Blackford Hill, two golf courses and two disused quarries (there are quarries all over Edinburgh) leave plenty of space for walking. Arthur and I walk often on the Braids when we visit his son and family on the far southern side, taking a route from Buckstone to Mortonhall and out onto the hillside, skirting the Mortonhall Golf Course on our way back. We are there on a sunny September Sunday, with Thomas and Gwen, their children Naomi and Alex, my daughter Gowan and grandson Leon. And of course the dog. We all agree how wonderful it is to have such an expanse of green slopes and wooded paths in the middle of a city. The children race, climb trees, throw the dog's ball for her to fetch.

West of the Braid Hills are the two Craiglockhart Hills, Easter and Wester, imposing breathing space between Morningside and Colinton. There are the remnants of a 14th-century tower on Wester Craiglockhart Hill, but the dominant buildings on the hills relate to the treatment of the disturbed. Old Craig House on the east hill dates from the 16th century, but was altered in 1878 to provide premises for the Royal Edinburgh Asylum. Craighouse was built some years later for the same purpose. On the west is the building that began life as a hydropathic hotel, making use of nearby spring water. In 1916 it was requisitioned by the army and became the Craiglockhart War Hospital where officers suffering from trauma were treated. In August 1917 the poet Wilfred Owen arrived there, where the man who was to become his friend and mentor, Siegfried Sassoon, was already a patient. Sassoon was a published poet, Owen younger and less confident about his writing. They formed a mutually sustaining bond. Sassoon's poem 'Sick leave' was written while he was at Craiglockhart – 'They come, the homeless ones, the noiseless dead' to disturb his rest and ask when is he going to return to 'the Battalion in the mud'. One of Owen's most famous poems, 'Dulce et decorum est', was also written at Craiglockhart, in which he describes the effects of a gas attack, 'the white eyes writhing', the blood 'gargling from the froth-corrupted lungs'. The poem ends by challenging

the old Lie: *Dulce et decorum est*
*Pro patria mori.*

Pat Barker's novel *Regeneration* (1991) explores the relationship between the two men, and their treatment by Drs William Rivers and AJ Brock, particularly the treatment of Sassoon by Dr Rivers. It evokes the feel of the hospital, its topography and routine, its sounds and smells, and its distance from the 'real' world – both the reality of war and the reality of 'normal' life. Whether Edinburgh was chosen by the authorities as a place of regeneration, or it was happenstance that suitable premises were found there for the treatment of trauma is not clear. But Scotland's capital was geographically a long way from the front line and beyond the sound of guns which must have been important. Many thousands of Scottish soldiers lost their lives in the conflict, including my uncle, 2nd Lieutenant Harry William Mackintosh Mackay, Gordon Highlanders and Royal Flying Corp, who was killed on 6 March 1918. I have his photograph. He was a handsome young man, sporting a moustache which made him look older than his 19 years.

The Craiglockhart Hills were, for a while, the location of two branches of Napier University, split between Craighouse and the former hospital. The Craighouse campus is now the site of a housing development. Captain Brock encouraged his patients to engage in physical and mental activity; Captain Rivers wanted his patients to talk. It seems appropriate for a university to inherit that legacy. The new residents of Craighouse may be less comfortable with the location's past.

From Craiglockhart you can look due south to the Pentland Hills. The city boundary now runs alongside the Lothian Burn to the Midlothian Ski Centre at Hillend and on up to Caerketton Hill. The little village of Swanston on the lower slopes was once a country walk from the outlying suburb of Morningside (where, wrote Muriel Spark in *Curriculum Vitae*, 'cleanliness and godliness shook hands with each other'). The Stevenson family had a rural retreat at Swanston Cottage where Louis spent many reflective and creative days. He struck up a kind of friendship with the local shepherd, John Todd, and learned something of the skills involved in herding sheep – 'the simple strategy of massing sheep upon a snowy evening, with its attendant scampering of earnest, shaggy aides-de-camp':

the shadow of the night darkening on the hills, inscrutable black blots of snow shower moving here and there like night already come, huddles of yellow sheep and dartings of black dogs upon the snow, a bitter air that took you by the throat, unearthly harpings of the wind along the moors.

In his unfinished novel *St Ives* Stevenson has his hero escape from imprisonment in the castle and make his way to Swanston, and then south to hoped-for safety in the company of drovers taking their cattle to England. You can still follow the drove road across the Pentlands. St Ives and his companions walk through 'a bare green valley, which wound upwards and backwards among the hills'. Soon they are 'ascending the side of a mountain by a rude green track'. The green track takes them south through

a continual succession of insignificant shaggy hills, divided by the course of ten thousand brooks, through which we had to wade, or by the side of which we encamped at night; infinite perspectives of heather, infinite quantities of moorfowl; here and there, by a stream side, small and pretty clumps of willows or the silver birch; here and there the ruins of ancient and inconsiderable fortresses.

St Ives has walked out of the city onto the Pentlands and along a drove road well-trodden by men and cattle from the Highlands. Nothing to do with Edinburgh, perhaps – yet the connection was there and is still there. For all the activity on the Pentland Hills, the ski slope, the firing range, the walkers and runners, the outlying car parks, there is still a sense of wildness, a wildness that lies partly within the city and is readily accessible, as any weekend visit will testify. There is still a sense of connection with the country that lies beyond. Climb to the top of Caerketton or neighbouring Allermuir and you can see the Highland hills, the Lammermuirs and Cheviots to the south, perhaps Goat Fell on the island of Arran. Edinburgh's hills and high towers are continual reminders of the Scotland that lies beyond the capital.

One June evening I climbed the steep slope up Allermuir and watched a blazing sun sink to the west. And then suddenly I was engulfed in mist and could see nothing. I was wrapped in cold, damp cloud. On the way down I slipped on loose scree and fell. No damage was done, but I had a vision of a broken ankle and a night on the hillside. The apparently benign green flanks of the Pentlands in minutes changed their character. Duality again.

Edinburgh is known for its seven hills – the twin Craiglockharts counting as one. But there is another hill lying within its bounds, a hill which seems to be known only to dog walkers. I visit it frequently, walking in from Standingstane Road that leads out of the village of Dalmeny, past the tank farm, and climbing up through the trees to the quarry's edge. This is Craigie Hill – Edinburgh's many craigs give the word to streets and districts all over the city. This is my neighbourhood hill, where there are snowdrops in February and sometimes a deer breaks out of the undergrowth. From the top you can look across the A90 buzzing with traffic to the firth, or towards the airport on the other side of the River Almond, vastly expanded from when I first knew it in the 1960s, when you could get a standby flight to London for £5. In the 1970s I often took the children to meet visitors. We would stand on the roof terrace and watch the plane land, and there was no charge for parking. We would watch and wave excitedly as the passengers descended from the plane and made their way across the tarmac.

Grandson Leon and I go to the airport to meet my nephew Ben and his small son. Now it costs more to park than a 1960s standby ticket to London. A few weeks earlier Leon had accompanied me when I dropped off his mother to get a flight to Gatwick. 'It's funner to meet someone than to drop them off,' he says now as we thread our way through the queues at the check-in desks to the arrivals area. But it was much funner in the days when his mother was his age, when the appearance of a distant shape in the sky was greeted with a shout of anticipation and the children leant on the rail, determined not to miss a moment of the drama of landing.

There is an Iron Age fort towards the southern end of Craigie Hill which was excavated in the 1860s by James Young Simpson, who as well as being a pioneer of anaesthetics was a keen amateur archaeologist. His archaeological interests extended beyond Scotland. In 1865 he donated to the Society of Antiquaries of Scotland a stunning limestone relief from the Assyrian city of Nimrud, now in the National Museum. There is no sign today of archaeological activity on Craigie Hill, but the fort is of a similar age to the slab of stone from Assyria, which depicts King Ashurnasirpal II who ruled from 883 to 859 BC. A connection perhaps, but we have no names of those early occupiers of Craigie Hill.

In winter the hill paths almost disappear under leaves and pine needles. The sense of suspended animation is pierced by birdsong. A large chunk of the hill has been gouged out for stone, leaving a wide rocky canyon where a few whins and birches cling to the steep sides. On the slope of the hill facing the city is West Craigie Farm. Before I had a garden big enough to grow my own I would go there to pick raspberries. Now it is the home of the flourishing Craigie's deli and café. We walk there sometimes, Arthur and I and the dog, and sit outside with our coffee, looking across to the water and the other city hills. James Robertson has described Edinburgh as 'land with a city draped and poured over it'. From any of Edinburgh's high points, you can understand why.

Dean Bridge. Rachel Calder.

9

Threaded by a complex stream

*My Water of Leith runs through a double city;*
*My city is threaded by a complex stream.*
Norman MacCaig, 'Double life'

*I have named, among many rivers that make music in my memory,*
*that dirty Water of Leith.*
RL Stevenson, 'The manse'


IN STEVENSON'S NOVEL *Catriona* (1893) his hero David Balfour makes his
way from the Lang Dykes, not yet Princes Street, to the village of Dean
beside the Water of Leith. He is in the country, skirting a field of barley, and
the people he sees on the road are country people. Later, he walks 'down
the glen of the Leith River, towards Stockbridge and Silvermills', both still
villages. The path takes him alongside the water, which 'bickered and sang',
and 'the sunbeams overhead struck out of the west among the long shadows
and (as the valley turned) made like a new scene and a new world of it at
every corner'.

The Water of Leith is a modest river that cuts through Edinburgh from
the Pentlands to the Firth of Forth. In 1751, the year when *Catriona* opens
and the year before the idea of the New Town was first projected, the river
was quite separate from the city. By the time Stevenson was born, in 1850
in Howard Place, close to Silvermills and Canonmills, names which are
a reminder that at one time the river was lined with mills, an expanding
Edinburgh had stretched beyond the river. Thomas Telford's 'handsome'
Dean Bridge arching high across the chasm below had joined older
bridges at Stockbridge and Canonmills. But David Balfour's walk beside
the river is far from 'the tall black city' which had not yet moved on from
the aftershocks of the Jacobite Rising of 1745. David himself is caught in
political manoeuvrings which put him at risk as he endeavours to assist the
escape of Alan Breck and bring justice in the case of the Appin murder, of
which he was a witness during the adventures related in *Kidnapped.*

In most major cities it is a river that has determined location, with
communities growing up around fords and crossing places. The Clyde
is essential to Glasgow's identity, London is unimaginable without the
Thames, Paris without the Seine, Budapest without the Danube. It is hard
to think of a capital city that isn't on a significant river. Edinburgh is an

exception. It didn't grow up as a riverside city and its character has nothing to do with the small river it now encompasses, and yet the Water of Leith has a distinctive and sometimes unexpected presence. Crossing the Dean Bridge on the top of a double-decker bus, you can look down at an often turbulent flow of water and see on the west side buildings that were once mills and warehouses, and on the east the grassy, tree-studded slope of the Dean Gardens. The houses of Randolph Cliff loom above.

Naomi Mitchison was born in 1897 round the corner in Randolph Crescent, 'built on the edge of a cliff above the Water of Leith', as she remembers in *Small Talk* (1973), the first volume of her memoirs. At the front it was five storeys high, at the back it dropped down through layers of cellars, where the six-year-old Naomi saw 'things that looked like ghosts'. The nearby bridge fuelled her imagination: 'I often hoped I would see a would-be suicide floating down from the Dean Bridge, parachuted by a petticoat.' In Peter May's novel *The Lewis Man* (2012), two teenage boys compete with each other in timed crossings of the bridge on an outside ledge, a highly dangerous undertaking which inevitably ends in tragedy.

The bridge's parapet was raised to deter suicides, but once when living in Buckingham Terrace just beyond the bridge we had a strange visitation. A man appeared at the door, dripping wet, saying he had jumped into the river. He can't have jumped from the bridge and survived to tell the tale, but we couldn't get a coherent story out of him. A happier memory of Naomi Mitchison's was watching pipers marching across the bridge – 'one rushed out onto the dining-room balcony to see them'.

Looking up from the Dean Village the bridge has a brooding magnificence. It seems to do more than link a divided Edinburgh. It echoes the earlier bridges that transformed the Old Town and made its expansion possible. It suggests the same sense of a layered city, of chasms and steep climbs and vertiginous connections. The bridge was the initiative of John Learmonth, owner of the Dean Estate north of the river, which he had purchased from the Nisbet family in 1825. He planned to develop housing on his estate and felt a high-level bridge was necessary access. There was an existing bridge upstream but he wanted a more direct connection with the city. Learmonth himself bore a large part of the cost. Thomas Telford was commissioned to design it and it was built by John Gibb of Aberdeen with stone from Craigleith quarry, which had provided material for much of the New Town. (The site of the quarry is now a retail park, skirted by the Queensferry Road as it heads northwest to Queensferry and the Forth Road Bridge.) The four-arch bridge was completed in 1831 and opened the following year. During its building members of the public were, for a penny, allowed on to the structure to admire the view.

It was some time before the residential development Learmonth hoped for materialised. It was the 1850s before Clarendon Crescent went up, and he had been dead for 15 years before Learmonth Terrace began to take shape in 1873. Nevertheless, the bridge unleashed a spate of building, which included churches, Daniel Stewart's School and the Dean Orphanage as well as residential terraces. The Dean Orphanage and John Watson's School, built before the bridge in 1825, are now the Scottish Gallery of Modern Art. The Orphanage was for many years the Dean Education Centre, where, as a Royal Scottish Museum education officer I attended many meetings. It is much more welcoming now as a gallery, though there is still a hint of the institution it originally was. The nature of the Orphanage, at least as it was in the late 1940s, is captured by Peter May in *The Lewis Man*, where the governor is portrayed as running a punitive regime with calculated sadism.

In *Crossriggs* (1908), by novelist sisters Jane and Mary Findlater, Alexandra Hope visits Edinburgh from her rural village an hour away by train. She has been at a house somewhere north of the Dean Bridge (not specifically identified) and is walking back to the station in rain and a howling wind. She pauses on the bridge:

> She stood looking down for a moment across the parapet of the bridge, held as always by the beauty of a scene that even the remorseless climate could not destroy. On either side of the blue gulf, high houses shone with lighted windows; in the yellow and stormy sky, great masses of vapour rolled above the town, and parted to a clearer space in the east. A darker point pricked out here and there from the mists, and far below between its gardened banks, the water ran like a ravelled white thread.

At this moment on the bridge, and in her personal life, the city is both threatening and beautiful. It is something that most Edinburgh residents and many visitors have probably experienced. There are times when weather and history seem to combine to reinforce Edinburgh's duality. On the Dean Bridge, a monument to human skill and effort, an individual is diminished by the nature of the city. The Water of Leith is 34 kilometres long and over the years

I have walked most of it. In the 19th century there were over 70 mills and tanneries along its length. Weirs and surviving mill lades are reminders. A walk upstream from Belford Bridge winds behind the solid mid-Victorian expansion of the city to the west, a network of streets and crescents, and Donaldson's School for the Deaf, which went up in the 1850s to a design by William Playfair – 'a proudly sited Jacobean palace' according to Gifford, McWilliam and Walker. Like so many of the Victorian-built schools in Edinburgh it is an eye-catching building, a bold statement not only of the value placed on education but of the kudos associated with providing institutions for those who could not afford to pay for it. The Victorians were less inclined to see education

Mill stones, Dean Village. Rachel Calder.

(and health) as commercial opportunities than many in the 21st century.

The money for Donaldson's came from James Donaldson, proprietor of the *Edinburgh Advertiser*, who left £240,000 in his will for the foundation of a school for poor children. His relatives attempted to challenge the will, on the grounds that such a bequest was a sign of insanity – clearly, not everyone believed that the underprivileged deserved to be taught, or that there might be more general social benefit if they were. The building was opened in 1850 by Queen Victoria who apparently thought it grander than some of her own residences. There were those who considered that the grandeur and ornamentation were far too good for the offspring of the poor. Later, Donaldson's became a school for the deaf. The school abandoned the building in 2008, to move to new premises in Linlithgow. There are plans to develop the site into 'luxury flats'.

Beyond Donaldson's is Roseburn and then Murrayfield. These were areas of mid-Victorian development – in the second half of the 19th century Edinburgh was expanding in all directions. The riverside path takes you through Roseburn Park and past the Murrayfield rugby stadium and the ice rink, and then bends south towards Gorgie and Slateford, where it is crossed by the Union Canal. Keep on going, and you'll find yourself walking through Craiglockart Dell. To the east are the two Craiglockhart hills, Easter and Wester. Beyond Craiglockhart is Colinton Dell and a stretch of river where there were once snuff and paper mills. By the 1830s there were 16 paper mills along the Water of Leith, producing paper for both Scotland and export.

If on your way upriver you divert to Colinton kirkyard you'll find the grave of James Gillespie whose snuff mill was successful enough to ensure a substantial fortune when he died – helped by his habits of parsimony and the fact that the American bid for independence interfered with tobacco imports and sent up the price. His snuff was sold in his brother's shop in the city's High Street. There's a plaque at the site, which is now the premises of Gordon's Trattoria. Muriel Spark described Gillespie as 'so satisfactorily and completely an Edinburgh character'. It's rare these days to encounter a snuff-taker, but I remember my uncle sniffing the stuff up with great satisfaction and sneezing gustily. The result was filthy handkerchiefs. In 1873 Gillespie built Spylaw House next to the mill (it is now divided into flats), and part of his fortune was earmarked for the foundation of a school for the sons of poor families, another school to add to those founded by successful businessmen. In its later manifestation it inspired Spark's *The Prime of Miss Jean Brodie*. Spark herself attended the school, and reflected later that 'my good schooling is partly due to the American War of Independence'.

When lawyer and novelist Henry Mackenzie lived in Colinton in the late 18th century, the village was no great distance from the metropolis but significantly distinct. Mackenzie's cottage – restored in 1996 – is modest. He would move later to the New Town, where in 1831 at the age of 86 he died at 6 Heriot Row, a few doors away from where my grandmother would later live. Scott, a much younger man and an admirer of Mackenzie, died the following year.

Colinton was still a village when the young Robert Louis Stevenson was a regular visitor to his grandfather in the manse. The Reverend Lewis Balfour had been there since 1823. RLS was born in 1850 and only knew his grandfather as an old man and never knew his grandmother who had died in 1844, but the house and its surroundings were an adventure playground. He had uncles who went to India, and the house contained the evidence, 'the bones of antelope, the wings of albatross... junks and bangles, beads and screens'. But it was the garden and its proximity to both river and graveyard that was the main appeal:

> It was a place in that time like no other: the garden cut into provinces by a great hedge of beech, and overlooked by the church and the terrace of the churchyard, where the tombstones were thick, and after nightfall 'spunkies' might be seen to dance at least by children; flower-pots lying warm in sunshine; laurels and the great yew making elsewhere a pleasing horror of shade; the smell of water rising from all round, with an added tang of paper-mills; the sound of water everywhere, and the sound of mills – the wheel and the damn singing their alternate strain; the birds on every bush and from every corner of the overhanging woods pealing out their notes until the air throbbed with them; and in the midst of this, the manse.

Much of what Stevenson evokes still lingers in the manse garden, or at least it did 30 or so years ago when I was in it. There is no sound or smell of mills, but the water still runs and there is still a sense of an enclosed and separate world.

Louis's mother, Margaret Balfour, had grown up in the manse with her brothers and sisters, and Louis, an only child, had cousins to play with which added to the adventure. Colinton would inspire some of the poems in *A Child's Garden of Verses* (1885):

> Over the borders, a sin without pardon,
>   Breaking the branches and crawling below,
> Out through the breach in the wall of the garden,
>   Down by the banks of the river we go.
>
> Here is the mill with the humming of thunder,
>   Here is the weir with the wonder of foam,
> Here is the sluice with the race running under –
>   Marvellous places, though handy to home!

Stevenson captures wonderfully the thrill of danger co-existing with the reassurance of home, such an important part of childhood experience.

The track that continues upriver was once the route of the railway to Balerno, opened in 1873 to service the mills and provide a passenger service for the increasing numbers who commuted to the city. There are still traces of the mill lades and sluices, and the weirs survive, all part of the need to control the flow of water. Too little, and the mill wheels would not turn; too much, and there was flooding. To solve this problem, the Pentland reservoirs of Threipmuir, Harlaw and Harperrig were created. Most of the mills themselves have vanished or been incorporated into new housing developments. The sites can be identified through names that indicate the activity of the past – Kinleith Mill (papermaking), East Mill (grain).

The riverside walk takes you through Juniper Green and Currie, where you get a view on the north bank of the beautifully proportioned Currie Kirk, built in 1784 when Currie was a village dominated by the mills and handweaving. And there are attractive waterside residences, but some of the new developments, heavily fenced with locked gates, intrude in their exclusivity on the pleasure of the walk. Beyond Balerno, the river diminishes, though fed by burns running off the Pentland Hills.

It is Christmas Day, sometime in the 1990s. Arthur and I walk downriver from the Dean Village. We had our Christmas meal the evening before and have driven my daughter back into town so she can cook a turkey for what she calls her 'waifs and strays', a collection of migrant friends who are a long way from home. The first part of the walk is very familiar to me, as we did it often as a family. Under the Dean Bridge, past the Dean Gardens on the other side of the water – Norman MacCaig's 'pretty boscage of Dean' – and the Moray Place Bank Gardens rising steeply on our right. We stop, as we always did then, at St Bernard's Well, which gets its name from a French 12th-century saint who was believed – rather unconvincingly – to have lived in a nearby cave. There is a dankness and darkness about it. The building, a circular structure echoing a Roman temple, was designed by the artist Alexander Nasmyth and put up in 1788 at the site of a mineral spring. Lord Gardenstone, a law lord, provided the funds – he believed he himself had benefited from the sulphurous waters. A statue of Hygeia, goddess of health, is surrounded by pillars, a tribute to the therapeutic powers, with a chamber underneath where the waters were sampled. The spring is now closed off. There was some controversy about its benefits. 'It cleans the intestines and an appetite gives while morbitic matters it quite away drives,' claimed the poet Claudero, rather tortuously. And a Dr Taylor recommended taking the waters after dinner. They were, he said, 'an excellent digester' and reviver of 'animal spirits': 'from being morose and sulky, we are all at once metamorphosed into gay and cheerful mood'. One wonders exactly what the water contained.

The neo-classical design – 'the chief ornament of this delightful valley', according to Alexander Campbell in 1801 – echoes the Georgian New Town, but the development of the Raeburn estate did not begin until nearly 30 years later. Henry Raeburn, the Stockbridge-born artist, acquired through his marriage to Ann Edgar Leslie the grounds of Deanhaugh, then later the St Bernard's estate. His plan was to build on these

St Bernard's Well, Water of Leith. Rachel Calder.

grounds, and the resulting streets and terraces form one of Edinburgh's most attractive areas. The river helps, of course, and the vegetation that lines it, and the gardens that front the houses in Ann Street, named for his wife. But it is also the scale and the variety that make it appealing. These are not the broad geometrical thoroughfares that sweep through the New Town, but narrower streets with kinks and curves and few right angles. The terraces are not so tall – the Ann Street houses are almost cottagey – and the effect much less grand.

Raeburn, born in 1756, painted some of the most notable figures of his time. In the Scottish National Portrait Gallery in Queen Street you'll find geologist James Hutton, Sir Walter Scott, musician and composer Niel Gow, businessman William Forbes, Colonel Alastair Macdonell of Glengarry festooned in full tartan regalia and anachronistic weaponry, Lord Braxfield staring belligerently, and a self-portrait of Raeburn himself who gazes out of the canvas with a look of thoughtful scepticism. His most famous picture –

although there has been controversy over whether Raeburn was indeed the artist – is probably the portrait of the Reverend Robert Walker, the skating minister, who has become an emblem of the National Gallery of Scotland. He is graceful, serious and nonchalant all at once.

Raeburn was born in what was still the village of Stockbridge, the son of a yarn-boiler. Both his parents had died before he was nine, and he was then looked after by his older brother. He attended Heriot's Hospital, founded in 1628 through a bequest from George Heriot, banker and jeweller who was a close associate of James VI. According to Scott, he spent his life in 'honourable and successful industry'. The school, 'a prodigy of Scottish Renaissance architecture', still survives on Lauriston Place, south of the castle. It was intended for the education of the sons of burgesses who had fallen on hard times. Duncan Thomson, former Keeper of the Scottish National Portrait Gallery, describes how Raeburn must have walked to school each day 'by tracks crossing the fields where the New Town was planned to rise, skirting St Cuthbert's where he had been baptised and climbing the 'Vennel' from the west end of the Grassmarket'. Raeburn's artistic career began with his apprenticeship at the age of 16 to James Gilliland, an Edinburgh goldsmith and jeweller. By the 1780s he was established as a portrait painter. Like Scott, Raeburn was struck by a financial crisis which left him bankrupt, and like Scott he pledged himself to work to pay off his debts. He had to sell his house and studio in York Place, though he retained the family home, St Bernard's House on the Water of Leith.

We reach Stockbridge and take the steps up to the street, cross the bridge and descend again on the other side. Our walk takes us along the back of the Stockbridge Colonies, built as artisan housing in 1861. The Colonies are neat, parallel rows of small but appealing terraces, each house divided vertically into upper and lower residences. There are similar terraces in other parts of Edinburgh, all built at around the same time to house artisan workers. My friend and former colleague Liz lived in Hugh Miller Place. Liz was petite, but even so I marvelled at how she managed to occupy so small a space – two rooms plus a tiny kitchen and shower room. But she had a garden, and enjoyed the sense of community the Colonies fostered. Across the road from Liz is the Glenogle Baths where I used to swim regularly after work. Liz often had a swim before breakfast.

We continue our walk to Canonmills. As the name suggests, there were once grain mills here, run by monks from Holyrood Abbey. Soon we are

Grassmarket. Alan Daiches. Courtesy National Library of Scotland.

skirting the back of Warriston Cemetery, a favourite haunt of Stevenson's, who was born not far away in Howard Place. His family considered it an unhealthy spot, too near the river and its noxious effluent from the mills and tanneries plus uncontrolled sewage. They flitted to Inverleith Terrace, just across the road, but it was damp and exposed, so in 1857 another move was made, this time to elegant Heriot Row in the heart of the New Town. Now the cemetery is, partly at least, a jungle, choked with vegetation and unkempt headstones. Across the road is the crematorium, with which over the years I have become all too familiar. In August 1977 my mother's funeral was held there, and I've attended many others since then.

We follow the river as it twists and turns on its way, trending northeast to the docks at Leith. Not far to the south is Pilrig House, another Stevenson/ Balfour connection. The house, built in 1638 by Gilbert Kirkwood, an Edinburgh goldsmith, on the site of an older house, was acquired by the Balfour family after the Treaty of Union. James Balfour had invested a large sum in the disastrous Darien venture, for which he was compensated as part of the terms of the Treaty. This enabled him to buy and improve Pilrig House. The Reverend Lewis Balfour, Stevenson's grandfather, was a direct descendent. Pilrig's connection with Colinton, linking the upper and the lower stretches of the river, also lies in the fact that Gilbert Kirkwood's grandfather was the Colinton blacksmith.

David Balfour of *Kidnapped* and *Catriona* is – intentionally – of the same family, although only in the latter novel does this become clear. In his mission 'for the sake of justice' David seeks out help from his cousin the laird of Pilrig. He does not follow the Water of Leith but sets off from the east end of the Old Town, down past Calton Hill where children are flying kites and on to Picardy where the 'whirr of looms' signals the presence of French weavers who 'wrought for the Linen Company'. A little further on he encounters a more disturbing sight, two figures hanging in chains from a gibbet:

They were dipped in tar, as the manner is; the wind span them, the chains clattered, and the birds hung about the uncanny jumping-jacks and cried.

Disturbing at the best of times, but the more so as David himself is a wanted man. At last he reaches his destination, 'a pleasant gabled house set by the walkside among some brave young woods'. James Balfour is not only Pilrig's laird but professor of moral philosophy at the university. He gives his cousin the help he needs, though rather grudgingly, and David continues on his risky enterprise.

The river winds in an s-bend and makes its way under Great Junction Street to the shore. We're in Leith now, once proudly separate from Edinburgh and still with its own identity. In 1636 William Brereton described Leith as 'a pretty little haven' which scarcely suggests that it was and had been for several centuries Scotland's busiest port. It traded on Edinburgh's behalf with France, the Low Countries and the Baltic. Large quantities of Scandinavian and Baltic pine beams and boards were imported for use in buildings, and hazel barrel hoops for coopers. The making of barrels was a crucial trade for a city so given to the consumption of wine. A fashion for painted wood ceilings increased the demand for imported timber. Thomas Gledstanes, who traded out of Leith, installed a splendid painted ceiling in Gladstone's Land in the Lawnmarket, and you can find Baltic ceiling timbers in the National Museum. Baltic timber was imported in such large quantity that space in Leith for storing it became a serious problem.

When New World markets opened up Leith traded also with the Americas. By 1779 there were 52 ships operating out of Leith, trading with Denmark, Norway, Russia, Prussia, Poland, Germany, Holland, France, Spain, Portugal, Guernsey, Ireland, Italy, North America and the West Indies. Those barrel hoops from the Baltic were essential for the barrels containing the vast quantities of wine from Europe. From the West Indies came rice, rum and sugar, the latter especially transforming the Scottish diet, and indigo, important for the burgeoning textile trade.

There was also constant traffic to and from London. By the late 18th century sailing smacks plied regularly between Leith and London, a faster and probably more comfortable way to travel than by road. In 1802 the Edinburgh and Leith Shipping Company began operation, and in the 1830s a steamer service was introduced. In the 1850s there were regular sailings to London, Newcastle, Hull and Liverpool in England, and to the Fife ports, Alloa and Stirling, Arbroath and Aberdeen, the Murray Firth ports and on to Cromarty, Wick and Thurso, and to Kirkwall in Orkney and Lerwick in Shetland. Edinburgh was connected.

It was in Leith that the Company of Scotland built its warehouse and assembled the trade goods for a commercial enterprise that, it was hoped, would make Scotland a key player in trade with Africa and the Indies. And it was from Leith on 12 July 1698 that the Darien Expedition's five ships set sail. Scotland's high hopes that Darien would give the nation a share of the spoils that were bringing so much profit to England came to worse than nothing. Thousands lost money in the venture, and Scotland was devastated and bitter. The bitterness found an outlet when in 1705 Captain Thomas Green of the *Worcester* along with his first mate and gunner were convicted of piracy and hanged on Leith sands. Captain Green may have had no involvement in the disaster but the *Worcester* belonged to the English East India Company which had played a part in ensuring the Darien scheme's demise.

There's not much to remind us of disaster as we emerge into an area of waterside eateries and luxury flats, but the maritime history lies not far beneath the surface. There are still docks at Leith, whose names signal a confident imperial past – Victoria Dock, Albert Dock, Prince of Wales Dock, Imperial Dock – and still warehouses not yet converted. The handsome Leith Custom House in Commercial Street no longer serves its original purpose (for many years it was a store for the National Museum) but it survives as testimony to past activity. Over the centuries Leith harbour, at first no more than an anchorage, was added to and extended. Quays and wharfs were built to facilitate loading and unloading. But there was a problem in ensuring water deep enough for large ships, not solved until John Rennie produced a scheme in 1799 for three new connected docks, though only two were built. There was further major expansion in the mid-19th century, but there remained a constant need for dredging.

The problem of keeping the channel clear was aggravated by the discharge of sewage into the Water of Leith, which must have somewhat counteracted the benefits of St Bernard's Well. Engineer James Rendel described the situation:

not only is the quantity of solid matter become so considerable as to cause growing expense in dredging

Leith docks. Alan Daiches. Courtesy National Library of Scotland.

to maintain the proper navigable Channel up to the new Dock, but its less solid products are deposited in such increased quantities in the higher part of the River... as to have become an intolerable nuisance.

Legislation to deal with Edinburgh's sewerage problems followed, but it was several decades before the Water of Leith became relatively clean. From at least the 16th century ships were built at Leith, and by the 1830s there were five shipyards in operation, clustered round the harbour area and along the Water of Leith. The last yard closed in 1984. Also on the river bank was Hawthorn's Engineering Works, which built locomotives. One of them, the *Ellesmere*, returned to Scotland after a life working in Cheshire and is now a conspicuous exhibit in the National Museum.

As the docks grew, medieval Leith was being overlaid by new streets and buildings. Lamb's House in Water's Close off Burgess Street, built by a merchant in the early 17th century, is a survival of an older Leith which has virtually disappeared. Warehouses made uncompromising statements about the port's commercial lifeblood. Public buildings reflected both its economic and its social status: the Custom House (opened in 1812), the Assembly Rooms in Constitution Street, Trinity House in Kirkgate. The Town Hall was completed in 1828. Trinity (the word is a corruption of 'Fraternity') House began as a charitable organisation dedicated to the care of destitute seamen, aware of the effects of 'hourly hazards and the fear of extreme poverty and beggary'. Funds were collected through a levy of 12 pennies on every ton of merchandise loaded or unloaded at Leith by Scottish ships. Its functions evolved, and in a charter of 1797 Trinity House was described as a 'Fraternity of Masters and Mariners' whose role was 'to promote, increase and further commerce and navigation'. The safety of seamen was central and the licensing of pilots a key function. Trinity House now houses a collection of maritime archives.

Leith was too exposed and too near Edinburgh to escape attack from the succession of hostile armies that threatened the capital. The Earl of Hertford marched on the town in May 1544; it quickly succumbed. Leith was burnt, and so were other ports on either side of the Forth. The army marched on to Edinburgh burning and looting, leaving the countryside devastated as the English army plundered it for supplies and spoils. That was just the way armies behaved. This was part one of what came to be called 'the rough wooing', Henry VIII's ruthless attempt to impose a union between his son Edward and the infant Mary, heir to the Scottish throne. Three years later the English were back for part two, defeating the Scots at the battle of Pinkie, fought near Musselburgh just along the coast from Leith. A huge number of Scottish ships in Forth ports were destroyed. In 1560 the Protestant Lords of the Congregation laid siege to Leith; in 1650 Cromwell's army was threatening Leith and Edinburgh. After the defeat of General Leslie's Scottish army at Dunbar there was no way of keeping Cromwell out of the capital. The South Leith Kirk records commented that 'the ministers and most part of the honest people [of Leith] fled out of the town for fear of the enemy'.

Until 1833 the port of Leith was controlled by Edinburgh, its vital gateway to overseas trade. But in that year Leith became an independent burgh. In spite of new building and the laying out of new streets, Robert Chambers was sniffily critical: 'The more ancient buildings in it are mean and inelegant, while the streets into which they have been huddled are narrow and dirty.' Perhaps he was implying that Leith should follow Edinburgh's example. But for Stevenson, Leith was a constant attraction: 'Leith camps on the seaside with her forest of masts; Leith roads are full of ships at anchor.' Ships and the sea always contained the promise of distant lands. Leith, wrote Robert Garioch, 'was a place for merchants' where in 'well-appyntit pubs' they 'cuid talk business', 'buirdly men with confident heids'.

For many, Leith represented not ships, not overseas trade, not a key player in Edinburgh's commercial life, but the races, conducted for over 300 years on Leith sands. Robert Fergusson's poem 'Leith Races' might suggest that the actual horse racing was incidental to the entertainment the crowds expected on race day. Downing 'hale bickers' of the ale offered by the 'browster wives', sampling the finnan haddies brought by 'Buchan bodies', gambling, playing 'rowly-powl', the 'flingin o' the dice', brawling, and finally 'hirpling hame like fools': a day at Leith Races was an opportunity for enjoying in well-lubricated fashion all the fun essential to the proceedings.

The earliest reference to horse racing at Leith goes back to 1504, during the reign of James IV. After the restoration of Charles II racing took place at Leith every Saturday, with prizes provided by the city and another by the king. (Some of the trophies are displayed in the National Museum.) When expansion of the docks brought racing to an end in 1815, the races moved along the coast to Musselburgh, but the event clearly lost in translation. In his *History of Leith* (1827) Alexander Campbell laments:

the Musselburgh races are utterly and wholly destitute of any portion of that reckless and thoroughgoing spirit of hilarity, which never failed to attend those of Leith. The former... are the coldest and most heartless things imaginable; and what they have gained in elegance and refinement, but indifferently supplies the place of the obstreperous interest, which the rough and round skelping on the plashy sands of Leith was wont to excite.

There were other forms of excitement at Leith. Crowds would assemble for royal arrivals and departures. James I arrived there from exile in England. Several royal brides from overseas stepped ashore at Leith, Mary of Gueldres, the wife of James II, and Margaret of Denmark who married James III were two. James V's first wife, Magdalen, also arrived at Leith. Mary, Queen of Scots disembarked at Leith when she returned to Scotland in 1561, to a mixed reception. George IV's arrival in 1822 to a bagpiping, tartan-bedecked welcome was a very different affair.

At the foot of Leith Walk there is a statue of Queen Victoria, but when she made her first visit to Scotland in 1842 she actually disembarked at the new Granton pier. There was a cheering crowd to greet her as she stepped off the gangway and entered a barouche which took her to Dalkeith House south of Edinburgh, where the royal party were the guests of the Duke and Duchess of Buccleuch, as George IV had been. She had porridge and finnan haddies for breakfast. This was the first of many visits to Scotland, though later she would usually travel by train. On a visit in 1872 the royal carriage took her over the Dean Bridge and on through Barnton to Granton and Leith, all in the pouring rain. Her journal records that at Leith 'there were numbers of people looking out for us in spite of the dreadful rain; but indeed everywhere the poor people came out and were most loyal... We stopped a moment to speak to the Provost of Leith, who said the people were very grateful for my coming; and I have since had repeated expressions of thanks, saying the good people felt my coming out in the rain more than anything'. She arrived back in Holyrood wet. None of Victoria's visits could match in scale or extravagance the arrival of George IV, but through her passion for all things Highland she did as much as Walter Scott to promote a tartan image of Scotland.

Ian Rankin's *A Question of Blood* (2003) takes Rebus to Leith, 'the same old Leith', he reflects, in spite of 'rejuvenation'. He sees a place of brothels, tattoo parlours, second-hand shops and 'uninviting bars': 'it could seem a spiritless place… where a smile might mark you as an outsider'. Rebus isn't much given to smiling. On our Christmas Day walk we see little of Rankin's underworld or of celebration. All is quiet. There are a few Christmas trees and coloured lights, but no thickets of flags, no bagpipes, no crowds on the streets and hanging out of windows. Arthur and I retrace our steps, following the Water of Leith upriver back to the Dean Village.

Union Canal, Rachel Calder.

1 0

# Sublime conceptions

*The idea which filled their imaginations was the sublime conception of
breaking down the barriers which Nature has reared.*
Robert Forsyth, *The Beauties of Scotland*

*It is sad that, under the exciting influence of what once upon a time
seemed the last word in human transport, the railways were allowed to
defile Edinburgh.*
Compton Mackenzie, *Edinburgh Evening News*

COAL CHANGED THE face of Edinburgh. It was not far away. The pits of the
Midlothian coalfield had been providing coal for the city from medieval
times. It was the essential fuel for domestic heating and increasingly for
industrial purposes. Anyone travelling south from the city could not fail
to notice the digging of coal and its cumbersome transport to where it was
needed. Names now familiar as city suburbs once signalled the production
of coal: Newcraighall, Duddingston, Gilmerton, Sherriffhall, Danderhall.
Gilmerton was described by James Grant as 'a village of colliers of a
peculiarly degraded and brutal nature, as ferocious and unprincipled as a
gang of desperadoes'.

In 1606 an Act was passed by parliament which bound colliers to their
employer and place of employment. In other words, they were in effect serfs,
who could not change their place of employment without a testimonial from
their master. This affected men, women and children. The men hewed the
coal, the women and children over the age of six or seven carried the coal
to the surface. It was a wretched and dangerous existence, but the system
was accepted by both church and state as a necessary means of ensuring
available labour in an increasingly important industry. But the miners were
relatively well paid, and their status is suggested by the fact that the kirks at
Dalkeith and Newton, near Danderhall, both had miners' lofts. The latter
survives. Painted panels record the names of the colliers responsible for the
loft's construction, and show picks, shovels and axes with the date 1732.
Fifteen years later a second loft was built, also commemorated with painted
panels.

In 1799 the Act was repealed, but for nearly two centuries there were
slaves at work on Edinburgh's doorstep providing the fuel on which the city
depended. The repeal of the act didn't make any difference to the nature of

the work, which was described in 1812 by the Alloa-born mining engineer Robert Bald. Here are women and girls at work:

> The mother sets out first, carrying a lighted candle in her teeth, the girls follow and in this manner they proceed to the pit bottom, and with weary steps and slow, ascend the stairs, halting occasionally to draw breath, till they arrive at the hill or pit-top... they go for eight or ten hours almost without resting. It is no uncommon thing to see them, when ascending the pit, weeping most bitterly from the excessive severity of their labour.

In 1812 physically punishing labour of all kinds was commonplace, but the toil of children in the mines is particularly shocking. It would be another couple of decades before this issue was addressed. Hugh Miller on his first visit to Edinburgh met men who had worked in mines before 1799. 'I regard it,' he wrote, 'as one of the most singular circumstances of my life, that I should have conversed with Scotchmen who have been born slaves.' He was particularly struck by the endurance of the women who 'carried all the coal from underground on their backs'. Their day's work, he was told, was 'equal to the carrying of a hundredweight from the level of the sea to the top of Ben Lomond'.

Meanwhile, coal had to be moved from pit to fire, whether domestic or industrial, and increasingly large quantities were required as cities expanded and industry developed. Steam was taking over from water power as the driver of manufacturing, and steam depended on coal. By the early 19th century Edinburgh was facing a shortage of coal, as coal owners sought higher profits by exporting much of the output of local mines. If coal was to be brought into the city from further afield, the Lanarkshire coalfield for example, an easier and cheaper form of transport was needed. Could a canal be dug from the Clyde to Leith?

The first sod for Scotland's first canal was cut in 1768 by Sir Lawrence Dundas (soon to build a splendid new house in Edinburgh's New Town) at the new port of Grangemouth on the Forth. The last was dug 22 years later. The canal was to join the rivers Forth and Clyde, the east coast and the west coast, and much research went into its route with the most notable engineers of the day consulted, including John Smeaton, James Brindley and James Watt. Alexander Campbell, who in 1811 published an account of a journey through 'North Britain', was impressed by the result: 'Of the many inventions and contrivances to facilitate the extension of commerce, none more interests the mind accustomed to reflection, than the constructing of navigable canals.'

For around four decades the canal carried large quantities of goods and materials, domestic and imported, as well as passengers. But it was 1822 before a link to Edinburgh was completed, the Union Canal, engineered by Hugh Baird and Thomas Telford. The prospect of high construction costs deterred any notion of connecting with Leith; the canal would terminate instead in the suburb of Fountainbridge. Much of the canal was dug by navvies from Ireland, including William Burke and William Hare who later turned to more lucrative activities. Horse-drawn barges now brought coal into the city, to the canal basin at Port Hopetoun just off the Lothian Road. And not only coal. Building materials for the ongoing construction of the New Town were also brought in by canal. But there were those who fiercely resisted its construction, especially local suppliers of coal who believed that making it easier to bring coal into the city would challenge their interests. They were right.

Work started at the Edinburgh end in 1818 and in January 1822 the first canal boat, the *Flora MacIvor*, named for Walter Scott's Jacobite heroine in *Waverley*, sailed as far as the tunnel still being cut under Prospect Hill just outside Falkirk. It was another five months before the tunnel was finished and the whole canal was navigable. Now coal could be brought in to Edinburgh from West Lothian and beyond.

The canal brought large-scale industry to Fountainbridge, most prominently the North British Rubber Factory in 1856, which spread its works over 20 acres alongside the canal and employed around 5,000 workers. Over the decades the factory made all kinds of rubber products from hot water bottles to car tyres. It was particularly noted for its wellington boot production – it was a key supplier of trench boots for the army during World War One, 1.2 million pairs in all. During World War Two it manufactured gas masks and fabric for barrage balloons. In the 1950s it became the first UK factory to manufacture traffic cones. By this time production was no longer linked with the canal for transport and the factory was gradually run down until it finally closed in 1973. Most of the original buildings are now gone. The surviving office building is to become an arts centre. Part of the site is now occupied by McEwan's Fountain

Brewery, also established in 1856, which moved from the other side of Fountainbridge, where you'll find an extensive leisure complex. Where once folk worked, now they play.

Not long after the canal was completed George IV made his unforgettable visit to Edinburgh, and the canal provided a route for visitors to get into the city to view the spectacle. Extra boats and horses were laid on. It was, according to the geologist Archibald Geikie writing rather later, a delightful way to travel. 'The boats were comfortably fitted up and were drawn by a cavalcade of horses, urged forward by postboys.' He enjoyed watching 'fields, trees, cottages, and hamlets flit past, as if they formed a vast moving panorama, while one seemed to be sitting absolutely still. For mere luxury of transportation, such canal-travel stands quite unrivalled.' But there was a downside. On a foggy day in March 1844, George Meikle Kemp, son of a Midlothian shepherd and designer of the Scott Monument, was making his way along the canal to his home in Morningside when he fell in. His body was found the next day. The Monument was completed two years later.

Today canal drownings still happen. But that doesn't deter from the fact that canal travel remains a 'delightful' and most relaxing way to move, not these days pulled by horses but propelled by a gently chugging diesel engine or perhaps by steam if you're lucky enough to get a sail in a steam launch. Almost as pleasurable is walking the towpath, though not recommended in fog. Over the years Arthur and I have walked most of the Union Canal's 31 miles. It takes a winding route from near Falkirk, winding because it follows the contours of the terrain, thus avoiding the need for locks. From the aqueducts spanning the Almond and

Aqueduct over the River Almond. Rachel Calder.

Avon Rivers you can look down vertiginously on the water running below, and on fields and sheep and tree tops. A short diversion from the Almond viaduct takes you to Almondell, once the home of the Erskine family. The estate came to the Erskines when in 1671 Katherine Stewart, who owned much of the land around Uphall, then the parish of Strathbrock, married Henry Erskine, 3rd Lord Cardross. Henry was a Covenanter who spent several years as a prisoner in Edinburgh Castle.

Henry Erskine's great grandson, also Henry, was a lawyer, twice Lord Advocate of Scotland, who defended Deacon Brodie though he was unable to save him from the gallows. Henry's older brother David was the 11th Earl of Buchan who was instrumental in founding the Society of Antiquaries of Scotland. Henry had a mansion house built to his own design, but there were some rather basic flaws. The roof failed to keep out the rain and the structure of the foundations hampered drainage. After a long-drawn-out deterioration the house was finally demolished in 1969. The estate is now part of Almondell and Calderwood Country Park, where Arthur and I often walk by the river.

The Almondell stables have become a visitor centre. Outside it is a stone pillar which once stood in nearby Kirkhill, David Erskine's estate. He had constructed a scale model of the solar system around his estate, and the calculations on which it was based are engraved on the pillar. The pillar eventually collapsed, but the stones were saved and re-erected at Almondell. A community art project created 11 pieces of art to represent Erskine's original idea and these are now distributed around West Lothian, with the Sun, Earth, Mercury, Venus and Jupiter in Broxburn, Pluto in Beecraigs Country Park, Uranus at Almondell, Neptune at Kingscavil Church and Saturn under the Union Canal's bridge 23. If you're not aware of the project, coming across these pieces is an unexpected pleasure.

One of our favoured routes through Almondell takes us to the handsome bridge built in 1800 to a design by the artist Alexander Nasmith and now restored after its collapse in 1973. Almondell projects seemed rather prone to collapse. We carry on beside the canal feeder, which brings water from the Almond to the canal at Lin's Mill. Burke and Hare reputedly worked on the feeder. Further on is a viaduct which once carried a railway line servicing the quarry and brickworks at Camps and the shale oil works at Pumpherston and Uphall. Thus was the capital connected with essential supplies, and essential products carried westward.

River Almond. Rachel Calder.

The canal enters today's city limits at Ratho, where stone from local quarries was once loaded – one of the quarries is now the site of the Scottish National Climbing Centre, a handy place for stopping for a coffee if you're walking the canal – and crosses the city bypass at Hermiston. It seems incongruous to imagine plodding horses hauling laden barges as you walk over a six-lane highway throbbing with traffic, with retail and business parks close by. Two sharp bends take the canal to Wester Hailes and Kingsknowe, and on to Slateford, where an aqueduct leaps the Water of Leith and Slateford Road. There are fewer bends now as it continues through Merchiston, past the site of the rubber works, to its current terminal at Lochrin Basin.

The canal was a highway that helped transform the city. It connected the capital with rapidly developing industrial projects in the Central Belt. Close to where the Union and the Forth and Clyde canals met were the Carron Ironworks, established in 1759. The works used local iron ore, smelted by coke, to produce, in the words of Sir John Carr, 'cannon, shot, shells, and anchors, to augment the desolations of war, and grates, pots, and pans, to

179

promote the comforts of the kitchen'. The most famous Carron product was the carronade, a cannon exported all over the world, and used by both sides in the Napoleonic Wars. At the peak of production about 5,000 were produced every year. 'The place was covered with cannons, mortars, bombs, balls, and these large pieces, short and expanded at the breech, which bear the name Carronades,' wrote a French visitor to the works in 1784. Perhaps he relayed favourable comment back to France, for when Nelson at Trafalgar and Wellington at Waterloo fired their carronades at the French, they replied in kind. You can see a carronade in the National Museum of Scotland.

Edinburgh had become the capital of a rapidly industrialising nation. Although the Carron Ironworks were 30 miles away, and 'the volumes of smoke, the spiry flames, and the suffocating heat of the glimmering air' did not touch the lives of city residents, nevertheless the Union Canal connected Edinburgh with the massive and rapid changes that were going on around it and which inevitably affected its commercial and professional life. William Cadell, one of the three founders of the Ironworks, also set up an ironworks at Cramond, now part of Edinburgh. A walk up the River Almond, once the city boundary, passes Caddell's Row and surviving workers' cottages as well as remnants of the 18th-century iron mills which transformed iron ore imported from Sweden and Russia into spades, shovels and nails. The forge hammers were powered by the river, which according to Robert Forsyth pounded away at the rate of 120 to 160 strokes a minute. Industry was on Edinburgh's doorstep. Further into the 19th century, the city grew around existing manufacturing works, as the developments in Fountainbridge illustrate.

The Union and Forth and Clyde canals also connected people. Travel between Scotland's two most important cities was easier and more comfortable. But 20 years after the opening of the Union Canal that connection was transformed. I once lived in a house close to the road that linked South Queensferry with Linlithgow and Bo'ness. Half a mile to the south was the Union Canal. A quarter of a mile away, running parallel, was the M9 motorway. And in between was the railway. The old road, the new road, the canal and the railway: a history of transport a short walk from our front door.

It was coal that fuelled the railways and it was coal that drove the building of Scotland's first steel tracks. Edinburgh's railway history began in the 1820s when a wagon way was constructed from Niddrie to St Leonards, with branches to Leith, Musselburgh and to the coalfields south of the city. The wagons, drawn by horses, though with a stationary steam engine to haul them up a particularly steep gradient, brought coal to the capital, but by 1831 they were also carrying passengers. It was known as the 'Innocent Railway' though any suggestion that it was without mishap is misleading – there were accidents. Part of the track bed survives as a walkway through the southern section of Holyrood Park. On a Sunday afternoon it's likely to be busy with walkers and cyclists.

Muriel Spark in her memoir *Curriculum Vitae* (1992) remembered the delivery of coal in the 1920s to her family's Bruntsfield tenement.

'Coal!' would come the cry from the streets every morning, and when we needed coal the coalman's horse would bring his cart to a clicking stop at my mother's bidding from the window. Then up the stairs would tramp the coal-black man with his hundredweights to tip them into our coal cellar which was built into the flat.

My own first acquaintance with coal was in Edinburgh in 1946. There were still horse-drawn coal carts in the streets and my grandmother had a coal fire in her Heriot Row flat. Sacks of coal were still carried up the stair. There was a coal bunker in a cupboard. Edinburgh in the 1940s and 50s was still reeking. And of course the train I had arrived in from London was fuelled by coal. You could smell it. You could see cinders flying past the window. A striking reminder of Edinburgh's heritage of coal is the National Mining Museum at Newtongrange, the site of the Lady Victoria mine which was first worked in the 1890s. Newtongrange itself was built to house the miners. When the shaft was sunk it was the deepest in Scotland. The adjacent railway line transported the coal into the city and out to the Border mill towns, part of the Waverley Line closed in 1969 but now reopened. The pit was closed in 1981. The museum's collections of tools, equipment, photographs and archives, and the site itself, are the closest we can get to mining history.

It is easy to overlook the fact that the city and its near neighbours manufactured a range of household goods which supplied the domestic market and contributed to commercial viability. The smell of coal, like the smell of tanning and papermaking, has vanished from the Edinburgh air. When

An Edinburgh brewer. Alan Daiches. Courtesy National Library of Scotland.

I first lived in Edinburgh in the 1970s the pungent, yeasty aroma from breweries in Roseburn, Fountainbridge, Slateford and Holyrood often filled my nostrils, but now the only remaining large-scale brewery is the Caledonian Brewery in Slateford Road. As a child of eight or so I was on an expedition with my father which took us past a paper mill. I'm not sure where we were – almost certainly somewhere to the south of the city, Penicuik, perhaps, or Polton – but the smell was overpowering.

Brewing was an essential activity in any community, especially where water supplies were dubious, as for centuries they usually were. In medieval times brewing was either a domestic task carried out mainly by women, or a monastic activity. But it inevitably became commercialised. By 1825 there were 29 commercial breweries in Edinburgh. The dominant names were William Younger and William McEwan – the latter left a permanent memorial in the shape of the university's McEwan Hall. Alcohol also fuelled the building of the Usher Hall, funded by a gift from Andrew Usher, whisky distiller and blender. There was a lot of money to be made in providing the populace with alcoholic beverages. Now small-scale artisan brewing is spreading, but that unmistakable smell has nearly gone.

Edinburgh's papermaking grew in tandem with printing and publishing. The city's first paper mill was set up in 1590 in Dalry, and by 1700 there were mills at Canonmills, Upper Spylaw and Restalrig utilising the Water of Leith. Later, mills were established to the south of Edinburgh on the River North Esk and on the Almond in West Lothian. For the residents of the New Town it may have been possible to pretend that there was no place for industrial development in Edinburgh, but it wasn't far away. Robert Heron writing in 1799 gives a hint when he described Leith:

The flourishing manufacture of bottle-glass, window-glass, and crystal, under the direction of gentlemen possessed of great ingenuity and opulence, well merits notice. Three glass-houses have long been employed in this business, and three others have lately been erected. A carpet, a soap work, and some iron-forges, are also worthy of being mentioned.

Leith's glass houses were those admired by Susan Ferrier's Bailie Broadfoot. The claret consumed at New Town dining tables needed good glassware. These tables may also have been graced with pottery made in Portobello or Musselburgh.

Industrial manufacturing and an acknowledgement of its transformation of middle-class domestic life could perhaps be ignored, but 'the last word in human transport' was another matter, especially when it came steaming through the very centre of the expanding city. A short walk from Robert Louis Stevenson's home in Heriot Row was Edinburgh's North Bridge, where he liked to pause and look down on the locomotives hissing steam in Waverley Station and dream of departure to far-off places. For all his love of Edinburgh, escape was always on his mind. He never knew the city before the railway, which came to Edinburgh in 1842 with a rail link to Glasgow, not distant enough for Stevenson's aspirations though many years later the Clyde would be a significant departure point for him. The Edinburgh to Glasgow connection wasn't the first chapter in the story of Scotland's railways, but it was the start of Edinburgh's role as a railway city. The impact was great and the response was mixed.

In 1842 the trains from Glasgow terminated at Haymarket. The original proposal had been for the trains to run along a cutting through Princes Street Gardens to a station at North Bridge. In spite of assurances that the trains would be out of sight and the smoke and steam hardly perceptible, not surprisingly the owners of property in Princes Street objected. But not for long. With an increasing number of shops and hotels in Princes Street, perceptions changed. The advantages to business of a station in the city's centre became more obvious and resistance was overruled. The Act of Parliament necessary to allow the construction of track through the Gardens was passed, and in 1847 the Edinburgh and Glasgow Railway reached the east end of the Gardens. Cockburn described it as 'a lamentable and irreparable blunder'. The previous year the North British Railway had opened a station at North Bridge, the end of its line from Berwick. On 17 May 1847 two new stations came into being, one serving Glasgow trains and the other connections to Leith and Granton. Seven years later the three stations became collectively known as Waverley Station, and in 1868 the North British Railway, having absorbed the other two companies, built a new station on the site. Stevenson, in his 18th year when the new Waverley Station was opened, must have been aware of its construction. But he would never have seen the present Waverley Bridge, on which work began in 1894, the year of his death in Samoa, or the North British Hotel above the station, now the Balmoral, which opened its doors in 1902.

Long before the first locomotives steamed through Princes Street Gardens the approach of the railways was causing indignation. The site for the North British Railway's station was occupied by the 15th-century Trinity College Church and Trinity Hospital. These had to go. Lord Cockburn was furious. He described the demands of the railway as 'an outrage by sordid traders, virtually consented to by a tasteless city, and sanctioned by an insensible Parliament'. Unappeased by a proposal to rebuild the church on Calton Hill he fulminated against 'this piece of desecration' and the people who 'would remove Pompeii for a railway and tell us they had applied it to a better purpose in Dundee'. The church was partially rebuilt. If you turn off the High Street down Trunk's Close, past Sandeman House where Scottish Book Trust is based, you will find it – it is now the home of the Brass Rubbing Centre. Although much was lost in the rebuilding the interior is still 'the noblest of any Scottish collegiate church', according to Gifford, McWilliam and Walker. Displayed in the National Gallery are two panels from an altarpiece in the original church, probably by Flemish artist Hugo van der Goes.

But the railway was unstoppable, and there had to be stations. In 1854 Alexander Smith was writing of 'great volumes of white smoke' surging from the railway station. And it wasn't just the major cities that were connected. There was a symbiotic development of suburban lines and the suburbs themselves. Living on the outer edges of Edinburgh became an increasingly attractive proposition with the knowledge that there were easy routes linking the outer communities and the centre. Barnton, Colinton, Morningside, Corstorphine became connected. My father, in the 1930s, used to catch a train near his family home in Newington to cross south Edinburgh to Morningside, connected by rail in 1884, where the woman

Waverley Station. Rachel Calder.

he would later marry lived. The suburban routes now survive as cycle paths and walkways. From time to time there has been talk of reopening them. My partner Arthur rarely walks a former railway line without muttering on its suitability for trams.

But taking a train from anywhere to Edinburgh today still offers an insight into the city's 19th and 20th-century expansion. Approaching from the west you pass the sprawl of Edinburgh Park, South Gyle and Sighthill, hard to navigate mazes of business and retail and manufacture interspersed with clots of housing. Another line to the south passes the unlovely concrete blocks of Wester Hailes, developed in the 1970s. There was once a mansion house at Wester Hailes. The line from Fife and points north skirts the Gyle Shopping Centre and the public park, then runs through the post-war development of Broomhouse to join the Glasgow line at Stenhouse. Then you're into 1920s Saughtonhall and late Victorian Balgreen, and passing Murrayfield Stadium, also 1920s, and slowing down for Haymarket Station. On the left, out of sight, are the solid Victorian villas of Wester Coates, many of them now hotels and guesthouses. On the right, the working-class housing of Dalry.

The main line from the south and England comes into Edinburgh from the east, past Monktonhall and Musselburgh, then parallel to Joppa and Portobello and the shore of the Firth of Forth. It crosses the Figgate Burn that Stevenson's David Balfour followed, through Craigentinny and Restalrig, described by Gifford, McWilliam and Walker as 'a natural dumping ground for inter-war housing'. Buried amongst them is the extraordinary Christie Miller Mausoleum, an overwhelming stone structure 'shocking the prim houses around it'. Designed by David Rhind it was built over the tomb of William Henry Miller of Craigentinny House who died in 1848. Its purpose was to commemorate, in the words of *The Scotsman*, 'the private virtues of the deceased, for, as a public character, he was unknown'. He can't have been entirely unknown as he was an MP for a number of years, successively Whig and Tory. He was also a keen book collector. He stipulated that he was to be buried 40 feet deep in a stone-lined grave, which prompted speculation on what he might be trying to hide. James Grant in *Old and New Edinburgh* suggests that he might have been 'a changeling – even a woman', something which his 'thin figure, weak voice, absence of all beard' seemed to reinforce.

The train continues, passing close to Piershill Cemetery where several members of my family are buried, and Meadowbank Sports Centre, then through Abbeyhill's Victorian tenements and terraces with Arthur's Seat beyond. On the flanks of Calton Hill is what was planned as an extension of the New Town, designed by William Playfair. The original plan was never completed, but Royal Terrace, Regent Terrace and Carlton Terrace partly circle Calton Hill. And on the other side of the track, out of sight, are the eastern end of the Canongate, Holyrood Palace and the Scottish Parliament. A journey from Newcraighall on Edinburgh's eastern edge to Dalmeny in what was once West Lothian takes you through Waverley Station and under the castle, and encompasses more than two thousand years of history.

Former villages, estates and country houses, Corstorphine, Gorgie, Dalry, Ravelston, Murrayfield, Roseburn, Bruntsfield, Liberton, Mortonhall, Colinton, Pilrig, Broomhouse give their names to areas absorbed by 19th- and 20th-century expansion. Other names are reminders of an earlier existence – Boroughmuir, Davidson's Mains and Oxgangs (both farms), Stockbridge, Comely Bank, Meadowbank. Hundreds of Edinburgh streets are named for people, mostly men, as a tribute to life and work. Some we remember – William Chambers, Thomas Guthrie (his street, connecting Chambers Street with the Cowgate, is easy to miss), the Duke of Wellington,

Viscount Melville, Queen Victoria, William Carnegie – but many others have little resonance. Edinburgh's street names are not only markers of notable individuals. They reveal a great deal about the way the city expanded, and contemporary perceptions of achievement and importance. A collection of streets in Newington, a 19th-century expansion of the city, commemorates prominent public figures. Cobden Road and Bright's Crescent are tributes to the two Liberal politicians who campaigned for free trade in the mid-19th century. Robert Peel, was a Tory prime Minister (Peel Terrace), John McLaren a Liberal politician (McLaren Road). Nearby are Queen's Crescent, Albert Place, Alfred Place and Ventnor Terrace, all celebrating the royal family. Nearby also is Waverley Park. Scott again.

Parallel to Ventnor Terrace is Crawfurd Road, where my father's family lived. John Crawfurd, from Islay, served as a surgeon with the East India Company and later as a diplomat, succeeding Thomas Stamford Raffles as administrator of Singapore. He served in Java under Lord Minto, who also has a street named for him. Crawfurd went on to have a multi-layered career, which included an extensive interest in the history, ethnology and languages of East Asia. It seems appropriate that Edinburgh's rabbi should have lived in his street. And also appropriate that a street in Brunstane, close to Jewel and Esk Valley College and the Brunstane Burn, should be named for my grandfather. Daiches Braes is a recent development (my father and uncle were present at the naming of the street). My rabbi grandfather would, I think, have appreciated the fact that across the A1, the main route south, are two areas of 1950s council house development, the Christians and the Magdalenes.

The original Brunstane House was owned by the Crichton family, who in the 16th century were strong supporters of the Reformation. George Wishart, in 1546 burned at the stake in St Andrews for heresy, and his follower John Knox stayed at the house. My grandfather, who probably never set foot in Brunstane, would have appreciated that connection too. A hundred years later the house, rebuilt, was the property of the 1st duke of Lauderdale, Charles II's representative in Scotland, and then went through a succession of aristocratic owners – the Duke of Argyll, the Earl of Abercorn – until in 1747 it was sold to Andrew Fletcher, Lord Milton, justice clerk and nephew of the Andrew Fletcher who so passionately opposed the Act of Union. He employed architect William Adam to remodel the house. Eventually in 1875 the land was sold to the Benhar Coal Company. There is a railway station at Brunstane, on the now reopened Borders line. Heading south from Newington takes you to Liberton, where you can find a clutch of literary streets: Robert Burns Drive and Clarinda Terrace, Walter Scott Avenue and many streets featuring Scott's novels and characters, among them Kenilworth Drive, Peveril Terrace, Claverhouse Drive, Dinmont Drive, Marmion Crescent, Ellangowan Terrace, Talisman Place, Redgauntlet Terrace. Edinburgh has imprinted literature and literature has imprinted Edinburgh. In the early years of the 20th century the North British Railway named over 40 locomotives after Scott novels and characters: *Redgauntlet*, *Jeanie Deans*, *Ivanhoe*, *Claverhouse* (in *Old Mortality*), *Jingling Geordie* (in *The Fortunes of Nigel*), *Dandie Dinmont* (in *Guy Mannering*), and many more. A later locomotive was the *Abbotsford*. Now you can get on a train at Waverley and alight a pleasant walk away from Scott's own tribute to the past.

My own children enjoyed, as I had done, standing on the footbridge in Princes Street Gardens to watch the trains. But for many the steam monsters were irreconcilable with the castle's rocky splendour and the New Town's ordered elegance. It wasn't just the loss of the material past but an unwelcome intrusion of the present. For Compton Mackenzie the railways were a desecration, an unwelcome, ugly, noisy clash with the city's richly layered past. To have a railway station at the very heart of an historic city was an aberration. But the railway now does not seem to trouble the castle, or the leisurely feel of the Gardens, or the crowds on Princes Street. Or the crowds that rapturously greeted the arrival of the *Flying Scotsman* when in May 2016, after long absence, it arrived gloriously at Waverley Station. The railway has become an organic part of Edinburgh's centre. And it is still the best way to arrive in the city.

11

Set spacious and sae noble

Forth Bridge. Rachel Calder.

*There's nane sae spacious and sae noble*
*As Firth of Forth.*
Robert Fergusson , 'Caller oysters'

*muscle straddling the Forth*
Stewart Conn, *'Forth Bridge'*

ON A COLD, grey January Sunday I am walking across the Forth Road Bridge. My daughter Rachel and her partner are with me, the dog of course, and seven-year-old grandson Leon on his bike. We've crossed to Fife on the train and are now walking back to the southern shore of the firth. From the rail bridge, *the* bridge, we gazed out over the steely water, looking east, to Hound Point and Inchcolm and the grey firth widening out to the North Sea. Minutes later we alighted at North Queensferry, at the station which dates back to when the bridge was opened in 1890. You can't buy a ticket there now, but there is a café and a gallery and a meeting room and many of the station's original features have been preserved. We walked up the hill, past the community centre. On our right, whin-covered slopes and, out of sight, a little loch. Leon insisted on a pause at the play park, climbed, jumped, climbed again and came down a very wet slide. He cheerfully pointed out that it didn't matter if he got wet as he had his waterproof trousers on.

We carried on down steps to the north end of the bridge. It's a few years since I last walked across the bridge. I have ambivalent feelings about the experience. I'm not comfortable with heights and the constant vibration caused by passing traffic makes me nervous. But today it's not so bad. There are no heavy goods vehicles on the bridge, which has reopened after a three-week emergency closure. The bridge had never been closed before and the sudden deprivation of the road crossing between the Kingdom of Fife and Edinburgh caused consternation and anger. For commuters it meant abandoning the car for the train or a lengthy detour via the Kincardine Bridge. Buses and trucks had no choice but the detour. Now the bridge is sufficiently repaired to allow cars and buses, but no HGVs. The walking is more comfortable, and the views, even on a murky day, are splendid.

We are walking on the east side of the bridge. We look down at North Queensferry and its harbour. There was once a station at the harbour, where people left the train to board a ferry which took them across the water to

South Queensferry at night. Rachel Calder.

Port Edgar, where they continued their journey on another train. Beyond the harbour is the quarry which is now the home of Deep Sea World. All the grandchildren have visited Deep Sea World. And above the village is the railway. Trains appear from the Ferry Hills tunnel, some stopping at the station before entering the approach to the bridge. It never ceases to fascinate. However many carriages there are, the trains look like toys on the massive structure of the bridge. That bridge, surely, will last forever.

The road bridge takes us on a gentle upward curve. We see only one other family on our walk but there is plenty of activity. The repairs are not yet complete. High above are men in orange, festooned in safety harnesses. I watch them, intrigued although it makes me ill to see them dangling there, catching the wind, tools in their cold hands. On our right are the impressive towers of the new bridge, the Queensferry Crossing, still under construction. The gaps between the spans are narrowing.

The view is impressive. To the west are South Queensferry's Port Edgar, Bo'ness and the fiery furnaces of Grangemouth, with Rosyth, Limekilns and Charleston on the north shore. Walking across the water helps to understand just how significant a divide the Firth of Forth is. The Carmelite friars on the south shore provided shelter for travellers benighted by bad weather, and St Mary's, the priory church, survives, sympathetically restored. From the bridge's vantage point you can see it and the ragged line of the High Street's buildings running parallel to the shore. The 15th-century church, put up on land and with money given by the Dundas family of nearby Dundas Castle, is the oldest building in Queensferry.

The old town is a thin strip backed by a ridge which accommodated 19th-century development, the substantial houses which marked the burgh's easy access, with the coming of the railway, to Edinburgh. It also accommodated the homes of those who built the railway and the bridge. Most of the latter have gone, notably Catherine Terrace which is now an empty space, although Rosshill and Forth Terraces, by Dalmeny Station, survive. Queensferry originally had its own station, on the branch line that led to Port Edgar. The footbridge that connected the upper level of the town to the old station still exists. I cross it every day on my early morning dog walk.

To the west of Port Edgar the road runs parallel to the shore to Society. It passes Inchgarvie House and the road up to Linn Mill, now intruded upon by the Queensferry Crossing. Inchgarvie House and Linn Mill both feature, thinly disguised, in Ian Rankin's *A Question of Blood* which centres on a Queensferry murder. The road leads to the gates of the Hopetoun estate and on to Hopetoun House, rising gently, the house itself gradually emerging from the landscape. Queensferry is flanked by three great estates, Hopetoun, Dalmeny and Dundas, which has ensured until now the survival of green space. Building is now under way on some of that green space. We reach the end of the bridge and Leon shoots off on his bike to get to the Inchgarvie play park before us. He wants time for another quick clamber before we catch up.

The Firth of Forth, wrote Walter Elliot, is the gateway to Scotland.

> It lies almost at the balancing point of Europe between the Mediterranean and the Baltic. Scotland is European, with its own sea-access to the springs of European thought.

The Firth was a gateway for Edinburgh, too. Without the connections that the waterway allowed, Scotland's capital would have been oddly isolated, perhaps would never have become Scotland's capital. (It is interesting to reflect that although Scottish mercenaries fought all over Europe, Scotland as a nation never had ambitions to invade continental Europe, as England invaded France.)

In November 1918, the German High Fleet was escorted into the Firth of Forth, where it finally surrendered at Rosyth on the Fife shore. This was a gateway that the ships of the 16th and 17th centuries, plying between Scotland's east coast and Northern Europe, can hardly have anticipated. A few years later, the British Grand Fleet lay at anchor in the Firth, and during World War Two allied shipping, including vessels of the United States after the Japanese attack on Pearl Harbour in December 1941, joined Royal Navy ships. Before the closure of the Royal Naval Dockyard at Rosyth it was not unusual to see a warship in the Firth, though more than one was a cause for excitement. Today, there is often no activity at all. The tugs neatly parked near the Hound Point tanker berth are sometimes the only clue that the Firth is still a functioning commercial waterway.

The huge expanse of water, commented on by so many observers, is strangely empty. The Firth of Forth described by Robert Heron in the 1790s was 'like a great lake, interspersed with islands and enlivened with a variety of shipping', and for Stevenson in the 1870s it evoked the promise of romance, the open sea and distant ports. He describes looking out over the Forth from Calton Hill:

> the sun picks out the white Pharos upon Inchkeith Island; the Firth extends on either hand from the Ferry to the May; the towns of Fifeshire sit, each on its bank of billowing smoke, along the opposite coast; and the hills inclose the view, except to the farthest east, where the haze of the horizon rests upon the open sea.

It is hard now to recapture that sense of busy shipping and international connection that was so important to Edinburgh's wellbeing. An occasional tanker passes under the bridges, and at weekends and summer evenings there may be a cluster of sailing boats, or one or both of Queensferry's skiffs may be out, energetically rowed. The activity now is more about leisure – huge gleaming cruise ships, and the *Maid of the Forth* and the *Forth Belle* plying between the Hawes Pier and Inchcolm – than the lifelines of trade. Three of the grandchildren, Naomi, Alex and Leon, had the opportunity to sample kayaking at Port Edgar. It was a cold April day, the intermittent sunshine barely enough to counter the northeast wind, which kept the kayaking close inshore. One of the adult kayakers overturned and was dumped into the water, where he thrashed helplessly for several minutes, although the water was shallow. Naomi, meanwhile, paddled like a pro.

Queensferry, designated a royal burgh in the 17th century, never rivalled the major Forth ports, like Leith to the east or Bo'ness to the west. Its description in the *Gazetteer* of 1844 is disparaging:

in spite of its antiquity and seemingly historical importance, [Queensferry] has always been of small extent, and has a mean appearance; nor has it ever been enriched by much commerce, or dignified by great events.

Some would argue with this. Queensferry, as the name suggests, was from at least the time of Queen Margaret the embarkation point for crossing the Forth. It was a crucial ferry link between Edinburgh and points north, at the narrowest point of the Firth before it widens out to join the North Sea. Travelling from Edinburgh, the first bridge across the Forth was at Stirling. The port may always have been small but in the mid-17th-century Queensferry shipmasters owned over 20 vessels. A century later trade was declining and Robert Forsyth rather condescendingly described the harbour's usefulness 'as a place of retreat to vessels in hard gales'.

By the early 19th century there was a turnpike road linking Queensferry and Edinburgh. It was on this road that Jonathan Oldbuck, Walter Scott's antiquary, travelled when the diligence departed late from Edinburgh's High Street. The handbill proclaimed that the coach would 'secure for travellers the opportunity of passing the Firth with the flood-tide'. But late departure and accidents along the way mean that:

when they descended the hill above the Hawes... the experienced eye of the Antiquary at once discerned, from the extent of the wet sand, and the number of black stones and rocks, covered with seaweed, which were visible along the skirts of the shore that the hour of tide was past.

(The black stones and seaweed-covered rocks are still there.) The antiquary resigns himself to the delay and quickly cheers himself up with the prospect of a 'snack' at the Hawes Inn – 'a very decent sort of a place' – and the anticipation of 'pleasanter sailing with the tide of ebb and the evening breeze'. The 'snack' consists of sea trout, caller haddock, mutton chops and cranberry tarts along with a magnum of wine.

Stevenson, writing at the other end of the 19th century, sets his description of Queensferry earlier, in 1751, five years after the Jacobite defeat at Culloden. Stevenson's hero David Balfour accompanies his Uncle Ebenezer to Queensferry. They are on foot, but they too breast the hill and look down on the Forth.

> The Firth of Forth... narrows at this point to the width of a good-sized river, which makes a convenient ferry going north, and turns the upper reach into a land-locked haven for all manner of ships. Right in the midst of the narrows lies an islet with some ruins, and on the south shore they have built a pier for the service of the ferry; and at the end of the pier, on the other side of the road, and back against a pretty garden of holly-trees and hawthorns, I could see the building they call the Hawes Inn.

The Hawes Inn, at the far eastern end of Queensferry, then known as Newhalls and separate from the town, is still there.

David walks down to the shore. 'Even so far up the firth, the smell of the sea water was exceedingly salt and stirring; the *Covenant*... was beginning to shake out her sails, which hung upon the yards in clusters; and the spirit of all I beheld put me in thoughts of far voyages and foreign places.' Stevenson was very familiar with Queensferry and the Forth shore, and often walked out to the Hawes from Edinburgh. The *Covenant* was bound for the Carolinas. By the 18th century the strong east coast connections with the Baltic, the Low Countries and Scandinavia were giving way to the pull of the New World.

There is no record of Stevenson commenting on the building of the Forth Bridge, although it was begun before he left Scotland for good in 1887. There were several false starts. In 1804 work began on a tunnel, but was abandoned when it flooded. Another tunnel proposal would have linked Rosyth Castle on the north shore with the Hopetoun estate on the south, but the Earl of Hopetoun objected. In 1817 there was an idea for a chain bridge. In 1863 Thomas Bouch proposed a bridge from Blackness to Charleston. Although the river was wider here than at Queensferry, it was not so deep. Bouch went on to build the ill-fated Tay Bridge, which collapsed in a storm a year and a half after it was opened in June 1878. Then came the suggestion of a double suspension bridge at Queensferry and finally, in 1873, the Forth Bridge Corporation began to apply itself to the proposal to bridge the Firth of Forth. A foundation stone was laid at Inchgarvie, Stevenson's 'islet with some ruins' which you now look down on from the train, but after the Tay Bridge disaster a halt was called. The bridge was eventually designed by Benjamin Baker and John Fowler for the Forth Bridge Railway Company. Work began in 1883.

'To see the Forth Bridge is rather like meeting a popular actress, but with this difference: it exceeds expectations,' wrote HV Morton in 1929. It took seven years to build its Aberdeen granite piers and its 54,000 tons of steel cantilevers. At one time there were 5,000 men working on it, many of them Irish. In the course of constructing the 2,528-metre-long bridge there were 500 accidents and at least 57 men died. Their names are recorded on a memorial near the Hawes Inn.

David Beveridge saw the bridge under construction and commented:

There seems little reason to doubt that it will display one of the most extraordinary and stupendous monuments ever achieved by human ingenuity and industry. Concentrating, as it does, the application of so much skill, energy and perseverance, there appears little risk in predicting that it is destined to figure as one of the wonders of the world.

Impressed as he was, Beveridge noted that such achievement came at a cost, though he was less worried at the death toll than at the fact that Inchgarvie's ancient function as a fortification site to guard the Forth had been overlaid by its use to assemble all kinds of equipment and materials. He reflected that Inchgarvie 'seems to be consigned to the fate generally meted out to all natural objects that either stand in the way of, or can be utilised for, the requirements of practical science'. He might have added that the demand for practical science to find solutions for the challenges of modern life would increase exponentially, as would the consequences for 'natural objects'. A consequence for Edinburgh was an increase in rail traffic and the need to rebuild Waverley Station.

*Black's Guide* described the bridge as 'this famous triumph of science' and recommended taking a sightseeing trip from Edinburgh. These were run by 'large brakes with their red-coated drivers, that ply frequently in the season from Princes Street, at a charge of 1s (return double) for the drive of 9 miles'. The bridge's symbolic distinction has survived the construction of the road bridge a mile or so upriver, opened in September 1964, and will survive the completion of the second road bridge which opened in 2017. Impressive as these bridges are, they lack that tangible sense of challenge contained in the very structure of the rail bridge and its bold message of new routes and connections. The Forth Bridge – which does not need the explanatory 'rail' – was designated a World Heritage Site in 2015. Once I encountered a young man hurrying along the path from Dalmeny station to the shore but not sure of his way. 'Where is the bridge?' he asked me. 'I have come to see the great bridge.' There was no doubt which bridge he was referring to.

To the east of Queensferry and the village of Dalmeny which lies to the south, is the Dalmeny estate, edging the shore as far as the River Almond which once marked Edinburgh's boundary. In 1662 the Earl of Rosebery acquired Barnbougle Castle, on the shore, from the Mowbray family. It wasn't until the 19th century that the present Dalmeny House was built, designed by William Wilkie. William Cobbett in 1833 was impressed by the estate, which he described as 'one of the finest in Scotland'. 'It has everything,' he went on, 'fine fields, fine pastures, fine woods, immense tracts of beautiful turnips, stack-yards with a hundred stacks in each': all the signs of modern farming and good husbandry. But, as he caustically pointed out, 'rendered mournful to me by the sight of a thrashing-machine and of the beggarly barrack, in which are doomed to live on oats, barley, peas and potatoes, those without whose labour all this land would be worthless, having neither woods, nor stacks, nor turnips, nor herds of cattle, nor flocks of sheep'.

Within the Dalmeny estate is Mons Hill from where you can see Edinburgh Castle and Arthur's Seat as well as the whole line of the firth's south shore from the Forth Bridge to the Bass Rock off North Berwick. A walk along the shore takes you past Long Craig pier, Fishery Cottage almost on the beach, Hound Point and the tanker berth, Barnbougle Castle, Dalmeny House itself looking out across the water, and on to the River Almond. Once, there was a little ferry that crossed the river to Cramond. Now that is gone, although there is talk of reinstating it. When the tide is out, it may be possible to wade across to Cramond, but I have never put that to the test.

On an April day in 1871 Thomas Stevenson and his son Louis walked to Cramond from Heriot Row in Edinburgh's New Town. They soon left the

Georgian terraces and their Victorian successors behind and were walking through pleasant farm land. There is now only a small area of surviving green as a reminder that father and son were enjoying a country walk. This particular occasion was memorable for the fact that Louis found the courage to tell his father that he did not want to pursue the paternal career of civil engineer, but hoped instead to be an author. But it was a walk they often took. The New Town to Cramond or Queensferry were favourite routes.

It was in Cramond parish that Stevenson set the House of Shaws in *Kidnapped*. 'The country was pleasant round about,' he writes, 'running in low hills, pleasantly watered and wooded'. And it was between Cramond and Queensferry that Stevenson and his friend Walter Simpson, son of James Young Simpson who discovered the anaesthetic properties of chloroform, paddled their canoes. Later they would make the canoeing trip in Belgium and France that provided material for Stevenson's first book *An Inland Voyage* (1878). Cramond had not yet become a suburb of Edinburgh, but there was little remaining evidence of its ancient history. People had lived where the River Almond empties into the Forth since at least 4,000 BC. The Romans had made it the centre of their first-century AD efforts to control Scotland, a convenient point for shipping men and materials west and north. A convenient point for fishing too – the Romans almost certainly enjoyed Cramond oysters. But there are signs of a more recent industrial past. The river powered grain mills which in the 18th century became the iron mills developed by Cadell of the Carron Ironworks.

When the tide is low you can walk out along a causeway to Cramond Island. The island is larger and rougher than it looks from the shore. It was described by Robert Heron in 1799 as having 'no other inhabitants than a few sheep, and a multitude of rabbits'. The rabbits are still there. From time to time a whale or a basking shark has been stranded there. If you go out to the island you have to watch the tide. Rachel and I were once somewhat negligent and found ourselves hurrying back across the causeway with the water up to our ankles.

A walkway from Cramond edges the shore and takes you to Granton. Up the hill on the right are Silverknowes, Muirhouse and Pilton, areas of council housing developed in the 1930s (Pilton) and 1950s (Muirhouse) as part of programmes of slum clearance. A quick tour through these areas reveals boarded up windows and shops – there aren't many – with steel shutters. It's hard to escape an air of sterility and desolation. If you read the novels of Irving Welsh, you get a vivid, and sometimes caustically comic, impression of squalid environments of deprivation and drugs. But walking by the water and looking up the green slope that stretches to Muirhouse suggests none of this. On a sunny weekend there will be families, walking and on bikes, and dozens of dogs racing across the sand.

Once a string of separate communities – Granton, Newhaven, Leith, Portobello, Joppa, Musselburgh – lined the Forth and served the capital city which had no coastline of its own. Now they merge into each other, and a coast that once bristled with quays and docks has been transformed. There are still identifiable remains of warehouses, railway lines and sidings, as well as handsome 18th- and 19th-century buildings which bear witness to a vigorous commercial past. Also surviving is evidence of an older history, though this is harder to track down. Almost in the shadow of what were once the gasworks in Granton (just one of the three gasholders remains) is Caroline Park House, a late 17th-century rebuilding of an older house on the estate of Royston. The estate had been bought by George Mackenzie of Tarbat, who later became the first Earl of Cromartie. Mackenzie had a chequered political career, supporting the Stewarts but later accepting William and Mary and supporting the Act of Union. He turned what had been a modest residence into something distinctly grand, which was later sold by his son to the Duke of Argyll, who named it Caroline Park after his daughter. The daughter's marriage into the Buccleuch family brought the estate into the ownership of the Duke of Buccleuch.

In 1834, the Duke, with 'patriotic munificence and liberality', instigated the creation of modern Granton. Work was begun on a deep water harbour, to a design originally by Robert Stevenson, Robert Louis's grandfather. Granton Square, designed by William Burn, and Lower Granton Road were also built in the 1830s and '40s as the area was developed. Like so many Forth harbours, Granton harbour was born out of coal. The Buccleuch estate included coal mines and the coal had to be shipped out. Not only coal, but all the products of the Forth valley were shipped out of Granton: iron, shale oil, paper, whisky. Among the many different cargoes coming in were the raw materials for some of these industries: esparto grass for paper, for example, and china clay for the thriving potteries which soon needed more material than local clay deposits could provide. Granton also became the base for the Northern Lighthouse Board vessels which inspected and supplied Scotland's lighthouses. Described at the time as 'the finest in the Firth of Forth', in 1862 Granton harbour was seen as a model. It was, according to James Lothian:

> one of the best equipped ports in the Kingdom, and large enough to shelter a fleet, where there are extensive wharfing for mineral traffic, an admirably worked patent slip, shipbuilding yard (Menzies of Leith), locomotive engine works (Hawthorne & Co), a railway from the wharf for the conveyance of minerals and goods to Slateford on the Caledonian line, and grain to the Caledonian distillery, and generally all the desiderata of a first-class port.

Granton was conceived as a means to an end, but it also, as the above quotation underlines, made a confident statement about commercial progress and Edinburgh's role in mid-century activity. The new development was handsomely and spaciously laid out, with Granton Road built to link this industrial development unashamedly with the city, flanked by villas and walled gardens. It is one of the few places within the city of Edinburgh where the intimate connection between industry and wealth was confidently paraded in a way that was more characteristic of Glasgow. In the 1890s a large tract of the Buccleuch estate was acquired for the construction of gasworks to supply the city. Existing gasworks in New Street near Waverley Station, and in Leith and Portobello, could not meet demand. The New Street works became subsequently a bus depot and is now the site of the much criticised Caltongate development.

From early in the 19th century a steamer service was operating out of Granton, taking passengers upriver to Stirling. Theodor Fontane, a visitor to Scotland, described the steamer with her 'black and scarcely moving cloud of smoke that issues from the funnel, a familiar roaring and snorting' followed by 'a rattling and scooping, as, after disengaging itself with an elegant turning motion from the side of the quay, the steamer begins to carry us through the bright sunshine upstream'. Granton harbour was also the southern end of the railway connection with Burntisland in Fife, which ferried trains across the Forth before the opening of the bridge in 1890. The *Leviathan* was crossing the Forth from 1850. It had a specially designed ramp, the brainchild of Thomas Bouch, which enabled the loading of goods wagons whatever the state of the tide. Passengers, though, still had to get off

Newhaven. Alan Daiches. Courtesy National Library of Scotland.

the trains, cross by steamer, and board a second train in Fife. A passenger ferry service to Fife continued until 1940, with the paddle steamer *William Muir* operating for over a half a century. In 1950 the ferry service was reinstated, and lasted for five years. An even shorter-lived attempt to re-establish a ferry connection between Edinburgh and Fife came in 1991 when the motorised catamaran *Spirit of Fife* was introduced, linking with a free bus service to central Edinburgh. The idea did not catch on.

Stone for the mid-century development of Granton was locally quarried. In 1856 the quarry was flooded by the sea, and later the flooded quarry provided the site for a barge which housed the Scottish Marine Station for Scientific Research, set up in 1884 by the Scottish Meteorological Society. The Antarctic explorer William Speirs Bruce studied there as a young student, as did the young Fridtjof Nansen, before going on to pursue a distinguished multi-stranded career as polar explorer, scientist and diplomat.

The scientific tradition is maintained by the National Museum of Scotland's Granton Centre, which provides storage and research areas for reserve collections, including a large part of its zoological material. The Granton Centre is part of the still developing Waterfront scheme, which aims to transform this once industrial limb of the capital. But Rankin's Rebus sees Granton's underbelly, 'in places ugly and brutal, region of harsh sea-wall views, grey industrial buildings and redundancy. Broken factory windows, spray paint, sooty lorries.'

To the east, Newhaven is some centuries older than Granton, although it too was created for a purpose. It owes its beginnings to the ambitions of James IV to transform Scotland into a major sea power, in competition with England. He spent £100,000 on building and equipping a navy, the flagship of which was the ambitiously large *Great Michael*, completed in 1511. The construction of the ship, of about 1,000 tons, required a new deep-water dock, a huge amount of timber – 'this schip tuik so meikle timber, that schoe waisted all the wood in Fife, save Falkland wood' wrote the historian Robert Lindsay of Pitscottie, who added 'she cumbered all Scotland to get hir to the sea'. The *Great Michael* is remembered now as a kind of floating folly. It was around 72 metres long, 36 metres wide, and could carry 27 cannon and around 300 crew. But it was involved in only one military encounter, and in 1514 was sold to France. One can think of 21st century grandiose schemes that have a touch of the *Great Michael*.

Newhaven did not sustain this dramatic start in shipbuilding. It became better known as a fishing port, and its 19th-century harbour was once packed with fishing boats. From the fish market dominating the quay, fishwives set off early in the morning with their loaded creels to sell fish door to door in Edinburgh. In their distinctive striped outfits they were familiar figures in the residential streets. The fish market survives, and Newhaven maintains its longstanding reputation for fish suppers.

Steam came to Newhaven before there was a harbour at Granton. In 1821 'an elegant chain pier' 150 metres long and suspended from four wooden towers was built for the use of steam vessels which plied up the Forth and across to Fife. For many years the chain pier was a favourite launching spot for bathers – 'that old resort of Edinburgh swimmers, where one could get a plunge in deep sea water at any hour or state of the tide, eg at daybreak of the New Year, as was the way with some hardy youths'. But with the passing of the steam boats it steadily deteriorated, until it was destroyed by a storm in 1898. *Black's Guide* of a few years later could still describe nearby Wardie as 'a democratic bathing place' and praise its 'airy promenade': 'swimmers get a capital early morning plunge when the tide suits'.

Portobello beach. Rachel Calder.

Starfish on Portobello beach. Rachel Calder.

The city's nearest stretch of coast was becoming a place of recreation as well as commercial connection. Beyond Newhaven and Wardie and the busy port of Leith was Portobello, which by the beginning of the 19th century was attracting attention as a healthful escape from Edinburgh. Now a dreary stretch of road flanked by used car dealers and carpet warehouses heads southeast from Leith to Portobello and beyond to Joppa and Musselburgh. For decades two landmarks dominated Portobello, the power station built in 1934 and the outdoor swimming pool which opened in 1936 with room for over 1,200 bathers. They reference two strands of Portobello's history, the industrial and the recreational. Portobello grew up on the site of a village called Figgate, situated at the mouth of the Figgate or Braid Burn.

The Figgate Whins upstream are described by Stevenson in *Catriona* (1893) as 'linky, boggy muirland'. The place acquired its change of name thanks to a resident who named his cottage after the battle of Puerto Bello when in 1739 Admiral Vernon defeated the Spanish at Panama. (Perhaps he was remembering the part Spain had played in the Darien disaster.) It wasn't until the 1780s that a small harbour was constructed at the mouth of the burn, which served the needs of the pottery works nearby. William Jameson, an Edinburgh builder who bought land in the area in order to build houses, set up first a brickworks and then, around 1787, two potteries. In the *Old Statistical Account* (1796) Portobello features as 'Portobello and Brickfield'. In the next century Portobello pottery became well known, with several factories producing earthenware and stoneware. Rathbone's, operating in the first half of the 19th century, was one of the most successful. As well as plates, bowls and jugs for which there was an increasing demand, the Rathbone family made fishwife and Highlander figures in response to the Victorian demand for decorative objects for the home.

There were local clay beds and local coal and nearby harbours for shipping out the finished products. Potteries were set up in Musselburgh and in Prestonpans further along the coast. But the harbour at Portobello gradually silted up and was eventually built over. For a while Portobello's industrial activity was paralleled by its growing reputation as a resort, but that inevitably changed.

In 1804, Groome's *Ordnance Gazetteer* highlighted 'the beauty of the beach, the fineness of its sands, and its general eligibility as a bathing place'. It began to attract the citizens of Edinburgh (the young Walter Scott was taken there for his health), and bathing machines appeared on the beach. In 1834 Robert Chambers commented that 'a great number of elegant new streets have been built... chiefly for the accommodation of genteel families of retired habits, or for valetudinarians who prefer a residence by the sea-shore on account of their health'. Villas sprung up, a pier where excursion steamers called was constructed in 1870 (only to be demolished in 1917). The two-mile promenade of 1898 signalled the victory of the recreational over the industrial, highlighted by the town being the birthplace in 1870 of one of Scotland's most famous entertainers, Harry Lauder (no relation, as far as I know, to my grandmother Janet Lauder). By the early 20th century Portobello was being described as

the miniature Margate of Edinburgh... a snug place... with some touches of pretension in the architecture of its long sea front; and its visitors are mostly of the tripper kind, yet some residents stand up with warm affection for its sands, donkeys, rowing-boats, and promenade pier.

With the demolition of the power station in 1983 the only evidence of Portobello's alliance with coal and manufacturing are two surviving kilns

on the site of Jameson's brickworks, close by the Figgate Burn.
'Portobello,' writes Alice Thompson in *The Existential Detective* (2009),
'is a place where you can find anonymity.' It is also a place that reflects
contrasting emotions: 'hope, despair, excitement and dullness', though I
suppose both the potential for anonymity and the contrast can be found in
any concentration of humanity. But Portobello and Leith, and their parent
city, feature ominously in this novel of layered deception and loss, real and
imagined.

*Black's Guide* isn't much concerned with the complexity of human
relations, and he considered next-door Joppa, with its Victorian terraces,
'a rather more choice suburb' than Portobello. Across the River Esk is
Musselburgh, now within the city limits. Stevenson gives us a glimpse
of this stretch of coast as he imagined it in the 1750s. David Balfour and
Alan Breck have spent the night under a whin bush and need to continue
their journey to Dirleton where Alan is to be picked up by the boat that
will take him to safety in France: 'so we went east by the beach of the sea,
towards where the salt-pans were smoking by the Esk mouth'. One of the
salt pans would later be managed by the father of William and Robert
Chambers.

Originally called Eskmouth, Musselburgh acquired its new name
on account of a mussel-bank near the river mouth. Fishing was its main
occupation – in Victorian times about 50 fishing boats were operating out of
the small harbour. Like the Newhaven fishwives, those from Musselburgh
carried heavy creels of fish to sell in Edinburgh. Robert Forsyth describes
them hurrying to make up time on occasions when the boats come in late: 'it
is not unusual for them to perform their journey of five miles by relays, and
shifting their burden from one to another every hundred yards, by which
means they have been known to arrive at the fish market in less than three
quarters of an hour'. Fishwives' Causeway still exists.

Forsyth also comments on what he calls the 'reversal of the character
of the sexes among the common people' in Musselburgh, with women
'engaging in more laborious employment than the men… long accustomed
to carry to Edinburgh vast quantities of salt, sand for washing floors, garden
stuffs, and other articles, which they sold there, and often brought back
heavy burdens of other goods'. According to him they could carry 200–250
pounds. (For comparison, the hardiest *voyageurs* in pioneering Canada
could carry two 90 pound packs.) 'Their manners are masculine,' Forsyth

Pottery kilns, Portobello. Rachel Calder.

writes. They played golf and football.

On Shrove Tuesday every year there was a football match between married and unmarried women 'in which the former are always victorious'. Chambers was less impressed. The Musselburgh fishwives, he said, were 'not only distinguished by a rude peculiarity of manners, but also by a comparatively grotesque dress'. Robert Fergusson was better disposed towards the fishwives, who supplied the 'caller oysters' he celebrated in a poem of that name.

> At Musselburgh, and eke Newhaven,
> The fisher-wives will get top livin,
> When lads gang out on Sunday's even
>         To treat their joes,
> And tak of fat pandours a prieven,
>         Or mussel brose.

Musselburgh profited by being on the main route to Edinburgh and at the crossing of the River Esk, but also suffered. Armies approached that way as well as travellers bringing commercial benefits. In 1547, the battle of Pinkie, a victory for invading English, was fought uncomfortably close (the battlefield is southeast of Inveresk, between the railway and the A1), with the wounded taken to Pinkie House, near the High Street, which belonged to the Abbot of Dunfermline and later became the home of the Seton family. Twenty years later another confrontation took place nearby, at Carberry Hill, where the defeat of Mary, Queen of Scots and the Earl of Bothwell led to her removal from the throne and imprisonment in Loch Leven castle. Bothwell went into exile and eventually had a miserable death in a Danish prison.

But battlefields meant nothing to my children when they were small. For them, Musselburgh meant one thing only, the obligatory stop after a day on the beach at Gullane for Luca's ice cream. We can get Luca's ice cream in Queensferry now, and often eat it sitting on a bench by the harbour, watching the tiny trains cross the massive rust-red bridge, the 'muscle straddling the Forth'.

World's End Close. Alan Daiches. Courtesy National Library of Scotland.

12

Built on history, built of history

*This rortie wretched city*
*Built on history*
*Built of history*
Sydney Goodsir Smith, *Kynd Kittock's Land*

*If we're lucky, our past will bear us company.*
Ron Butlin, 'Kickstarting History'

SYDNEY GOODSIR SMITH's long poem *Kynd Kittock's Land* drew on his experience of Edinburgh in the 1960s and also on the photographs of Alan Daiches, my brother, who photographed particularly the Old Town and the Rose Street pubs with which Goodsir Smith was very familiar. The poem and the pictures were commissioned by the BBC for a television programme that was aired on 28 February 1964 and repeated the following year. The poem was read by Iain Cuthbertson.

Goodsir Smith's poem is textured like the city itself, stony, craggy, dark, two-faced, woven with dreams and memories. And although written five decades ago, the poem still expresses a recognisable Edinburgh – and suggests that if Goodsir Smith were alive today he could well write another poem in similar vein. There have been huge changes, destructions, renewals and overlays, but under the surface and at the margins the wretched and the rortie – a word of Australian derivation meaning rowdy (Goodsir Smith was born in New Zealand) – are still there. Goodsir Smith's Edinburgh was

Sair come doun frae its auld hiechts
The hauf o't smug, complacent,
Lost til all pride of race or spirit,
The tither wild and rouch as ever
In its secret hairt
But lost alsweill, the smeddum gane,
The man o' independent mind has cap in hand the day

Edinburgh is an 'empty capital'. It dreams of freedom but the dream is

Indulging an auld ritual
Whase meaning's been forgot owre lang

Sydney Goodsir Smith. Alan Daiches. Courtesy National Library of Scotland.

Today, the capital is not so empty. It is home to Scotland's parliament and the location of multiform social, political and cultural expressiveness. But it is still a place whose history and character allow an indulgence in old rituals. As I write this the festivals of 2016, which transformed the streets of central Edinburgh in an almost saturnalian spirit, have gone but the tourists still crowd the pavements, the bagpipes still lustily resound, the cameras silently record. The tourists are there because Edinburgh's 'granderie in auld lang syne' is still palpable, it still speaks. But they may also catch a sense of Goodsir Smith's 'dour gurlie [stormy, growling] city...That sells itsel for greed'. The greed is more conspicuous than ever, as are the objects that it feeds on. And greed and its collaterals are responsible for some of the damage inflicted on the city. But geography and geology as well as history and the written word defy these ravages.

Who was Kynd Kittock and what was her land? Kind Kittock's story is told in a ballad attributed to William Dunbar. She was devoted to drinking, but died of thirst and went to heaven. There she found 'the ale of heaven was sour' so slipped out to an alehouse just on the other side of heaven's gate, where 'she ran the pitchers to pour, And for to brew and bake'. She appears again in Eric Linklater's story *Kind Kitty* (1935) which locates Kitty firmly in Edinburgh and tells of her inebriated adventures with her 'little flat bottle of whisky'. So for Goodsir Smith she represents Edinburgh's underworld, and indeed the World's End, the name of a High Street pub once at the Netherbow Port which marked the town limits – brass studs in the street are a reminder. This is how the poem ends:

> This is mine, Kynd Kittock's land,
> For ever and aye while stane shall stand –
> For ever and aye till the World's End

Land is also the name given to Old Town tenements, so the word doubly anchors Kynd Kittock to the old city. But Edinburgh is an idea as well as a location, and both survive to be appropriated, embraced, experienced. Writers and artists and historians can batter away at the old stones, but they still – for the most part – stand and retain that sense of immortality if not immutability.

Goodsir Smith's poem is irreverent, uncompromising, comic, affectionate. His words have lost none of their chiselled vigour. Alan's photographs convey an almost tender empathy, towards stone and cast iron as well as people. When the poem was published in 1965 they were without the photographs, and although the poem retains its impact I feel the separation. The photographs came before the words, so Goodsir Smith was responding to images that were themselves an individual's response to the city, as well as to his own experience and observation. These images and the poem itself are now a part of the fabric of history. And so the layers accumulate, and are never lost if you know where to look. The city is interpreted over and over again – in the half century since the creation of *Kynd Kittock's Land* there have been thousands more images and many thousands more words. Histories, reminiscences, poems, stories, tourist brochures, newspaper articles – there has never been a lack of attempts to put Edinburgh into words. It is hard to resist the temptation.

You can argue that every structure is built on history. I live in a bungalow built in 1935. Its original owners were the Nardini family who ran South Queensferry's first fish and chip shop. The house was built on farm land at the end of a row of substantial Victorian villas that backed onto the railway and faced towards the Ferry Muir, the scene of witch burning in the 17th century. The land was part of the Dalmeny estate – the lane outside the house still belongs to Lord Rosebery. Nearby is Queensferry's bowling club, founded in 1877, and Station Road Park, where once there was a reservoir supplying the burgh with water. Life is enriched by knowing these things.

And everywhere is built *of* history, my own history now part of the house I live in, as the house is part of more than 20 years of my life and the life of my partner Arthur, although he spends half his time in Argyll with its own environment of the past.. From the house, a frequent Sunday morning walk takes us through Easter Dalmeny Farm. Today, the middle of August, there is a giant combine harvester in the yard. The sun is shining and the harvest is about to begin. The track divides a field of ripe wheat. Fifty yards in front of us, two young foxes cross the track and disappear. Our Labrador pauses to sniff the spot where they crossed but otherwise shows no interest. We see deer sometimes, in Craigie Woods and running across the fields. We are within the city limits. This, too, is Edinburgh, this place of wheat and barley and oil seed rape and buzzards overhead and deer and properly rural foxes.

We go under the A90, throbbing with traffic. A few miles away the Edinburgh festivals are in full swing, a hectic and serendipitous transformation of the city. 'Welcoming the world to Edinburgh', the 2016 Edinburgh International Festival programme says. There are performances in French, German, Italian, Russian and many varieties of English. There are performers and audiences, in the main Festival, the Fringe, the Book Festival, from every continent. On the street a multitude of languages weaves in and out of the music, the drumbeats and the acrobatics that flow around and through the crowds. For a few weeks Edinburgh is transformed, light and sound and spectacle take over, and, for the resident, everyday life is hampered. The real world is overlaid. Getting to work or the shops, going to school, most quotidian activities, all take extra time. People grumble.

Some escape for the duration. But for many residents the Festival is a golden opportunity for boosting income. The millions of visitors festival Edinburgh attracts need to sleep, eat and drink as well as attend shows. They buy postcards and tartan and books and shortbread. Some may buy a rare single malt whisky. Recent research indicates the Edinburgh's festivals, including the Tattoo and the events at Hogmanay, in 2015 brought in £313 million. They sustain over 6,000 jobs.

The Edinburgh Festival was a conscious attempt at post-war cultural regeneration, a deliberate statement that creativity not only survived war but was capable of renewing the spirit and making the world whole again. And it was a statement also specifically about Scotland, staking Edinburgh's claim to be at the centre of renewal. Edinburgh, as Angela Bartie writes in *The Edinburgh Festivals. Culture and Society in Post-War Britain* (2013) was 'casting off the shadow of John Knox and finding a new cultural confidence that paved the way for debates over devolution and Scottish independence'. Lord and Lady Rosebery of Dalmeny played a part in the Festival's inception. Lord Rosebery, the 6th earl, was chair of the Scottish Tourist Board at the time, and Eva, countess of Rosebery, a musician herself, was chair of the Scottish National Orchestra. Dalmeny House was the scene of early discussions.

Kathleen Ferrier was one of the performers at the first Edinburgh Festival in 1947. 'It was unforgettable,' she wrote later.

The sun shone, the station was decked with flags, the streets were gay. Plays and ballet by the finest artists were being performed, literally morning, noon and night, and the hospitality was showered upon guests and visitors by the so-called 'dour' Scots! What a misnomer!

My grandmother, Flora Daiches, also remembered the first Festival, which came just two years after she had lost her husband. She talked of walking home on warm summer evenings after attending concerts. For her the concerts must have been particularly welcome, as she had been a talented pianist and her love of music stayed with her always. Her grand piano was the focal point of her Heriot Row living room. It is part of my earliest Edinburgh memories.

The Festival Fringe – or the outlying performances that became the Fringe – was also born in 1947. It was an almost accidental birth, arising from the eight professional and amateur theatre groups that decided, though not invited to participate in the Festival, that they would perform anyway. It seemed there was an appetite for Shakespeare, Strindberg, Maxim Gorky, James Bridie and Robert MacLellan, among others, and so the Fringe began. Now for most of August almost every inch of Edinburgh has become a potential performance space, and the Fringe itself has fringes. Edinburgh's visitors, packing the pavements of Princes Street, battling their way through the High Street crowds, become part of the performance.

Not everyone was happy, or convinced that 1947 heralded the start of a new cultural era. Bruno Walter could claim the Festival as 'one of the most magnificent experiences since the war' but Scotland's own Hugh MacDiarmid was not persuaded. 'It is to my mind absurd that a city which has always treated the arts so meanly can suddenly blossom forth as a great centre of world-culture,' he wrote in a letter to *The Scotsman*. It would not have seemed absurd to the literati of the 18th century, or to Walter Scott who orchestrated his own version of absurdity to honour George IV. Scott's jamboree may not have been high culture, but it certainly demonstrated that Edinburgh was neither mean-spirited nor repressed.

Twelve years after the Festival began its annual metamorphosis of the city, a former junk shop in Charles Street – a street that no longer exists – was transformed into a bookshop. Sometime around then, 1959, a tall and charming American friend of my brother's visited us in the family house near Cambridge. This was Jim Haynes, an American living in Edinburgh and the begetter of the Paperback Bookshop. You couldn't miss it – there was a horned rhino head looming out of the outside wall. Charles Street and the shop were long since swallowed up by the university's expansion but a small replica of the rhino head marks the spot. Inside the shop the shelves were packed with books, many from writers and publishers outwith the United Kingdom and hard to find in conventional bookshops. You could browse and read over a cup of coffee and very likely find yourself having a conversation with someone interesting.

Four years later came another landmark in Edinburgh's journey of cultural experiment. In January 1963 the Traverse Theatre opened in a former brothel in James Court, just off the Lawnmarket. I remember it as dark and cramped, creaky and crowded, but it rapidly became a focus of experimental drama and challenging debate. It was, wrote the cultural journalist Joyce McMillan, 'at the epicentre of an intellectual ferment that

Paperback Bookshop. Alan Daiches. Courtesy National Library of Scotland.

rocked the capital's prissy façade and put it on the international map'. Jim Haynes was also a key player in founding the Traverse, along with Richard Demarco. It was Alan who introduced me to both the Paperback and the Traverse, and to smoke-filled pubs that were homes to the folk music revival, all of it contributing to a spine-tingling world of bohemian daring and counter-culture. It coexisted with an older, sadder Edinburgh. When in 1969 the Traverse moved to the east end of the Grassmarket it was still a place where the destitute congregated. When it moved in 1992 to its custom-built premises in Cambridge Street it lost that gritty consanguinity, though it remains a focus of new drama. Success, almost inevitably, involves a separation from the circumstances that generate it.

So two decades after Edinburgh's post-war cultural blossoming – to appropriate MacDiarmid's word – the city became the locus of not only the classical and established in music, words and art but also of experiment and challenge. Perhaps it was no accident that two of the leaders in this transformation had origins outwith Scotland, Jim Haynes from the US, and Richard Demarco whose antecedents were from southern Italy and Ireland. But there were plenty of others ready and willing to assist and who brought both a Scottish and an international perspective to the party, writer and publisher John Calder among them. And it was the partnership of Jim Haynes and John Calder that brought into being, with the help of Sonia Orwell, the International Writers' Conference of August 1962. It was 'the first time literature would play a part in the Festival...what we wanted to do was to return literature to its proper place in the Edinburgh arts, and to fertilise the Scottish scene with a big international presence,' John Calder wrote in *The International Writers' Conference Revisited* (2012). Calder went on:

Had George Thomson of the Edinburgh Review not commissioned songs from Haydn and Beethoven, articles and new work from Goethe and Stendhal and Edinburgh a European centre when London was provincial? Bookshops flourished in Scotland when there was hardly a publisher in London and bookshops there had to subscribe a new book to its customers before it could be printed.

What followed were five days of heated discussion and contentious exchange to packed audiences and with extensive press coverage. Subjects covered included contemporary Scottish writing, censorship and the future of the novel. The Scottish session, chaired by my father, was particularly fiery. It ended in near-chaos with an outbreak of anti-Polaris songs. I remember the tensions and the histrionics – writers, in Nick Phillipson's words, 'making an exhibition of themselves'. But I also remember the geniality and goodwill, if not harmony, that emerged afterhours at one of the smoky, boozy parties that I was lucky enough to attend as a wide-eyed 20-year-old.

The following year there was another conference, this time focused on the theatre – the Traverse had been on the go for less than a year. Edinburgh's citizens may have muttered disapprovingly of the writers in 1962 discussing drugs and homosexuality, but the 1963 conference provoked vociferous moral outrage. On the last day, when the theme was 'The Theatre of the Future', a naked young woman was wheeled on a trolley across the McEwen Hall organ gallery. Most of the audience could have had no more than a glimpse of nudity but the mere fact of an unclothed young woman was enough. 'I knew,' wrote one member of the audience in a letter to *The Scotsman*, 'the organisers believe in avant-garde theatre and no censorship. This idea is contrary to our heritage.' Well, perhaps. But Edinburgh, and Scotland, also have a heritage of free thinking and free expression. How else would Presbyterianism have arrived on these shores? Or the Enlightenment taken root?

The fact that the young woman, Anna Kesselaar, was an 18-year-old unmarried mother fuelled the flames. She was denounced from the pulpit of St Giles. She was brought to trial, accused of 'acting in a shameless and indecent manner'. She was found not guilty. The case against the perpetrators of the 'happening' was dropped. For Anna that wasn't the end of the story. She lost her job with Basil Spence's architecture firm – Spence was regretful, apparently, but couldn't risk the possibility of moral contamination – and there was an attempt to remove her child from her. 'Any woman who has a child out of wedlock', thundered the minister at St Giles, 'is not morally fit to bring that child up.' She had to leave Edinburgh.

There is still a lingering feeling that Edinburgh's festivals are an aberration, a heady and uncharacteristic mix of culture and excess that when the performers have departed subsides with relief into a 'strange silence' and 'rather chilling dignity and reserve' as described in Elspeth Davie's novel *Coming to Light* (1989). At the end of the novel Davie describes the Festival's concluding firework display. When the spectacular 'bursting and hissing' colour fades, the crowd moves away. 'The shuffle of hundreds of boots and shoes moving homewards could be heard down the main street like the sound of the tide drawing out from a stony beach.' It's all over. 'Even the irrepressible Fringe has been pressed back into its Pandora's box.' People are departing, the stations 'echoing with goodbyes', and Edinburgh heaves 'a great sigh of relief'. Davie, like so many others, writes about the city's doubleness. It cannot be ignored.

Thirty years on, the sense of a return to grey normality after festival excitement is less apparent. Most of the street performers have gone. George Street, for four weeks closed to traffic and filled with pop-up outdoor eateries, is again choked with car fumes. The Charlotte Square tents have disappeared leaving the grass so scarred it's hard to believe that it will recover – but it will and next spring will see the green grass spangled with gold and purple crocuses. But the strange figure who has occupied the corner of the Lawnmarket and George IV Bridge throughout the Festival, apparently floating in mid-air bowing and swooping at passers-by, is still there three weeks after it's all over. There is still a lingering hint of theatre.

My four grandparents were all incomers to Edinburgh. They arrived just after the First World War, and it is thanks to them that Edinburgh has become a part of my history as well as theirs. 'If we're lucky, our past will bear us company,' poet and former Edinburgh Makar Ron Butlin says. And our past reaches beyond our birth, which in my case was in another country, and beyond the birth of parents and grandparents. I grew up with a sense of Edinburgh, absorbed through my parents' memories of childhood and student life in the city and punctuated by my own childhood visits. It was inevitable that members of my family, including the younger generations that my parents and grandparents never knew, would become key players in the pages of this book.

In 1963 my soon-to-be parents-in-law, Peter and Mabel Ritchie Calder, Scots who had spent most of their adult life in the south of England (though in Peter's case also in many other parts of the world) bought a flat in Edinburgh's Randolph Place. It was a spacious top floor flat with splendid views to the north. It became the focal point of the many visits to Edinburgh made by me and husband Angus, and our initial base when we arrived from Kenya in 1971 to make our home in Scotland. Not an ideal base for a family with three small children, one an infant who had to be carried up and down three flights of stairs, but nevertheless a very comfortable and much-appreciated refuge while we settled into Edinburgh life and looked for a place of our own.

Those three children all attended Stockbridge Primary School, down the hill from Buckingham Terrace where we eventually settled. Every day we walked through the Dean Gardens alongside the Water of Leith, to Dean Terrace and on past Stockbridge Library to the school in Hamilton Place. The school itself was typical of those built in the wake of the Education

Act of 1872, which provided a national system of education for children up to the age of 13. There are many similar schools all over Edinburgh. Stockbridge School was designed by Robert Rowand Anderson. Anderson designed a number of schools and also worked on church restorations, but he is best known for some of Edinburgh's most prominent buildings – the Scottish National Portrait Gallery, the Edinburgh Medical School and the McEwan Hall, and outwith Edinburgh, Mount Stuart on the Isle of Bute and the lovely Govan parish church in Glasgow. Stockbridge School is a solid, Gothic, gabled building intended to accommodate 600 children. It's a handsome if rather severe structure, but its concrete playground was no deterrent to the noisy and imaginative games that erupted at playtime.

Along the road from Stockbridge School, in Henderson Row, is Edinburgh Academy, completed in 1824. Lord Cockburn was among those who perceived a need for a new school to offer more opportunity for a classical education. He and Leonard Horner, merchant and educational reformer, set up a committee to raise funds for its construction. Walter Scott was one of its first directors. The original building is low and rather plain with Doric pillars, reflecting the institution's classical aspirations. The building in its low-key location on the northern edge of the New Town is very different from the independent schools that appeared later in the century. Daniel Stewart's College (now Daniel Stewart's and Melville College) went up in 1848 to a design by David Rhind. It was built with money left by Daniel Stewart, a Perthshire-born crofter's son whose fortune stemmed initially from India and later from property development. His intention was to fund a school for underprivileged boys, but the splendid Jacobean building, which opened its doors in 1855, looks – like Donaldson's School – far too imposing for its purposes and in 1870 became a fee-paying institution. The building stands on a rise overlooking Queensferry Road. You can't miss it.

Fettes College, built in the 1860s, was also designed to be viewed from a distance in all its grandiosity. The architect was David Bryce, a leading proponent of the Scottish Baronial style. The building is a heady mix of Scottish Baronial and French Gothic described by Gifford, McWilliam and Walker as 'superbly confident in organisation, lively and scholarly in detail'. There is no doubting its statement of authority, but, like Daniel Stewart's, Fettes was originally intended for the impoverished or orphaned. William Fettes, twice lord provost of Edinburgh, made his money from selling the

Fettes School. Rachel Calder.

much-desired beverages, tea and wine. After the 1872 Education Act all children had access to basic schooling. The boys and girls making their way each morning to Stockbridge Primary must at times have shared their journey with children going to the Academy. They may also have caught glimpses of Fettes College or Daniel Stewart's – neither school was far from Stockbridge.

My mother and father had bursaries to George Watson's Ladies College and George Watson's School respectively. I have some of my mother's school reports, on heavy paper headed Report of Progress and Conduct and signed by the headmistress, GE Ainslie. 'Very good and helpful' is a repeated comment. My mother was 'conscientious', 'very good in all subjects', 'an excellent worker'. The only negative note is 'must guard against forgetfulness'. I think she was a dreamy child. So was I. From 1921–22, when she was 12 and 13, she was class captain. In the second term of that year she was absent for 36 days. I know that she had diphtheria as a child, which perhaps accounted for this absence.

George Watson, born in Edinburgh in 1654, was a merchant and banker, the first accountant of the Bank of Scotland, founded in 1695. When he died in 1723, he, like George Heriot before him and others later, left money for the education of the deprived – 'the sons and grandsons of decayed merchants'. George Watson's Hospital opened in 1741 just off Lauriston Place, on a site which was later absorbed into the Royal Infirmary. It moved first to nearby Archibald Place, then, in 1932 (shortly after my father's time) to Colinton Road. In 1870 Watson's became an independent day school, and the following year a school for girls, George Watson's Ladies' College, was opened in George Square. Edinburgh's earliest girls' school, and one of the world's oldest school for girls, was the Merchant Maiden Hospital founded in 1694 by Mary Erskine, an Edinburgh business woman, entrepreneur and philanthropist. The school, originally in the Cowgate, was for the daughters of city burgesses who had fallen on hard times. It is now the Mary Erskine School in Ravelston.

One of George Watson's Ladies' College's most distinguished alumnae was Cecily Fairfield, who would in later life become the novelist and commentator Rebecca West. She was 17 years older than my mother, so they can't have coincided, but perhaps my mother read her novel *The Judge* (1922) which draws on her Edinburgh childhood. Cecily's mother, Isabella Mackenzie, had grown up in Edinburgh, in Heriot Row. When in 1901 she returned to her native city as an impoverished single parent the family lived first in Hope Park Square, then in Buccleuch Place. In *The Judge*, Buccleuch Place is 'a street of tall houses separated by so insanely wide a cobbled roadway that it had none of the human, close-pressed quality of a street, but was desolate with the natural desolation of a ravine'. What was once modest Georgian elegance had become by the early 20th century shabby and run-down, a far cry from Heriot Row.

Today, Buccleuch Place has been absorbed by the university, and the centre of the 'insanely wide' street is a car park. *The Judge* also pictures Hope Park Square, 'the queerest place, hardly 40 paces across, on three sides of which small squat houses sat closely with a quarrelling air'. Then a near-slum, it is now a rather delightful corner tucked away off a lane at the east end of the Meadows, and the home of the university's Institute for Advanced Studies in the Humanities.

Cecily, or Cissie as she was called, did not have far to go to school in George Square, presided over by the same headteacher who signed my mother's reports – Miss Ainslie. Cissie didn't get on with Miss Ainslie.

It would be interesting to see her reports. At the age of 17 she left school and left Edinburgh to study at what would become the Royal Academy of Dramatic Art. She was not sorry to say goodbye to Edinburgh and what she described as 'the Scottish blight that ruined my early life'. The 'blight' was the result of having an alcoholic and absent father and living on the wrong side of the tracks in a city highly conscious of social status.

In Elspeth Davie's novel *Creating a Scene* (1984) her central character, Foley, reflects that he has been too long in beautiful Edinburgh:

> I've only to pass half a dozen litter tubs inscribed: 'This city is beautiful...' to feel like crowning the railing spikes with paper bags. There's a smug element in a city which has been admired over centuries. The people tend to rely heavily on the skyline like a woman on her profile – never mind if the rest goes to pot.

Edinburgh's smugness and sense of moral righteousness were also a part of Rebecca West's perceived 'blight', as they were a part of Robert Louis Stevenson's yearning to escape. People do leave Edinburgh. My parents did, although in their case it was a reluctant departure and they always intended to return. And each of their children for a time made Edinburgh their home. Alan began his photographic career in Edinburgh in 1960, first in Castle Wynd, then in the Torphichen Street flat he shared with his wife Jean. I and my family came to Edinburgh in 1971. For a while my sister Liz lived in the same Edinburgh street as me. After a seven-year sojourn in West Lothian, I returned within the city limits in 1984. My middle child returned to Edinburgh after several years away and now lives close to me. My elder daughter's photographs of the city feature in this book. My son and his family in Wales visit often. Edinburgh has imprinted us all.

Goodsir Smith attacked the city's self-righteousness, as did MacDiarmid and many others. He exposed the underbelly on which it still rests. Christine De Luca, an Edinburgh Makar, in her poem 'Edinburgh volte face' catches the flavour of the city's concern with appearances:

> City of venerable skylines;
> each morning you un-do yourself
> like someone more anxious to save the wrapping
> than enjoy the gift.

Steps of the Royal Scottish Academy. Alan Daiches. Courtesy National Library of Scotland.

Edinburgh's wrappings can be dazzling. On my way to see a dramatised version of Alice Munro's story 'The view from castle rock' I walk up Castle Terrace with my daughter Gowan. The sky is a brilliant blue. Outlined against it are the round and square and spiked towers of George Heriot's School. On my left is the dark backside of the castle. Below me is the Grassmarket with all its grim associations of death and destitution. Somehow it all seems both solid and illusory. We are early, so we sit with a coffee in the sunshine outside the Traverse Theatre. Half a century ago I might have been drinking coffee in the original Traverse, unaware that the floor under my feet might collapse at any time. When in Alice Munro's story, the young Andrew and his father look out from the castle ramparts across the Firth of Forth, they see the illusion of a promised land. Sometimes it is hard to be sure of reality.

It's a Saturday afternoon in February, grey but with glimmers of sunshine. Six adults are walking along the Dalmeny shore of the Firth of Forth, and three children and a dog are running, all brandishing sticks. Anna, my niece, is carrying a bag. In the bag is a plastic urn containing the ashes of her father, my brother Alan, who died suddenly in January 2006. We are going to scatter his ashes in the firth.

We stop on the beach just beyond Hound Point, opposite the tanker berth and St David's on the north shore. From the low grassy cliff above the beach we can see the bridges to the west and Cramond Island to the east. A mile or so away is Barnbougle Castle and beyond that Dalmeny House. The children write their names in the sand. Alan goes into the water that connects to the city he loved and to the North Sea, which perhaps will take him up Scotland's east coast and round into the Moray Firth with all its associations of happy family holidays. We toast him in malt whisky. The shouts and laughter of the children, his grandchildren and his great nephew, are the best possible accompaniment.

His photographs of children in Edinburgh's streets have become part of my Edinburgh. It's personal.

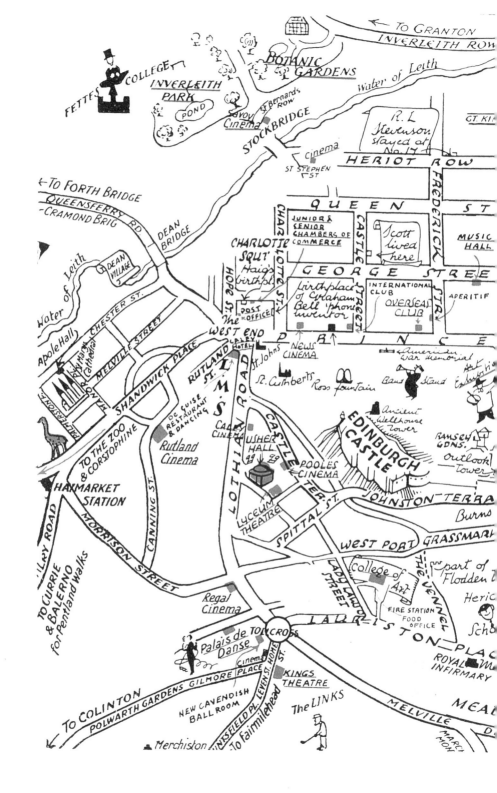

# Timeline
## of some key events in Scotland's and Edinburgh's past from 1100

| | |
|---|---|
| 1107 | Succession of Alexander I |
| 1124 | Succession of David I |
| 1128 | Holyrood Abbey founded |
| 1130s | Edinburgh Castle's St Margaret's Chapel built |
| 1153 | Succession of Malcolm IV |
| 1165 | Succession of William I 'The Lion' |
| 1214 | Succession of Alexander II |
| 1243 | Dedication of St Giles church |
| 1249 | Succession of Alexander III |
| 1263 | Battle of Largs and retreat of the Norse |
| 1292 | Succession of John Balliol |
| 1295 | Franco-Scottish alliance against England |
| 1296 | English army captures Edinburgh Castle |
| 1297 | William Wallace resists English invasion |
| 1305 | Execution of Wallace |
| 1306 | Succession of Robert I 'the Bruce' |
| 1314 | Battle of Bannockburn |
| 1320 | Declaration of Arbroath |
| 1329 | Royal charter granted to Edinburgh by Robert the Bruce |
| | Succession of David II |
| 1334 | English army recaptures Edinburgh Castle |
| 1371 | Succession of Robert II |
| 1385 | English army besieges Edinburgh Castle |
| 1390 | Succession of Robert III |
| 1406 | Succession of James I |
| 1437 | Succession of James II |
| 1460 | Succession of James III |
| 1482 | English army occupies Edinburgh |
| 1488 | Battle of Sauchieburn |
| | Succession of James IV |
| 1507 | Edinburgh's first printing press |
| 1513 | Battle of Flodden |
| | Succession of James V |

| | |
|---|---|
| | Construction of Flodden Wall begins |
| 1542 | Battle of Solway Moss |
| | Succession of Mary, Queen of Scots |
| 1546 | George Wishart executed for heresy |
| 1547 | Battle of Pinkie |
| 1559 | John Knox returns to Scotland |
| 1560 | Reformation Parliament |
| 1561 | Mary, Queen of Scots, returns to Scotland |
| 1564 | Construction of the 'Maiden' beheading machine |
| 1565 | Marriage of Mary, Queen of Scots and Henry Darnley |
| 1567 | Murder of Darnley |
| | Abdication of Mary |
| | Succession of James VI |
| 1570 | Murder of Regent Moray |
| 1573 | Final defeat of Mary, Queen of Scot's supporters |
| 1581 | Execution of James Douglas, Earl of Morton |
| 1582 | Foundation of the University of Edinburgh |
| 1603 | Union of the crowns of Scotland and England |
| 1625 | Succession of Charles I |
| 1629 | Birth of Mary Erskine |
| 1633 | Edinburgh formally becomes capital of Scotland |
| 1637 | Introduction of the Scottish Prayer Book |
| 1638 | Signing of the Covenant |
| 1639–40 | Bishops' Wars |
| 1640 | New parliament building completed |
| 1643 | Signing of the Solemn League and Covenant |
| 1644 | Scottish invasion of England |
| | Battle of Marston Moor |
| 1645 | Battle of Philiphaugh |
| 1646 | Surrender of Charles I |
| 1649 | Execution of Charles I |
| | Succession of Charles II |
| 1650 | Battle of Dunbar |
| | Cromwell's army in Edinburgh |
| 1651 | Battle of Worcester |
| | Start of Cromwell Protectorate |
| 1659 | George Heriot's School opens |

| 1660 | Restoration of the monarchy |
|------|------|
| 1661 | Execution of Archibald Campbell, Duke of Argyll |
| 1665 | Holyrood Palace rebuilt |
| 1666 | Pentland Rising |
| 1674 | Piped water supply to Edinburgh |
| 1679 | Battle of Bothwell Brigg |
| | Advocates Library founded (or 1680) |
| 1684 | Birth of Allan Ramsay, poet |
| | Robert Sibbald's *Scotia Illustrata* published |
| 1685 | Succession of James VII and II |
| 1689 | Succession of William III and Mary II |
| | Battle of Killiecrankie |
| 1690 | Presbyterianism established |
| 1692 | Massacre of Glencoe |
| 1694 | Merchant Maiden Hospital (school for girls, later Mary Erskine's) opens |
| 1695 | Bank of Scotland founded |
| 1698 | Darien expedition |
| 1702 | Succession of Queen Anne |
| 1706 | Daniel Defoe in Edinburgh as government spy |
| 1707 | Act of Union |
| | Death of Mary Erskine |
| 1711 | Birth of David Hume |
| 1714 | Succession of George I |
| 1715 | Jacobite Rebellion |
| 1723 | Birth of Adam Smith |
| 1726 | Birth of James Hutton |
| 1727 | Succession of George II |
| 1728 | Birth of Robert Adam |
| | Birth of Joseph Black |
| 1736 | Porteous Riots |
| 1738 | Building of Royal Infirmary begins |
| 1739 | David Hume's *A Treatise of Human Nature* published |
| 1741 | George Watson's College opens |
| 1745 | Jacobite Rebellion |
| | Birth of Henry Mackenzie |
| 1746 | Battle of Culloden |

| 1750 | Birth of Robert Fergusson |
| 1753 | Birth of Dugald Stewart |
| 1754 | Select Society founded |
| | Mons Meg taken to London |
| 1756 | Birth of Henry Raeburn |
| 1758 | Death of Allan Ramsay, poet |
| 1759 | Drainage of North Loch begins |
| | Robert Burns born |
| 1760 | Succession of George III |
| 1762 | St Cecilia's Hall completed |
| 1763 | North Bridge completed |
| 1766 | Adam Smith's *The Wealth of Nations* published |
| | James Craig's plan for the New Town approved |
| 1770 | Birth of James Hogg |
| 1771 | Birth of Walter Scott |
| 1772 | North Bridge completed |
| 1773 | Birth of Francis Jeffrey |
| 1774 | Death of Robert Fergusson |
| 1776 | Death of David Hume |
| 1779 | Birth of Henry Cockburn |
| 1780 | Society of Antiquaries of Scotland founded |
| 1781 | Construction of the Mound begins |
| 1783 | Royal Society of Edinburgh founded |
| 1785 | South Bridge foundation stone laid |
| 1786 | Robert Burns's first visit to Edinburgh |
| 1788 | Deacon Brodie hanged |
| | South Bridge completed |
| 1789 | Foundation stone of University of Edinburgh's Old College laid |
| 1790 | Death of Adam Smith |
| | Birth of William Playfair |
| 1792 | Death of Robert Adam |
| 1795 | James Hutton's *Theory of the Earth* published |
| | Birth of Thomas Carlyle |
| 1797 | Death of James Hutton |
| 1799 | Death of Joseph Black |
| 1803 | Third and successful launch of the *Edinburgh Review* |
| 1811 | Birth of James Young Simpson |

| | |
|---|---|
| 1814 | Scott's *Waverley* published |
| 1817 | Tolbooth demolished |
| 1818 | *Blackwood's Magazine* launched |
| | Scott's *The Heart of Midlothian* published |
| | Edinburgh Gas Lighting Company established |
| 1820 | Succession of George IV |
| 1821 | School of Arts of Edinburgh founded, later the Watt Institute |
| 1822 | George IV's visit to Edinburgh |
| | Union Canal opened |
| | William Burn's plan for the Moray Estate produced |
| | Royal Botanic Garden moves from Leith Walk to Inverleith |
| | Royal Bank of Scotland founded |
| 1823 | Death of Sir Henry Raeburn |
| 1824 | Observatory on Calton Hill opens |
| | Edinburgh Academy opens |
| | Hugh Miller's first visit to Edinburgh |
| 1826 | Work on National Monument begins, never completed |
| | Royal Scottish Academy opens |
| 1828 | Death of Dugald Stewart |
| 1829 | Succession of William 'IV' |
| | Mons Meg returns to Edinburgh from London |
| | William Burke executed |
| 1831 | Dean Bridge opens |
| 1832 | Reform Act |
| | Death of Sir Walter Scott |
| | Death of Henry Mackenzie |
| | Melville College opens |
| 1835 | Death of James Hogg |
| 1836 | Discovery of miniature coffins on Arthur's Seat |
| 1837 | Succession of Queen Victoria |
| 1842 | Edinburgh and Glasgow Railway opens |
| 1843 | Disruption of the Church of Scotland |
| 1846 | North Bridge railway station opens |
| | Daniel Stewart's School opens |
| 1850 | Birth of Robert Louis Stevenson |
| | Death of Francis Jeffrey |
| 1851 | Donaldson's Hospital (later school) opens |

| 1854 | National Gallery of Scotland opens |
| | Death of Lord Cockburn |
| | Waverley Station created through the amalgamation of three |
| | existing railway stations |
| 1856 | Death of Hugh Miller |
| 1857 | Death of William Playfair |
| 1860 | Hospital for Sick Children opens |
| 1862 | Edinburgh International Exhibition |
| 1864 | Last public hanging in Edinburgh |
| 1870 | Death of Sir James Young Simpson |
| | Fettes College opens |
| 1871 | George Watson's Ladies' College opens |
| 1872 | Education Act |
| 1874 | Heart of Midlothian football club founded |
| 1881 | Death of Thomas Carlyle |
| 1883 | Royal Lyceum Theatre opens |
| 1888 | St George's girls' school opens |
| 1890 | Forth Bridge opens |
| | Edinburgh Central Library, funded by Andrew Carnegie, opens |
| 1892 | Birth of Hugh MacDiarmid (Christopher Grieve) |
| 1895 | Electric lighting permanently installed in Edinburgh |
| 1896 | Empire Palace Theatre, Edinburgh's first cinema, opens |
| 1897 | Birth of Naomi Mitchison |
| 1901 | Succession of Edward 'VII' |
| 1902 | Watt Institute becomes Heriot-Watt College, later university |
| 1906 | King's Theatre completed |
| 1910 | Succession of George V |
| | Birth of Norman MacCaig |
| 1913 | Zoological Park opens on Corstorphine Hill |
| 1914 | Usher Hall opens |
| 1914–18 | First World War |
| 1915 | Birth of Sydney Goodsir Smith |
| 1918 | Birth of Muriel Spark |
| 1925 | Advocates Library gifted to the nation and National Library of |
| | Scotland set up |
| 1926 | General Strike |
| 1929 | Union of the Church of Scotland and the Free Church |

| | |
|---|---|
| 1936 | Succession of Edward 'VIII' |
| | Succession of George VI |
| 1939–45 | Second World War |
| 1947 | First Edinburgh International Festival |
| 1948 | National Health Service introduced |
| 1952 | Succession of Elizabeth 'II' |
| 1961 | Scottish National Gallery of Modern Art opens at Inverleith House |
| 1962 | International Writers' Conference |
| 1963 | Traverse Theatre founded |
| 1964 | Forth Road Bridge opens |
| 1975 | Death of Sydney Goodsir Smith |
| 1978 | Filmhouse opens |
| | Death of Hugh MacDiarmid |
| 1979 | First Edinburgh Jazz Festival |
| | First Edinburgh Folk Festival |
| 1980 | City Art Centre opens |
| 1983 | First Edinburgh Book Festival |
| 1984 | Scottish Gallery of Modern Art moves to Belford Road |
| 1989 | First Edinburgh Science Festival |
| 1994 | Festival Theatre opens |
| 1996 | Death of Norman MacCaig |
| 1999 | Death of Naomi Mitchison |
| 1999 | Restoration of Scottish Parliament |
| 2006 | Death of Muriel Spark |
| 2017 | Queensferry Crossing opens |

# Copyright Acknowledgements
## for books quoted in the text

Bartie, Angela, *The Edinburgh Festivals. Culture and Society in Post-War Britain*, Edinburgh University Press, 2013

Bateman, Meg, 'Moray Place Gardens, Edinburgh', in *Edinburgh, An Intimate City*, ed Bashabi Fraser and Elaine Greig, City of Edinburgh Council, 2000

Broster, DK, *The Flight of the Heron*, Heinemann, 1925

Bruce, George, 'City Inscape', in *Edinburgh, An Intimate City*; *Festival in the North*, City of Edinburgh Council, 2000

Butlin, Ron. *The Magicians of Edinburgh*, Polygon, 2012

Davie, Elspeth, *Creating a Scene*, John Calder, 1984; *Coming to Light*, Hamish Hamilton, 1989

Donati, Colin, 'Sic Itur ad Astra', in *Edinburgh, An Intimate City*, City of Edinburgh Council, 2000

Galbraith, Gillian, *The Road to Hell*, Birlinn, 2012

Garioch, Robert, *Collected Poems*, Macdonald, 1977

Gifford, John, McWilliam, Colin and Walker, David, *The Buildings of Scotland: Edinburgh*, Penguin, 1984

Glen, Duncan, 'Edinburgh's Botanics', in *Edinburgh, An Intimate City*, City of Edinburgh Council, 2000

Linklater, Eric, *Magnus Merriman*, Jonathan Cape, Newnes, 1934; *Edinburgh*, 1960; *The Survival of Scotland*, Horizon Press, 1968

MacCaig, Norman, *Collected Poems*, Chatto and Windus, 1990

McCall Smith, Alexander, *44 Scotland Street*, Abacus, 2005; *The Careful Use of Compliments*, Abacus, 2007; *The Lost Art of Gratitude*, Abacus, 2009

McDermid, Val, *Out of Bounds*, Little, Brown, 2016

MacDiarmid, Hugh, *Complete Poems*, Martin Brian & O'Keefe, 1978

McKean, Charles, *Portrait of a City*, Century, 1991

May, Peter, *The Lewis Man*, Quercus, 2012

Mitchison, Naomi, *Small Talk*, The Bodley Head, 1973

Mitchison, Rosalind, *A History of Scotland*, Routledge, 1970

Morgan, Edwin, *Collected Poems*, Carcanet, 1990

Morton, HV, *In Search of Scotland*, 1929

Muir, Edwin, *Scottish Journey*, Heinemann/Gollancz, 1935

Munro, Alice, *The View from Castle Rock*, Chatto and Windus, 2006

Rankin, Ian, *Set in Darkness*, Orion, 2000; *The Falls*, Orion, 2001; *Resurrection Men*, Orion, 2001; *A Question of Blood*, Orion, 2003
Robertson, James, *The Fanatic*, Fourth Estate, 2000; *Joseph Knight*, Fourth Estate, 2003; *Voyage of Intent*, Luath Press, 2005; *And the Land Lay Still*, 2010
Smith, Sidney Goodsir, *Kynd Kittock's Land*, M Macdonald, 1964
Spark, Muriel, *The Prime of Miss Jean Brodie*, Macmillan, 1961; *Curriculum Vitae: A Volume of Autobiography*, Constable, 1992
Thompson, Alice, *The Existential Detective*, Two Ravens Press, 2010
Waterston, Charles, *Collections in Context*, National Museums of Scotland, 1997
Yee, Chiang, *The Silent Traveller in Edinburgh*, Methuen, 1948

# Some Other Useful Books

Arnot, Hugo, *The History of Edinburgh*, 1779
Bald, Robert, *A General View of the Coal Trade in Scotland*, 1808
Barker, Pat, *Regeneration*, 1991
Barr, Pat, *A Curious Life for a Lady: The Story of Isabella Bird*, 1970
Bartie, Angela and Elaine Bell (ed), *The International Writers' Conference Revisited*, 2012.
Beveridge, David, *Between the Ochils and the Forth*, 1888
Bird, Isabella, *Notes on Old Edinburgh*, 1869
*Black's Guide to Edinburgh*, 1910
Bone, James, *The Perambulator in Edinburgh*, 1926
Buchan, John, *Huntingtower*, 1922; *Midwinter*, 1923
Burns, Robert, *Complete Works*, 1986
Calder, Jenni, *RLS: A Life Study*, 1980; *Robert Louis Stevenson and Victorian Edinburgh* (ed), 1980; *The Wealth of a Nation in the National Museums of Scotland* (ed), 1989; *St Ives* by RL Stevenson (new ending), 1990; 'Professions, proles and profits' in *Hugh Miller in Context*, ed Lester Borley, 2002
Campbell, Alexander, *History of Leith*, 1927
Cant, Malcolm, *Villages of Edinburgh*, 1999
Carlyle, Alexander, *Autobiography*, ed J Hill Burton, 1910
Carlyle, Thomas, *Historical Sketches*, 1898

Carr, Sir John, *Caledonian Sketches, or a Tour Through Scotland in 1807*, 1808

Chambers, Robert, *Traditions of Edinburgh*, 1825

Cobbett, William, *Tour in Scotland*, 1833

Cockburn, Henry, Lord, *Memorials of His Time*, 1856

Coghill, Hamish, *Lost Edinburgh*, 2008

Conn, Stewart, *The Luncheon of the Boating Party*, Bloodaxe, 1992; *Stolen Light*, 1999; *Ghosts at Cockcrow*, 2005

Crawford, Robert, *The Beginning and the End of the World. St Andrews, Scandal and the Birth of Photography*, 2011

Daiches, David, *Two Worlds*, Macmillan, 1956; *Scotland and the Union*, 1977; *Edinburgh*, 1978; *A Traveller's Companion to Edinburgh*, 2004

Defoe, Daniel, *A Tour Through the Whole Island of Great Britain*, vol 3, 1727

Doyle, Arthur Conan, *Memories and Adventures*, 1924; *The Firm of Girdlestone*, 1890

Duff, David (ed) *Queen Victoria's Highland Journals*, 1983

Edwards, Owen Dudley, *Burke & Hare*, nd

Fergusson, Robert, *Selected Poems* (ed James Robertson), 2000

Ferrier, Susan, *Marriage*, 1818

Findlater, Jane and Mary, *Crossriggs*, 1908

Fletcher, Andrew, of Saltoun, *The Political Works of Andrew Fletcher, Esq of Saltoun*, 1749

Forsyth, Robert, *Beauties of Scotland*, 1805

Fraser, Bashabi and Greig, Elaine (eds), *Edinburgh, an Intimate City*, 2000

Fry, Michael, *Edinburgh. A History of the City*, 2010

Galt, John, *Ringan Gilhaize*, 1823

Geddie, John, *Romantic Edinburgh*, 1900; *The Fringes of Edinburgh*, nd

Geikie, Archibald, *Scottish Reminiscences*, 1904

Gilbert, WM, *Edinburgh in the Nineteenth Century*, 1901

Grant, James, *Cassell's Old and New Edinburgh*, 1880–83

Gray, W Forbes, *A Literary Centre of a Literary Capital*, 1946

Gray, JM, (ed), *Memoirs of the Life of Sir John Clerk of Penicuik*, 1892

Grierson, Flora, *Haunting Edinburgh*, 1924

Groome, Francis H, *Ordnance Gazetteer of Scotland*, 1882

Heron, Robert, *Scotland Described*, 1797

Hogg, James, *The Private Memoirs and Confessions of a Justified Sinner*, 1824

Hume, David, of Godscroft, *History of the Houses of Douglas and Angus*,

1643
Irving, Washington, *Correspondence*, 1907
Jardine, Quentin, *Skinner's Rules*, 1994
Lockhart, John Gibson, *Memoirs of the Life of Sir Walter Scott Bart*, 1837–38
Lothian, James, *The Banks of the Forth*, 1862
Lownie, Ralph (ed) *Auld Reekie: An Edinburgh Anthology*, 2004
MacDougall, Carl, *Painting the Forth Bridge. A Search for Scottish Identity*, 2001
MacGregor, Alastair Alpin, *Auld Reekie*, 1943
McHardy, Stuart and Smith, Donald, *Arthur's Seat. Journeys and Excavations*, 2012
Mackenzie, Henry, *The Man of Feeling*, 1771
McLevy, James, *McLevy: The Edinburgh Detective*, 2001
Maitland, William *The History of Edinburgh from its Foundation to the Present Time*, 1753
Massie, Alan, *Edinburgh*, 1994
Masson, David, *Edinburgh Sketches*, 1892; *Memoirs of Two Cities, Edinburgh and Aberdeen*, 1911
Masson, Rosaline, *Edinburgh*, 1904
Miller, Hugh, *My Schools and Schoolmasters*, 1854; *Edinburgh and its Neighbourhood*, 1864
Miller, Karl (ed), *Memoirs of Modern Scotland*, 1970
Miller, Philip *The Blue Hotel*, 2015
Nicholls, David, *One Day*, 2014
Owen, Wilfred, *Poems*, 1960
Power, William, *Literature and Oatmeal*, 1935
Prebble, John, *The King's Jaunt: George IV in Scotland, 1822*, 1988
Ramsay, Allan *Poems by Allan Ramsay and Robert Fergusson* (ed Alexander Manson Kinghorn and Alexander Law), 1974
Rankin, Ian, *The Black Book*, 1993; *The Hanging Garden* 1998; *The Naming of the Dead*, 2006; *Exit Music*, 2007; *Saints of the Shadow Bible*, 2013
Ruskin, John, *Lectures on Architecture and Painting*, 1854
Royle, Trevor, *Precipitous City*, 1980
Sassoon, Siegfried, *Collected Poems 1908–1956*, 1961
Smith, Donald, *The English Spy*, 2007
Scott, Walter, *Waverley*, 1814, *Guy Mannering*, 1815; *The Antiquary*, 1816; *Rob Roy*, 1817; *The Heart of Midlothian*, 1818; *The Abbot*, 1820, *Journal*

(ed WEK Anderson), 1972

Sibbald, Robert, *Scotia Illustrata*, 1684; *Autobiography*, 1833

Sinclair, Sir John (ed) *The Statistical Account of Scotland*, vol VI, 1793

Smith, Adam, *The Wealth of Nations*, 1766

Smith, Alexander, *A Summer in Sky*, 1865

Smollett, Tobias, *Humphrey Clinker*, 1771

Spence, Lewis, *Collected Poems*, Serif Books, 1953

Stevenson, Robert Louis, *Edinburgh, Picturesque Notes*, 1879; *Familiar Studies of Men and Books*, 1882; *Strange Case of Dr Jekyll and Mr Hyde*, 1886; *Kidnapped*, 1886; *Catriona*, 1893; *St Ives* 1897; *Letters*, vols I–VIII (ed Bradford A Booth and Ernest Mehew), 1994-95; *Collected Poems* (ed Roger C Lewis), 2003

Topham, Edward, *Letters from Edinburgh*, 1776

Welsh, Irving, *Trainspotting*, 1993

Wesley, John, *Journal*, 1827

West, Rebecca, *The Judge*, 1922

Wilson, Daniel, *Memorials of Edinburgh in the Olden Time*, 1891

Wodrow, W, *History of the Sufferings of the Church of Scotland*, 1721

Wordsworth, Dorothy, *Recollections of a Tour in Scotland*, 1823

Youngson, AJ, *The Making of Classical Edinburgh 1750–1840*, 1966

# Map

Every effort has been made to trace the copyright holders of the map on pages 226–27. The firm of CJ Cousland and Sons Ltd was wound up in the early 1970s. The map first appeared in 1947 in *Edinburgh at Work and Play*, a booklet published to mark the inaugural Edinburgh Festival.

# Acknowledgments

Warmest thanks to all those individuals and institutions who have contributed to this book, knowingly or unknowingly, through companionship, conversation and the written word. I am grateful also to all those living writers whose published work I have quoted from, and to the departed also. All are listed in the bibliography.

Special thanks to Arthur Blue and Cookie, Sheila Brock, Gowan Calder, Kristian Calder, Christine De Luca, Edinburgh Central Library, Fiona Graham, Val Greaves, Katrina Hazell, Diana Lary, the late Charles McKean, the late Iseabail Macleod, Leon Matthews, Museum of Edinburgh, National Library of Scotland especially Sally Harrower and Ioannis Vasillos, National Museum of Scotland especially Hugh Cheape, George Dalgleish and David Forsyth, Vina Oberlander and the late Jon Oberlander, Queensferry Heritage Trust, James Robertson, the late Elizabeth Robertson, Scottish National Portrait Gallery, South Queensferry Library, The Writers' Museum. And thank you Alice Young, for enthusiastic editing and constructive suggestions.

Most of all, a profound thankyou to Rachel Calder, who took many of the photographs, to David Daiches and Anna Daiches who gave permission for me to include photographs taken by their father Alan, and to John Burnett who read the first draft and whose knowledgeable, thoughtful and sympathetic comments and corrections have helped to make this a better book.

# Index

# Luath Press Limited

*committed to publishing well written books worth reading*

LUATH PRESS takes its name from Robert Burns, whose little collie Luath (*Gael.*, swift or nimble) tripped up Jean Armour at a wedding and gave him the chance to speak to the woman who was to be his wife and the abiding love of his life. Burns called one of the 'Twa Dogs' Luath after Cuchullin's hunting dog in Ossian's *Fingal*. Luath Press was established in 1981 in the heart of Burns country, and is now based a few steps up the road from Burns' first lodgings on Edinburgh's Royal Mile. Luath offers you distinctive writing with a hint of unexpected pleasures.

Most bookshops in the UK, the US, Canada, Australia, New Zealand and parts of Europe, either carry our books in stock or can order them for you. To order direct from us, please send a £sterling cheque, postal order, international money order or your credit card details (number, address of cardholder and expiry date) to us at the address below. Please add post and packing as follows: UK – £1.00 per delivery address; overseas surface mail – £2.50 per delivery address; overseas airmail – £3.50 for the first book to each delivery address, plus £1.00 for each additional book by airmail to the same address. If your order is a gift, we will happily enclose your card or message at no extra charge.

**Luath** Press Limited
543/2 Castlehill
The Royal Mile
Edinburgh EH1 2ND
Scotland
Telephone: +44 (0)131 225 4326 (24 hours)
Email: sales@luath. co.uk
Website: www. luath.co.uk